Trust

Trust: Reaching the 100 Million Missing Voters (and other selected essays)

By Farai Chideya

Cover design by Nicola Ginzler, ginzlerdesign.com
Cover model: L. Dewey

Published by Soft Skull Press
71 Bond Street, Brooklyn, NY 11217

Distributed by Publishers Group West
www.pgw.com | 1.800.788.3123

Printed in Canada

Library of Congess Cataloging-in-Publication Data available
from the Library of Congress.

ISBN: 1-932360-26-3

To my grandmother, Mary Catherine Stokes,
who lived, learned, loved, and left a lasting legacy.

Contents

Trust

Selected Essays

Campaigns, Voting, and Down and Dirty Politics

War and Terror

Sex, Drugs, and Hip Hop

C.R.E.A.M. (Cash Rules Everything Around Me)

Media and Technology

Race and Justice

Beyond Our Borders

Preface: Why This, Why Now

As I finished writing this book, I learned that my eighteen-year-old cousin had been dispatched to fight in Iraq. He is tall, handsome, and freckled. The way I see him and will always see him is as kind. When my grandmother was dying, he came to the hospital and posed for her in his high school graduation cap and gown, the kind of embarrassing display most teens would avoid at all costs. Once she returned home for her final days, he spent many of them with her, taking a much older man's responsibility for her care. He is bilingual and brilliant. And he is fighting a war that I and many other people around the world are convinced that America should never have entered in the first place.

I hear that my cousin is a machine gunner on a Bradley tank. He can hear rockets and mortars exploding just a few hundred yards away. I wonder if he got the care package I sent him. I wonder that from the relative safety of New York, a city remarkably recovered from the terrorist attacks of September 11, 2001. While some, including the president of the United States, seemed to take the attacks as a personal insult, New Yorkers girded themselves and began to forge new lives. New in the sense that, while the city has always had its dangers, this was the last thing we expected.

No more.

For months after the attacks, although I was out of the city, I would tense up at the sound of airplanes overhead. I can only imagine what it meant for my friends who were closer to the center. One literally sped away from the crumbling towers in a taxicab, watching a man on foot behind him become engulfed in the billowing rubble. A couple who lived a few blocks away from the towers had to flee their home posthaste. Still more friends emerged from subways or looked out of office windows and watched the towers fall.

The fall of those towers accelerated a chain of sociopolitical calamity: one that began with a presidential election marred by bungling, voter intimidation, and the Supreme Court's suspect fiat, along with the failed promise that tax cuts for the rich would revive the economy and continued with the wars in Afghanistan and Iraq, more tax cuts, the worsening of poverty and medical access and America's schools, and the revelation that our rationale for going to war in Iraq was a sham.

There is another war going on right now, a war to revive and redefine American democracy. The biggest threat we face is failing to acknowledge that this war is being waged. Yet every day we see evidence that America is falling apart.

Right now I am sitting in my office. It's on the tenth floor of a high-rise owned and largely occupied by a bank. The building is 70 percent empty. The bank accelerated layoffs after 9/11.

Many of my friends are un- or under-employed. These are not slackers (God bless the endangered slacker) but college-educated overachievers who are humbled, financially and emotionally, to realize that their skills are disposable.

Subsequently, many of them are without healthcare or paying exorbitant rates, particularly if they are freelancers or have the financially deadly "pre-existing condition."

One friend works full time as a "freelancer" and needs a physical therapist. She pays $450 out of pocket per month, and considers it a bargain.

My sister, a doctor in a community health clinic in California, sees a steady stream of the uninsured, ranging from homeless individuals to working-class families.

My mother recently retired as a Baltimore City Public Schools teacher. The city schools, always vulnerable, are now running a $25 million deficit. The system laid off a thousand workers and is asking teachers to agree to pay cuts and unpaid furlough days. In Portland, Oregon, where several friends live, the city schools closed two weeks early in 2003 due to budget deficits.

This country needs help—all of our help. For me, saving this country is personal. And you?

Maybe you vote. Perhaps you're satisfied with the service you get from our government because you vote. Perhaps, on the other hand, you feel as though you can only vote for a series of "least-worsts," candidates who are the lesser of two evils.

Or perhaps, like half of eligible Americans, you don't vote. Our government calls people who have been unemployed so long that they have stopped looking for work "discouraged workers." We do not report these discouraged workers as unemployed; thus, our accounting of unemployment in America is a fraud. For example, if America's reported workforce were the same size as it was three years ago, unemployment would be 7.3 percent instead of 5.6 percent. Instead, millions of Americans have just stopped looking.[1] Many

Americans have stopped participating in politics as well. But we cannot discount the discouraged voters in America. Some of them are what we might call classically apathetic—"passionless" or "indifferent," according to the dictionary definition. But many more have been without adequate political representation so long that they simply cannot bear to vote.

If you're one of those "discouraged voters," there's no reason to be ashamed or embarrassed. But there is a reason to change. The political system as it stands right now is structured to discount your input. You deserve to be heard. More than that, there are literally thousands of individuals and organizations working to make sure that you *can* be heard.

This book is about making sure that every citizen's vote is valued and that voting can actually change the system. This is about reclaiming a space for ourselves in the life of the country and being proud to do it.

I am writing not just as a reporter or a political analyst but as an American citizen, with all the joys, responsibilities, and perils that that entails. I ask you to sit with me a while and think about our future.

Voting as Personal Power

It's time for a movement.

It's time to stand up and rebuild American democracy.

We deserve political parties that respond to our needs.

We deserve to not have to choose between the lesser of two evils.

We deserve to feel good, not dirty, about participating in a system which we build, pay for, and empower—the government of the United States of America.

I won't let the people who say my vote doesn't matter brain-wash me. I know my vote matters. History proves it. Now it's my turn.

I pledge to:

> Vote in all elections;
>
> Educate myself so I can make the best choices for myself and my community;
>
> Join with others to make parties and politicians hear my voice;
>
> Encourage others to register and vote.

Consider it done.

Trust

1. Trust

What if, one morning, you woke up to find the person sleeping next to you was missing? What if parents rose to find their children gone or children clambered out of bed to find their parents absent? What if half of America simply disappeared?

On one day every four years, this disappearing act happens. Only half of Americans voted in the 1996 and 2000 elections, continuing a slow but steady decline in voting over the past half century. And that's the good news. In midterm elections, three-quarters of eligible voters routinely stay home.

It's easy to paint the millions of missing voters as self-sabotaging losers. It's a lot harder for us to critique an American political system that has itself been failing voters. In *Why Americans Still Don't Vote: And Why Politicians Want It That Way*, Frances Fox Piven and Richard A. Cloward write:

> Americans generally take for granted that ours is the very model of a democracy. Our leaders regularly proclaim the United States to be the world's leading democracy and assert that other nations should measure their progress by the extent to which they develop electoral arrangements that match our own. At the core of this self-congratulation is the belief that the right to vote is firmly established here. But in fact the United States is the only major democratic nation in which the less-well-off, as well as the young and minorities, are substantially underrepresented in the electorate.[1]

In other words, American democracy is highly overrated, not necessarily in its concept but in its execution. We pride ourselves on being a beacon of hope for the world. In reality, there is much we could learn from other democracies—*if* we want to change.

Piven and Cloward's subtitle says it all: many politicians don't want the system to change. The two-party system, the authors argue, is structured to play a game of "keep away" with voters and potential voters who want reform. Within the past century and a half, those underserved voters have included women, poor Southern whites, and African-Americans. They were kept out of the system by restrictive and now-illegal methods including the poll tax and literacy tests; by political maneuvers that contained emerging third parties; and by outright voter intimidation. In fact, the authors go so far as to argue "the United States was not a democracy, in the elementary sense of an effective universal suffrage, during the twentieth century."

Provocative. But even if you accept it—and how could you accept such a heretical statement?—those days have passed, right?

Alright, then: let's take a look at the 2000 presidential election. According to that year's U.S. Census, America had 281 million occupants. Not all were eligible to vote. Some were under the age of eighteen. Others were disenfranchised for being felons. Still more were not citizens.

And yet, this left a total voter pool of roughly 200 million. Officially, the 2000 election was decided by 537 votes. That's the last legal count that tipped Florida into the Republican column, and thus the country into an electoral college, but *not* popular vote, victory for George W. Bush. The 2000 election was marred by error (dimpled, hanging, and pregnant chads), voter intimidation (African-Americans being asked for multiple forms of ID and being purged from voter rolls), media manipulation (the Republican party flew in congressional aides who helped storm the recount office in Dade County, Florida), and a conservative-led Supreme Court's decision to intervene on behalf of George W. Bush.

Election 2000 was also a prime example of how every vote counts. Those 537 votes were one ten-thousandth of the total votes cast in Florida. They were two hundred-thousandths of the total votes cast in the United States. In visual terms, the votes that decided the presidency were the size of one tiny dot of ink on a billboard. Granted, that 537-vote margin may not have been precise. But it highlights the critical absence of the 76 million eligible voters who stayed away from the polls in 2000.[2]

Americans were already cynical about politics, and the 2000 election didn't do much to reassure us. In 1966, fully 76 percent of Americans felt they could trust the federal government. That dropped to an all-time low of 21 percent in 1994, and has risen to roughly 40 percent today.[3] According to one 2004 study, most Americans—already cynical—didn't get any more so after the 2000 election. But some groups are less trusting and more fed up. Independents, who often do not vote because they don't like either major-party candidate, are more likely to want new leadership in Washington. And between 2000 and 2004, African-Americans who thought "people like me don't have any say about what the government does" rose from 34 percent to 58 percent.[4]

Let's also be honest here: politics can be as boring as watching paint dry. It seems as if parties, politicians, and even political journalists go out of their way to make the issues seem obscure and your chances of affecting our country's future remote. Most of the time, when the government makes headlines, it's because something is screwed up—a corruption scandal, thousand-dollar toilet seats, or dirty campaigns. In our celebrity-saturated culture, politicians generally look and act extremely un-hip. (Shallow, yes, but it makes a difference.) And political events can be as white as Klan rallies. In my more than ten years as a political reporter, I've often been the youngest and brownest person in the room. Time passes; the faces stay the same. New blood is rare. Many of us have an almost instinctive revulsion when it comes to government. We're so turned off by its trappings that we can't bear to participate.

Good government relies on an implicit contract of trust. Citizens must trust politicians to create stable institutions and right-minded policies. In turn, politicians must trust the leadership (expressed, most of all, via voting) of citizens.

That contract of trust is broken. It didn't happen all at once. In fact, it traces at least as far back as the post–Civil War era called Reconstruction, when both political parties colluded to disenfranchise African-Americans and poor whites. In recent years, citizens have been pushed aside by the growing power of corporate interests in shaping policy. For example, the office of Vice President Dick Cheney is still fighting to keep secret what went on at special closed-door meetings with energy companies, including the failed energy giant Enron. The playing field has changed in the past century and a half but the fundamental issue has not: Americans need to have a citizen's basic trust in their government, a basic belief that, even if they do not always get what they want, their voice matters and can be heard.

The right to vote is something we now take for granted. But for much of our history, women, African-Americans, and other people of color were simply denied the vote. Once enfranchised, African-Americans in particular were barred from voting via new laws and physical threats. As the 2000 election illustrates, voter intimidation is not just a thing of the past.

Just as critical, the rise in the twentieth century of television-driven multimillion dollar presidential campaigns highlighted those campaigns' dependence on big donors. (Check out Charles Lewis's bestselling book, *The Buying of the President, 2004*, for appropriately gory details.) In order to win and keep winning, politicians have to get paid not only by us, the taxpayers who provide their salaries, but by the corporations and rich donors who fund their campaigns.

On a personal level, many Americans no longer expect their government to be accessible. When citizens do reach out to government officials, it's usually on the local level and runs along the lines of, "I have a pothole on my street and it needs to be fixed." There are much larger "potholes" in state and federal policy, but it's often difficult to reach out and get a response. In fact, the White House actually changed the design of www.whitehouse.gov in order to make it more difficult for citizens to email! The best way to reach political leaders has been and still is to form a coalition with like-minded citizens, something we'll discuss later in the book.

Finally, in order to trust that they can shape government, citizens need transparency. We need the ability to be able to see and understand the workings of government so we can make the best possible decisions. That's where the media comes in. Most government publications are written in, well, government-ese. So most of us rely on the news media to inform us about political decisions and events and even to help shape our opinions.

But in recent years, the media has devoted less time to "hard" news like political news. The political news that does make air is often filled with just as much jargon and gobbledygook as any government press release. And the rise of conservative media outlets including Fox News have made all the networks scramble to assess the tone of their reporting. This could have been positive if television media in particular had taken a fresh look at how they serve their audience. But political news has remained an insider sport. Most national political news comes from a handful of reporters and commentators. Their ranks do not come near representing the racial, gender, or even ideological diversity of the American people.

In order to reinvigorate American democracy, we will have to work on rebuilding our trust in government and our ability to shape it. The remainder of this book focuses on examining why this trust has corroded, then highlights the ways in which innovators are trying to rebuild faith in America's political system.

2. A Brief History of Voter Turnout

I don't want everyone to vote; our leverage in the election quite candidly goes up as the voting populace goes down.

Conservative activist Paul Weyrich, director of the Committee for the Survival of a Free Congress, speaking at a 1980 fundraiser for Ronald Reagan[1]

Winning the Vote

The history of voting in America is a lot more action-packed than textbooks imply. It involves a series of revolutions in the way we think about political participation. Often these were real revolutions, filled with battles and bloodshed and strong ideas on both sides about right and wrong. Today, we think of the universal franchise, or right to vote, as a fait accompli, something we've always had and always will. To the contrary, our idea of a universal voting right is a relatively new concept.

Forgive me if I use a little bit of this chapter to go over old history. I was never taught it well in school. Instead, I spent years listening to history as a recitation of dates. But political history is a series of thrusts and parries in an ongoing duel between leaders who try to consolidate powers in the hands of the few and people who believe in democracy for the many.

Let's start with the American Revolution. According to the textbooks, a group of freedom-seeking pilgrims came to the Americas and overthrew the tyranny of British taxation. True, America was created in 1776 as an experiment in freedom and democracy. But the franchise, or right to vote, was far from universal. It only extended to white, landowning males, who openly distrusted the ability of poorer men (let alone women or people of African descent) to make political decisions. During the 1800s, a variety of political movements and protests overthrew property, religious, and literacy requirements that blocked male voters. In some states, even men who were not citizens could vote.

Women only received the right to vote in 1920, less than a hundred years ago. African-Americans technically received the right to vote with the adoption of the Fourteenth Amendment in 1868, after the Civil War. But it took the civil rights movement of the 1950s and 1960s to break down a wall of legal barriers (and a pattern of violence) that blocked the black vote. All of these changes came about because people didn't sit around and wait: they put their lives on the line to achieve change.

Perhaps we in the United States felt smug because we were the leaders of the democracy pack. Most European nations were even slower to give their citizens the right to vote. For example, compare the United Kingdom and America during the nineteenth century. In the United States in 1848, 2.9 million men cast their votes for the presidency. This reflected 13 percent of the total population and 73 percent of eligible voters.[2] In 1832 and 1867, the British added small landholders to the list of the wealthy and privileged who could vote. But even after 1867, only 16 percent of British men, or roughly 8 percent of the total British population, had the right to vote. British women only gained the same rights to vote as men in 1928. (For further comparison, Switzerland, which now has a higher percentage of female legislators than the United States, only granted women the right to vote in 1971!) In other words, even in Western democracies, the vote is not something which has been given, but which the people consistently fought for.

And how did Americans go about getting the vote? It usually involved a large portion of protest and an equally generous amount of behind-the-scenes negotiating. In 1842, a Rhode Island state legislator named Thomas Dorr led a ragged insurgency of poor citizens to protest the requirement that voters be landowners. After all, our Declaration of Independence said "All men are created equal." Dorr (who was a landowner) and his non-landowning supporters wanted to put some substance behind the words. They commandeered a couple of cannons—which failed to fire. Dorr served time in prison for the insurrection. But gradually, states yielded to pressure to drop the requirement on owning property.

The suffragist movement put women in a position to exercise their voting rights. In 1848, women organized the first Women's Rights Convention in Seneca Falls, New York. In 1890, Wyoming gave women the vote; Colorado followed three years later. But a decade after Washington State's decision, most American women still could not vote. A suffragist named Alice Paul helped organize protests in front of the White House, for which the women were jailed. President Woodrow Wilson eventually endorsed a suffrage amendment. Finally, after two-thirds of states ratified the

Nineteenth Amendment, all American women gained the right to vote in 1920.

The struggle of African-Americans to vote is remarkable because it has been waged at least twice and continues today. People of African descent were barred from voting when America was founded. Then, after the Civil War and the abolition of slavery, African-Americans gained the right to vote by constitutional amendment. Next, that right was effectively taken away when hostile politicians and racist activists waged a campaign of legal barriers and violence. The civil rights movement led politicians to pass the Voting Rights Act of 1965, which protected not only the black vote but all voters.

Yet widely documented instances of voter intimidation targeting African-Americans occurred in 2000, 2002, and beyond. In one example, the district attorney of Waller County, Texas, (which is predominately white) said he would prosecute students for "falsely" registering to vote in the district. The district happens to contain the predominately black Prairie View A & M University. In fact, American students have the right to vote where they go to school because plaintiffs from Prairie View A & M won a 1979 Supreme Court decision.[3]

But let's back up a bit. The first phase of black enfranchisement began after the Civil War, when, in 1866, the Congress passed the Fourteenth Amendment to the Constitution. (It was ratified in 1868.) It states: "No state shall make or enforce any law which shall abridge the privileges or immunities of citizens of the United States; nor shall any state deprive any person of life, liberty, or property, without due process of law; nor deny to any person within its jurisdiction the equal protection of the laws." During the post–Civil War Reconstruction era, the federal government protected black voting rights. Several Southern states sent African-American legislators to Congress.

I remember walking into a small gallery in a black history museum in Selma, Alabama, near the Edmund Pettus Bridge. In March 1965, police beat and tear-gassed civil rights marchers on the bridge. The event was televised throughout the country and came to be known as Bloody Sunday. A gallery off the museum's main hall displays portraits of black, Reconstruction-era congressmen. Did these proud, dignified men understand that their participation in the United States government was a limited-time offer? Did they understand that local politicians, Klansmen, and everyday citizens would deprive African-Americans of the right to vote and them of the ability to serve? And once they were disenfranchised, did they understand how long it would take our political system to recover from what had happened? After all, the first post-Reconstruction black senator was not elected until 1967.

With Reconstruction, the federal government pushed Southern states to give African-Americans full property and citizenship rights. But the two parties colluded in a secret compromise that ended reforms. Southern Democrats, who were mostly wealthy white planters, said they would back a Republican president. In exchange, Republicans ended Reconstruction.

Between 1876 and 1892, after the end of support for Reconstruction, an average of 60 percent of black men and 69 percent of white men in the South voted in the presidential election. By the period spanning 1900 to 1916, as the federal government ended its push to reform Southern politics, that number dropped to 2 percent of black men and 50 percent of white men. By 1924, the percentages were zero for black men and 32 percent for white men.

Not only did the end of Reconstruction disenfranchise black voters, it sharply cut down on the participation of white voters as well. The imposition of poll taxes and literacy tests blocked poor whites from voting almost as effectively as blacks.[4] In 1890, Mississippi enacted a $2 poll tax on every voter. In today's terms, that means you would have to cough up nearly $40 to vote.

Ironically, many poor whites opposed the civil rights movement of the 1950s and 1960s although it offered them, as well as African-Americans, a greater chance at political participation. For centuries, politicians have successfully pitted poor whites and African-Americans against each other, although the two groups have many common political goals. African-Americans gained leverage in national politics from the Great Migration north in the early twentieth century, when they became a key voting block in cities like Chicago. President Harry Truman then endorsed a civil rights platform at the 1948 Democratic National Convention, and some Southern Democrats (or Dixiecrats), including Strom Thurmond, walked out of the convention. The Democratic Party was then effectively split between acquiescing to Southern white leaders and playing to a racially diverse urban electorate in the North, a schism which lingers to this day.

After the assassination of President John F. Kennedy, President Lyndon Johnson signed the Voting Rights Act of 1965, which made the federal government accountable for enforcing voting rights. It was by and large a success. In Mississippi, only 5 percent of African-Americans were registered to vote in 1960. In 1968, that number rose to nearly 60 percent. [5]

Recently, however, there have been several examples of race-based voter intimidation. During the 2000 election, African-Americans were asked, illegally, for multiple forms of ID. A computer system run by a private company with Republican ties, ChoicePoint, "scrubbed" thousands of voters from the rolls. They were wrongly listed as felons and far more likely to be African-American than white.[6] Black Florida voters also complained of police roadblocks near polling places.

Florida isn't the only example of voter intimidation. In Kentucky in 2003, the Republican Party announced plans to put election-day "challengers" in fifty-nine predominately black voting precincts. Challengers are private citizens, deputized for election day, who can ask any voter who looks suspicious to sign an affidavit saying he or she is a registered voter. Most of the GOP challengers lived outside the urban areas targeted by the party.[7]

Using the Vote

Voter intimidation doesn't rate much news coverage these days. By all appearances, adult American citizens of every race, creed, and income level have the right to vote. So why do so few people exercise their rights?

In *Why Americans Still Don't Vote*, Piven and Cloward argue that nonvoters are mainly poor and working-class Americans who are largely ignored by both major political parties. The Republican Party has become heavily indebted to its big business donors. But the Democratic Party has re-aligned itself with business interests too. This means that a lot of American policies end up favoring corporations over real people. In his book *Spoiling for a Fight: Third-Party Politics in America*, Micah Sifry writes:

> Substantial numbers of Americans—in some cases majorities—support aid to poor children, cuts in corporate welfare, reductions in military spending, universal health care insurance, alternatives to the drug war, labor and environmental protections in trade agreements, tougher measures to guarantee

clean air, water and food, a living wage, more democratic over-
sight of federal banking policy, burden sharing with our overseas allies, more investment in energy conservation and alternative fuels, and a comprehensive overhaul of the campaign
finance system, to take some of the major issues that were not
raised in the 2000 presidential election.[8]

And yet, these issues are virtual untouchables, a third-rail of politics that
mainstream officials consider career suicide. Given that, many nonvoters
see elections as a choice between a Democratic Party that cares little for them
and a Republican Party that cares even less.

Poor and working-class voters tend to mobilize when politicians speak
to their needs, and politicians usually speak to their needs only when they
absolutely have to. Often, that means times of massive economic crisis.
Take the rise in voting during the 1920s and 1930s. The country was in an
economic depression. Americans began protesting for jobs. Democratic
President Franklin D. Roosevelt responded with New Deal policies creating
more government jobs, job relief, and the Social Security program. This
era also marked the beginning of class-based divisions between Democrats
and Republicans, as new poor and working-class voters began supporting
the Democrats.

But that didn't last. Piven and Cloward argue that during the next forty
years, the Democratic Party built new alliances with big business. They let
their old labor coalitions fade away. The unions were in trouble: they did-
n't know what to do with new working-class and poor constituents, who
tended to be women and people of color in the service industry. And the
Democrats didn't seem in any hurry to reach out to these workers either. Or
as Piven and Cloward put it, "The unions did little to enroll new black and
Hispanic voters, or the poor and working-class women who were entering
the workforce. Nor did the local Democratic parties. Instead, local officials
who presided over voter registration used these procedures to maintain *a
narrow and reliable electorate. . . .*"[9]

In other words, the game's been fixed. Half of voters have been shut out
from the get-go, and the two parties can haggle over who's left. The most
generous way to look at this is that the two parties don't know how to market

to new voters. It's as if they're only broadcasting on AM radio in a cable and Internet world.

If the two major parties aren't interested in reaching half of Americans, who will try to get them to the polls? For one, Piven and Cloward didn't just write about the problems with voting; they actually tried to solve them. The two worked on a program called Human Serve designed to register Americans through social service agencies like unemployment offices. Human Serve eventually morphed into the National Voter Registration Act (NVRA), or Motor Voter bill. The NVRA allowed people to register when they got their driver's license or visited other government agencies. In 1992, President George Bush vetoed the bill, which was pushed heavily on MTV by Rock the Vote. Republicans feared that new, less affluent voters would vote Democratic. Ten months later, in the early days of his first term, President Bill Clinton signed the Motor Voter bill into law.

So what happened then? "The NVRA reforms produced an unprecedented increase in voter registration," write Piven and Cloward. "Turnout, however, did not rise."[10] In fact, between 1994 and 1998, voting fell 2.8 percentage points. Among the possible reasons: Americans are less plugged in to social networks like family and church that help mobilize voters, and Americans are disillusioned with their political choices. Or as Steven J. Rosenstone and John Mark Hansen put it in their book *Mobilization, Participation, and Democracy in America*, voters "have lost their confidence in the effectiveness of their actions."[11] In other words, we're so sick and tired of politics as usual that we've just given up.

Is there still hope? Could Motor Voter still bring new voters to the polls? If that happens, write Piven and Cloward:

> it is not likely to be because the dynamic of electoral compe-
> tition itself prods the major parties to reach out to new vot-
> ers. It is more likely to be because *a new surge of protest, perhaps
> accompanied by the rise of minor parties* and the electoral cleavages
> that both movements and minor parties threaten, forces
> political leaders to make programmatic and cultural appeals,
> and undertake the voter recruitment, that will reach out to
> the tens of millions of Americans who now remain beyond
> the pale of electoral politics.[12]

Piven and Cloward identify two major factors that could reshape American politics: protest—likely coming from new activist organizations—and minor parties.

The rest of this essay examines how these two factors—protest and third-party politics—could influence American elections in 2004 and beyond. First, I lay some groundwork by examining the political events of the last four years and how they've further eroded the trust of the American public. Then, the book turns to the kind of outreach Piven and Cloward are talking about—innovative attempts to reach new voters in 2004. One of them is hip hop generation political organizing. Can it change the American electorate? And finally, how are third-party movements reshaping the political landscape?

America is at a crossroads. We can continue to content ourselves with the illusion that America is a fully participatory democracy. Or we can look for groundbreaking solutions to half the country feeling left out. The good news is that many different groups are looking for these solutions. Will millions of Americans heed their call?

3. The 2000 Election

A Devastating Blow to American Democracy

The perfect façade of American democracy suffered a devastating blow during the 2000 presidential election. The question today is whether the bad taste left by election 2000 will depress voter turnout in the 2004 election. The terrain of election 2004 is largely the same as four years ago: a key state, Florida, whose voting machines are deeply flawed; a divide between the cultural conservatism of the South and Midwest and the social liberalism of the coasts; and the economy as a key issue, one which could trump social issues and unite a populist voter block. Have we learned lessons from the 2000 election, or will politicians and the media go on to repeat the same mistakes?

I will not go into a comprehensive accounting of the election—others have done that sufficiently. What I will do is give my impressions of the campaign season, election, and aftermath from the standpoint of a citizen and political analyst. I'll take a look at the experience of Al Gore's campaign manager Donna Brazile, and also at the views and experiences of a variety of nonvoters I found in Florida during the long election debacle. The constituencies mobilized and disenfranchised during the 2000 election are, in large part, the same players who will determine the outcome of election 2004. If anything, ideological rifts between liberals and conservatives have deepened in the last four years. The two major parties may not change many minds, but each has a chance to mobilize new voters.

Campaign 2000 had an oddly fuzzy quality. Vice President Al Gore battled for the Democrats, Texas Governor George W. Bush for the Republicans, and consumer advocate Ralph Nader for the Green Party. Perennial conservative candidate Patrick Buchanan ran on the Reform Party ticket, but won only one half of one percent of the vote. Both Gore and Bush tried their best to triangulate, or play to the center by taking the other side's issues. For example, Gore supported missile defense and Bush heavily pushed education reform. Maybe this allowed them to score a few extra voters from the other side. But as interviews with nonvoters demonstrate later this chapter, the muddying of candidate and party differences discouraged many from voting.

There were a few flashy attempts to woo new voters. In July and August 2000, two shadow conventions paralleled the Democratic and Republican National Conventions. Speakers included Arizona Senator John McCain, comedian/commentator Al Franken, musicians DJ Spooky and Chuck D, and columnist Ariana Huffington, who helped organize the events. The shadow conventions brought together everyone from button-down academics to teenage activists. Topics that wouldn't get a smidgen of time at the major conventions were given intense scrutiny, including the effects of the War on Drugs. The Republican governor of New Mexico, Gary Johnson, spoke about the need to end the drug war. Gus Smith spoke about his daughter Kemba, a battered woman who received a twenty-four-and-a-half-year prison term for transporting drug money for her abusive boyfriend. She was later pardoned by President Clinton in the waning days of his term. (I moderated one panel on the drug war, which costs U.S. taxpayers roughly $40 billion per year.)

The energy at the shadow conventions was raw and inspiring. The young people who came to the event seemed dismayed by politics-as-usual, but inspired that they could find their voice in this context. Inside the Republican and Democratic National Conventions—spaces that I was privileged to work in and visit—the atmosphere was very different: coordinated, buttoned-down, and ready for prime time. Outside each venue, a series of protesters tried to garner attention.

2000 Election Timeline

November 7
Election Day

7:48 PM Voter News Service announces Al Gore has won Florida (before the close of all state polls).

10 PM Florida race is once again "too close to call."

November 8

2:16 AM Fox News calls Florida for George W. Bush. Decision is made by Bush's first cousin.

Between 3 and 4 AM Gore calls Bush to concede. Networks then say race is too close to call. Gore calls Bush to withdraw concession.

November 9

Florida results show George Bush leading by 1,784 votes. The narrow margin automatically triggers a machine recount in all of Florida's 67 counties.

The mainstream media couldn't be bothered to take the protesters seriously. Often they were portrayed as buffoons and only the most outrageous of them were shown on television. Rarely were they ever given a chance to speak. I remember talking to one CNN anchor who agreed that the protesters were being given short shrift.

The buzzword on protests was "1968," the year that police and antiwar activists clashed violently at the Democratic National Convention in Chicago. Although there were some arrests and strong-arm tactics used against protesters, the Republican convention in Philadelphia and the Democratic convention in Los Angeles were relatively calm. In the first place, no single issue unified the protesters. It was a case of a thousand flowers blooming—and few of their messages registering.

Then, on November 7, election day, I went down to Washington, D.C., to do on-air analysis for CNN. I had been fighting off a cold, which was rapidly turning into a fever. My illness added a layer of the surreal to an evening that had more twists and turns than anyone could have predicted.

After doing a live pop (guest appearance) with conservative analyst Tucker Carlson, I hung out in the green room waiting to see if they'd need me again. It was filled with an array of analysts and commentators, including future *Crossfire* co-hosts James Carville and Carlson, who came with his wife.

The Voter News Service (a joint polling effort by ABC, CBS, NBC, Fox, CNN, and the Associated Press) declared that Vice President Al Gore had won the state of Florida at 7:48 PM.[1] Carlson's wife began to cry.

November 10
First recount shows George Bush ahead by 327 without counting absentee ballots. The Democrats request hand recounts in Miami-Dade, Broward, Palm Beach and Volusia Counties.

November 11
Palm Beach announces it will recount. Bush goes to federal court to bar the recount.

November 12
Volusia County begins recount. Democrats file suit in Seminole County against Republican absentee ballots.

November 13
Federal court refuses to stop recount. Florida election officials announce that they will certify the election the next day. Democrats appeal.

Perhaps the prediction that Gore won Florida was a curse instead of a blessing. The television networks promised not to announce winners until the polls closed in each state, but the Florida call occurred just before the close of polls in the western part of the state. That gave Republican organizers time to urge last-minute voters to turn out. Of course, it was far from the networks' only blunder that night.

I was let off duty by CNN and went to an election-night party filled with people convinced that Al Gore was going to win. Being a bunch of good Washington liberals, they had broken out the champagne. But then, at 10 PM, the networks announced that the race was too close to call. To add to partygoers' misery, the vice president also lost his home state of Tennessee. (If he had won in Tennessee, he would have had an undisputed victory in the presidential race.) Next, at 2:16 AM, the Fox News Channel named Bush the victor in Florida. In order not to be scooped, other networks named Bush the winner, too. Without any conclusive poll data, Fox relied on an employee named John Ellis to make the decision. Ellis is George W. Bush's first cousin and had been in contact with his cousin all night.

Gore called to concede to Bush. Bush prepared for his victory speech. Then, an hour later, the networks reversed themselves again and said that Florida was too close to call. Gore called to un-concede, a bit like putting a genie back into a bottle. George W. Bush reportedly snapped at him; Gore told Bush not to get "snippy."

2000 Election Timeline (con't)

November 14
District court upholds the deadline but states further recounts can continue and may be included. Katherine Harris, Florida secretary of state, certifies results with a 300-vote Bush lead in an attempt to stop the recount.

November 15
Broward County continues a hand recount. Secretary of State Harris refuses to accept additional votes based on recount.

November 16
State supreme court says manual recount can continue.

November 17
Florida circuit court judge Terry Lewis says Harris can certify results, but the state supreme court puts a hold on that decision.

November 18
Overseas ballots are counted, giving Bush a 930-vote lead.

I went to bed at a time when voters thought Bush would be the next president of the United States. I woke to find pandemonium, no clear winner. Over the course of the next thirty-seven days, the campaigns would fight over whether or not to recount ballots, which ballots to count, and how to count them. There were three basic problems with the voting in Florida. First, there was the "butterfly ballot" used in heavily Democratic Palm Beach County. Given the way the candidates' names were placed, over five thousand voters ended up punching holes both for Gore and for conservative Patrick Buchanan. Even Buchanan admitted these were not likely to be his voters. These votes were disqualified, and they totaled ten times the number of votes with which George W. Bush claimed victory.[2] Second, punch-card ballots used in several counties were delivered partially punched. To count or not to count them? That's the whole "dimpled chad," "hanging chad," "two-corned chad," "pregnant chad" controversy. Third, different counties use different voting systems. The most old-fashioned and error-prone systems were concentrated in counties with more poor, working-class, and African-American voters. In some counties, 3 percent of all votes were discarded because they were improperly punched or marked.

So several counties started recounts. And then things really got ugly. On November 22, a group of Republican congressional staffers flew from Washington, D.C., down to Florida. They put out the message on conservative radio to meet at Miami's county hall, where workers were hard at work hand-recounting ballots. The group of Republicans then stormed the recount office, assaulting workers and shutting the recount down.

November 20

Arguments before Florida high court.

November 21

Florida high court rules that recount can continue and should be certified on November 26 at 3 PM.

November 22

George Bush appeals to the U.S. Supreme Court to stop the recount. Republican congressional staffers fly to Florida from D.C. Using alerts on conservative radio to get participants, they build up a mob that storms the recount office in Miami's county hall.

November 26

Secretary of State Harris certifies Bush victory at 537 votes (the final certified figure). This does not include recounts in Palm Beach and Miami-Dade.

November 27

Gore officially contests the results.

The chaos of election 2000 divided Americans into those who felt the recount should continue and those who thought it should end. But the way it ended eroded many Americans' confidence in our political process. President George W. Bush took office because the U.S. Supreme Court decided, by a vote of 5 to 4, to stop the Florida recounts. Did the Justices have a hard deadline for making their decision? Well, the federal deadline for counting ballots is January 6, but the Court decided to stop the recount on December 12. The decision broke down not only on ideological but personal lines. Two of the conservative justices who declared Bush the winner had personal ties to the Texas governor and his family. After the Supreme Court selected the president, Justice Clarence Thomas's wife got a job taking applications for people who wanted to work in the Bush administration. Two of Antonin Scalia's nine children, both lawyers, went to work for Bush.

In 2004, reports revealed that Justice Scalia went duck hunting with Vice President Dick Cheney. Scalia came under pressure to recuse himself from (that is, refrain from ruling on) the case where Cheney tried to keep the public from seeing notes on a secret White House energy meeting. Scalia *did* recuse himself from a case involving the use of "God" in the Pledge of Allegiance because he had made public comments on his views, but he did not recuse himself from the energy meeting case (which, in 2004, the Court ruled should return to a lower court). And neither Thomas nor Scalia recused themselves from the 2000 election case. If both had, the Florida recount would have continued, and Vice President Al Gore, winner of the

2000 Election Timeline (con't)

December 1

U.S. Supreme Court hears arguments on the earlier extension of the date for recounts by Florida.

December 2

Circuit court judge N. Sander Sauls hears case on whether Miami-Dade and Palm Beach should hand-recount votes.

December 4

The U.S. Supreme Court orders clarification of earlier Florida Supreme Court decision.

December 5

Judge Sauls rules against Gore.

December 6

Gore appeals to Florida supreme court.

December 7

Oral arguments before Florida supreme court.

December 8

Florida supreme court orders a manual recount of all votes in the state that could not be read by a machine.

popular vote in America, may well have become president. Today, not surprisingly, most Bush supporters believe the justices made the right call. Many Gore supporters, on the other hand, are still smarting from the way the election ended. But even among Gore's supporters, one question remains: was there anything Gore could have done differently?

An Insider's View of the 2000 Election: Donna Brazile

For most of us, trust in the political system is not unconditional or unlimited. Our government and politicians have to reaffirm and renew their worth through positive action. (Of course, the definition of a positive action varies depending on who you are. Not surprisingly, Democrats tend to trust government more during a Democratic presidency, while Republicans trust government more when a fellow Republican is in office.)3 You would think that those who work in politics would have the greatest belief in the system. But even political insiders can become disillusioned.

Former Al Gore campaign manager Donna Brazile won't say outright that Gore would be president now if only he'd listened to her. She doesn't have to. Instead, she talks about the point where their relationship—an opposites-attract partnership of the passionate organizer and the cerebral politician—broke down.

"My sister lives in Seminole County (Florida). She called me and said, 'How many forms of ID do you need to vote?' And that's when I broke."

December 9

U.S. Supreme Court halts counting without hearing appeal.

December 10

Lawyers file briefs before Supreme Court.

December 11

Oral arguments before the Court.

December 12

At 10 PM the Supreme Court rules that no further recounts can take place. Justices Clarence Thomas and Antonin Scalia have personal contacts with the Bush family but do not recuse themselves from the 5-to-4 decision.

December 13th

Gore concedes.

It was election day. Since dawn, Brazile had been on radio stations across America, listening to black callers complain of police roadblocks, problems with the voter rolls, and being asked, illegally, for more than one form of ID. (Her sister had to show three before she was allowed to vote.) "This was not isolated to a specific state or a specific region," Brazile says. "Black people were catching hell."

When she went to the vice president, says Brazile, "I got froze out." Gore decided to pursue a legal strategy to fight the suspicious activity in Florida. Brazile wanted to get activists into play and focus on civil and voting rights. "The Republican talking points were all about, 'Stop the count. Declare victory.' And ours were all about, 'Here's why we gotta have the count.' It was not based on the Voting Rights Act. It was all blah-de-blah. It was all bullshit."

Brazile's kind face and salt-and-pepper hair clash with her sometimes salty language. But she's always had a take-no-prisoners philosophy when it comes to defending civil rights. Brazile, the third of nine children, grew up in Kenner, Louisiana, near New Orleans. When Rev. Martin Luther King, Jr., was assassinated, she snuck out of the house to hear a preacher from the SCLC. "I got an ass-whipping for leaving the house," she says. "But I had to go."

Brazile was only eight, but she learned that the antidote to political oppression was political action. The very next year, she rode her bike through the neighborhood to campaign for a local candidate. And of course, there's the time she started a riot in her newly integrated school to protest the way the black kids were left to stand in the sun while white kids had shade.

"I've had one of the best seats in history," says Brazile, who recently completed the political memoir *Cooking with Grease*. "Working on the bill to make [Martin Luther] King's day a holiday. I was there when Harold Washington was first elected. I was there when Jesse Jackson launched his campaign. I was there when Mondale selected Ferraro. I was there when Shirley Chisholm launched the first black women's political party. I was there with Hands Across America, and the fight for housing and homelessness, because my own family had experienced that. . . . All the way down to working on the Hill, what it was like being on the largest plantation in America." All of these positive, if hard-won, experiences with government as a social-change agent gave Brazile the strength and motivation to continue her work.

It seems physically impossible for Brazile to have just one job. She lectures at Georgetown and the University of Maryland. She heads the Democratic National Committee's Voting Rights Institute. She writes for newspapers and magazines and co-hosts a show on CNN. She is a fierce Southern-foods cook who delights in crafting dishes for friends like D.C. congresswoman Eleanor Holmes Norton. But there's one job she's not aiming to have again—campaign manager. "Al Gore cured me. I would never get involved in another presidential campaign on that level again. I'm cured," she cries. "I'm still cured!"

The tortured denouement of the Gore campaign left Brazile "weary." "I was so beaten down—not broken, 'cause it takes a lot to break me—but I was so beaten down," she says. "I went to church . . . [and] I went to confession because I'm Catholic. I say 'Bless me Father for I have sinned.' And he says 'What is your sin?' And I said, 'You know, I do my job and something happened and I think I could have fought just a little harder in terms of what was going on in the campaign. . . . I could have fought harder on Tennessee.'" Brazile had pushed to put more money and voter mobilization troops into the South, particularly Gore's home state of Tennessee, which he lost. Then, she wanted to rely on civil rights and advocacy groups to help fight for the recount. Gore chose a more hands-off legal strategy. His running mate Joe Lieberman, on the other hand, advocated pushing civil rights.

The Gore legal strategy didn't succeed. "I finally broke down and cried the day that . . . the Supreme Court decision just enraged me," says Brazile. "If I could have found Clarence Thomas's phone number that night, I would have cussed him out. I was so pissed. And because they used civil rights statutes to stop the count, I was so angry. I live right down the street from the Supreme Court, a couple blocks from where Frederick Douglass had his Capitol Hill home. And I was on a rampage. I wanted to have a rally that night at midnight. But nobody was up [for it]. Everybody was just shocked."

"The mainstream press were so busy trying to figure out the legal ramifications and the constitutional crisis. And I was dealing with downright racial discrimination at the ballot box," says Brazile. She sent out media advisories on the voting rights violations. "And I was evil," she says. "I thought that everybody in the campaign had abandoned the struggle. Here black people got out and voted, and they got abandoned. It was very personal because here I played a major role in the campaign for almost three years of my life, and during the time when I thought the campaign should have listened to me, I was totally marginalized because—the race stuff. Nobody cared."

For Brazile, as for many Americans, the great shame of election 2000 was not simply the failure of the system, but the lackluster response of the media, government, and public. Few responded as outrages came to light, particularly given the racial politics of the situation, and the public's muted response reflects the pervasive lack of trust in the system. After all, if you think government is wrecked, you won't be surprised when it fails you.

Today, Brazile is kinder in judging both herself and the campaign she managed. She didn't endorse a Democratic candidate in the 2004 primaries. Instead, she's focusing on the need for voters to define their issues and choose the candidate who speaks to them. The top political issue today, hands down, is "jobs and the economy," says Brazile. "Since President Bill Clinton left office, unemployment has skyrocketed. The 2004 electoral season will be the most important political season in our lifetime."

Florida's Nonvoters

In late November 2000, I flew to Tallahassee, Florida, to see for myself what was going on. I traveled with my fellow reporter Dani McClain, who is also African-American. Coming from New York, we immediately had to adjust to seeing Confederate flags everywhere, from the back of pickup trucks to the signage on local convenience stores.

Tallahassee is Florida's capital and the home of two major universities. In the center of town, reporters clustered near the courthouse where Leon County Circuit Judge N. Sanders Sauls was hearing Gore's request to continue recounts. Scores of television cameras crowded in to get tight shots of a few protesters. The camera angles made the few seem like many. What people at home generally could not see was that the protesters were a small and motley crowd. The atmosphere near the courtroom was more like the end of a family barbecue, with a dozen Bush supporters and eight or nine Gore supporters leaning against the walls and chatting amiably with people on their side. Unlike the instance of Republicans organizing Bush supporters to storm the recount offices in Miami-Dade, the Democratic protesters, in particular, seemed to have little awareness that their actions would be taped and replayed.

My main reason for coming to Florida was to interview nonvoters about how they made the decision to stay away from the polls, and whether they regretted it given how close the race was. I found plenty of voters as well, stalwart Bush and Gore voters with a long list of reasons for their decisions. Many of them felt that they'd just participated in the race of a lifetime.

First stop: a public housing project where all or most of the residents were African-American. Twenty-year-old Shawenda Please, a college student with a two-year-old son, tried to register twice: once with her mother and once at school. She wanted to vote for Gore, but when it came time to vote, her name wasn't on the rolls. Another resident had just moved from out of state and failed to re-register. And then I ran into a group of men shooting the breeze on a stoop. I ended up going out for a bite to eat with Marcell Thompson, a long-haul truck driver who was visiting his family.

Thompson, the kind of good, hard-working man who would get the girl in a Terry McMillan novel, was thoroughly disillusioned by politics. He would have voted for Gore, he said, but he was on the road. Then he added, "I pretty much couldn't care less about voting any way because I truly believe that what runs the country, and what's always run the country, is money and power. . . . Even though we fought as women and men and blacks to vote, regardless of how much we've been through to get to the position where we are now, we can vote all we want to. It's who has the money and who has the power who gets the say-so. That's just how the country has always been run and how it always will be run."

If Thompson were president, what issues would he focus on? "Everyday life," he said. "I mean, you have single mothers out here who are really struggling. There are certain programs that help certain mothers, but you have certain mothers who have an honest job that doesn't pay enough to reach up to their means of what they really need. And then whenever they get to the point where they have no choice but to ask for certain assistance, then you got other people looking at them and saying, 'People always got to get your hand out.'"

Just a few miles away at Florida State University, a group of teenage students had a different take on voting. The students who voted tended to have a strong family history of following politics and also felt confident in their ability to make decisions. Those who did not vote either had trouble registering (particularly as students who lived outside their home states) or didn't have a history of political engagement in their families.

Jessica Smith, age nineteen, didn't vote. "I don't even think my parents vote," she said. On the other hand, eighteen-year-old Cynthia Copeland voted via Ohio absentee ballot. "My parents were always like, it's a responsibility," Copeland said. "They always vote." Their experiences reflect national patterns. According to the National Association of Secretaries of State, young adults whose parents vote are twice as likely to go to the polls as ones whose parents don't vote.[4] In other words, we can't blame young people alone; we have to look at the examples set for them.

The students also took issue with the quality and style of political information they received. Eighteen-year-old Amber Waters chose not to vote because, she says, "I didn't know which way one person was going with it as opposed to another. . . . I didn't want to cast a wrong vote." She mused for a moment. "I didn't have the information I needed. [After the election] in class for the next two weeks everyone was talking about how they voted for Bush and how they voted for Gore. And I was hearing more and more things and so, now, if I were to vote now, I know exactly what I would do. I now know what I need to know to make an informed decision."

Marie Wilson, former president of the Ms. Foundation for Women, adds that women often don't trust their political instincts. "We have to help women understand that they can trust their own intuition," Wilson says. "Politics is a rough intelligence." In 2004, Wilson published *Closing the Leadership Gap: Why Women Can and Must Help Run the World*. She believes the lack of female elected officials further alienates potential female voters, a powerful bloc. Twenty-two million single women alone are likely nonvoters in the 2004 election.

As I continued my trip through Florida, I got yet another perspective on voting in a town near Tallahassee called Havana. This cluster of 1,700 people, more than half of them black, was really two different worlds.[5] There was the charming white southern town, with quaint vintage shops and restaurants, and the economically depressed black town with a grimy community center. In the dim confines of the community center, twenty-one-year-old Michael Terry spent his day with other men who seemed cut out of the mainstream economy. Asked about Gore and Bush, Terry said, with a bitter laugh, "They're the same. Both of 'em white." Did Terry think voting could change his life? "It ain't gonna change anything," he said. He pointed to the state of the town's schools. "Oh, they're garbage." After desegregation the white parents put their children in private schools. Havana's public schools are almost all black and underfunded.

Another Havana resident, Ray Miller, pulled his car up beside me and Dani McClain after we'd unsuccessfully approached some white residents to get them to talk to us. Smiling through a mouth full of gold fronts, he said he'd picked us as outsiders because we both had braids or dreadlocks. Miller, who can't vote because of his felony record, was amazed at the outcome in Florida. "They just messed this up. All the people who don't have a felony on their record, they should at least count them," he said. "It's bad enough that people [with records] can't vote."

To many people, it sounds perfectly logical to keep convicted felons off the voter rolls. But most Western democracies return voting rights to people who have served their sentences. And, perhaps more important, the laws aren't equal across America. States have widely different policies. Forty-six states forbid prisoners to vote; thirty-two bar felons on parole from voting; twenty-nine block prisoners on probation; and fourteen states block people who've served their whole sentence for a felony—over a million Americans—from ever voting again.[6] Not surprisingly, the states most likely to take away felons' voting rights forever are states with high black and Latino populations, and they've used these laws to shape the voting pool. Although now the laws are defended as race-neutral, they were instituted during the Reconstruction-era backlash against what one Alabama lawmaker described as "the menace of negro domination."[7]

Eighty percent of Americans favor reinstating the voting rights of felons who have served all of their sentences. A bipartisan panel led by former presidents Gerald Ford and Jimmy Carter recommended the same thing.[8] And as he left office, outgoing president Bill Clinton made the same suggestion. (See the essay "On Felons Reclaiming the Right to Vote" later in this book.) This may reflect the fact that most felons aren't convicted for violent crimes: only a fifth of felons convicted in state court committed an act of violence, while a third were sentenced on drug crimes.[9] But current legislators are too afraid of backlash—or too concerned that former felons could tip the vote in states like Florida—to change the laws.

In fact, Florida has one of the highest rates of felony disfranchisement in America. Political observers are now questioning why so many Floridians become felons in the first place. State Senator Daryl Jones, of Miami, told the

Nation, "Every year the Florida legislature is trying to make more [minor] crimes felonies. Why? So they can eliminate people from the voter rolls." In the year 2000, 187,000 Floridians were disenfranchised for their felony records.

The Republican-run state was so eager to strike felons from its rolls that it hired a private company, ChoicePoint, to cross-check the Florida lists for felons who had moved from Texas. The deeply flawed lists they produced relied on inexact matches—for example, two people who had the same last name and similar social security numbers or birth dates. False matches included an employee of the Monroe County election supervisor's office and a black minister from Leon County, Rev. Willie David Whiting. Whiting arrived at his Tallahassee polling place and was told he could not vote. Turns out he'd been mixed up with someone named Willie J. Whiting, whose birthday was two days from the minister's. "I felt like I was slingshotted back into slavery," Rev. Whiting later told a federal civil rights commission investigating the election.[10]

Today, not only have we failed to learn from the Florida fiasco; we are in danger of repeating it or even making the problem worse. For two years, politicians didn't take much action on voting reform. Then, in 2002, Congress passed the Help America Vote Act, or HAVA. It authorizes $3.86 billion to update machinery and improve staffing for federal elections. HAVA also puts new requirements on people registering to vote, in particular making them show ID or give out their social security number. In a commentary for the legal magazine *Writ*, Grant Hayden writes, "This wouldn't be the first time in our history that an attempt to disenfranchise voters masqueraded as an 'anti-fraud' measure. Southern Democrats in the late nineteenth century employed a variety of similar devices in order to keep blacks and lower-class whites away from the ballot box."[11] The biggest impact from HAVA is that its call for new machinery is being turned into a push for electronic voting. This may not cure America's voting problems. In fact, electronic voting could spark a new and bigger crisis in voter confidence.

Electronic Voting Machines: Florida 2000 All Over Again?

Two years after a presidential election marred by controversy and confusion, voters in Florida's Miami-Dade County might have expected they could rest easy. After all, their government had just purchased a system of brand-new touch-screen voting stations, "voting ATMs."

But after the polls had closed, confusion reigned again. Some precincts in Miami-Dade and Broward showed that no one had voted for governor—this despite scores of voters passing through.

The culprit? Touch-screen machines manufactured by Election Systems & Software. The company blamed poll workers for not properly inserting cartridges that would read the votes when the polls closed. Election Systems & Software insisted the votes *were* registered. They performed a data extraction on the machines in question, pulling out what they said were the correct votes. No one else could check for sure. Why? Because Election Systems & Software and virtually all other electronic voting companies do not make machines that print a paper record of each voter's actions. This, say critics, could lead to tampering and fraud.[12]

Miami-Dade's 2002 election was a clear case of putting technology before the needs and limitations of people. The poll workers, many of them elderly long-time volunteers, were given only a brief training; the county didn't get its voting machines until June and was setting them up as late as the day before the election; and a complicated boot-up procedure (the ballots are trilingual) meant that not all machines were ready by the time polls opened.[13]

Technology is now being touted as the solution to voting problems, but flawed systems already caused trouble in election 2000. Volusia County, Florida, used optical scanners—computers that count paper ballots—manufactured by the Diebold Corporation. Just days after the 2000 election, the *Washington Post* ran a front page article that began:

> Something very strange happened on election night to Deborah Tannenbaum, a Democratic Party official in Volusia County. At 10 PM, she called the county elections department and learned that Al Gore was leading George W. Bush 83,000 votes to 62,000. But when she checked the county's Web site for an update half an hour later, she found a startling development: Gore's count had dropped by 16,000 votes, while an obscure Socialist candidate had picked up 10,000—all because of a single precinct with only 600 voters.[14]

Florida election officials later claimed they'd been able to retrieve the correct vote count. Luckily, in this case, they had the original paper ballots to refer to.[15] But with most new electronic voting systems, there is no paper trail recording the original votes.

Touch-screen voting does have its advantages. It's easier for the disabled and for non-English-proficient voters to use. But if the new voting machines are like ATMs, who holds the password? And just as important, who can *access* the password? Last year, scientists at Johns Hopkins and Rice universities discovered security flaws in the Diebold corporation's voting machines. The source code that ran the machine also contained the password to access it, a definite no-no.[16]

Diebold has 40,000 voting machines in thirty-seven states. It is also run by a fiercely partisan leader.[17] Diebold's chief executive, Walden O'Dell, hosted a $1,000-a-plate Republican fundraising dinner in the summer of 2003. In his invitation, he said that he was "committed to helping Ohio deliver its electoral votes to the president next year." Around the time of the fundraiser, the Ohio secretary of state was working to help Diebold qualify to sell Ohio voting machines for use in the 2004 elections.[18]

The fallout from the 2000 election and the push for paperless electronic voting machines threaten one of the pillars of public trust: enfranchisement, or the right to vote. (Interestingly, "enfranchisement" can also be defined as "freedom from political subjugation or servitude," something we Americans have come to take for granted.) Electronic voting machines are *the* story to watch in the 2004 elections. Many municipalities are committed to using paperless ballots in 2004, though the flaws in electronic voting machines continue to emerge. For example, in October 2003, during the recall election that ultimately put Arnold Schwarzenegger in the California governor's office, machines in Alameda County started marking votes for Democratic Lieutenant Governor Cruz Bustamante as votes for the socialist candidate.[19] The machines were Diebold's.

An equally troubling example of e-voting occurred in George W. Bush's home state of Texas. As Ben Tripp of the watchdog organization CounterPunch wrote:

> Computerized voting machines in the 2002 election did
> all kinds of weird things: if you pressed the Democrat's

name in some counties in Texas, for example, the Republican's name was chosen. And in Cormal County, Texas, three Republican candidates won by exactly 18,181 votes apiece. There's the kind of coincidence the FBI loves. But it gets even more amazing: in two *other* races elsewhere in this great nation, Republicans won by—wait for it—18,181 votes. The odds of this are similar to the odds of waking up on the surface of Mars with your underwear on your head and a bowling trophy gripped between your knees. These results were eventually 'adjusted', proving it was all just a wacky coincidence. But how can we know? Because there is no physical evidence of how a vote was cast. [20]

Just as disturbing as the voting malfunctions is the fact that most major-media outlets ignored stories like these, leaving the connect-the-dots to independent investigative reporters in the United States and as far flung as the United Kingdom and New Zealand. (Some of the best reporting on the 2000 election was actually published in the U.K., apparently because U.S. news editors were too afraid to reflect the chaos and controversy of the election.)

Electronic voting without a paper trail is a recipe for disaster. Despite growing awareness of the problem and public protest, many municipalities will certainly use this flawed system in 2004. Voters and civil rights groups will have to come up with smart, innovative ways to track the vote and hold e-voting companies accountable for failures. Of course, municipalities could research ways to keep an independent paper trail of votes or even dump the paperless systems before November. The problem is that many counties have already paid for this flawed technology, and any change would be costly. Nonetheless, there's a notable backlash against the paperless voting machines. First, the California secretary of state announced that as of July 1, 2005, no county or city can use electronic voting machines that do not leave a verifiable paper trail. Of course, this will not be implemented until after the next presidential election.[21] Then came public hearings on whether Diebold machines—which were not, as the company claimed, federally approved—had failed California voters in a March 2004 primary. After Diebold machines malfunctioned in Alameda and San Diego counties, thousands of voters in San Diego County were turned away from the polls. During the hearings, company president Bob Urosevich apologized, saying he was "sorry for the inconvenience of the voters." The chief counsel to the state's election division said, "Weren't they actually disenfranchised?" Urosevich said, "Yes, sir." Consequently, the state banned four counties from using electronic voting machines and ordered ten others to improve security before the November 2004 election.[22]

Electronic voting companies have never explained their resistance to creating a paper trail, something that would be simple enough to do by attaching printer technology to the existing machines. In fact, an ideal system might provide two printouts—one that is double-checked for accuracy by the voter and saved by election officials and a second that the voter could keep as a record or receipt. The need to track these e-votes puts voters in a tough position: they either have to trust a deeply flawed and partisan system or find ways of independently corroborating their votes. This is a huge barrier to trust in the system and political participation. No matter what happens in 2004, reform advocates must demand that all e-voting have a paper trail in future elections.

4. The Red and the Blue: A Divided America

One legacy of the 2000 election is a system of new voting machines that could be even more dangerous to democracy than the old ones. Another is a national political deadlock—the Red States vs. the Blue States.

During the 2000 election, as results trickled in from across the country, networks showed Republican-won states as red and Democratic-won states as blue. The map filled up in a clear pattern, with coastal and Great Lakes states in the Blue camp and the central and southern states falling in the Red camp. George W. Bush won a higher number of states, but Al Gore won populous states with a high value in the electoral college, the somewhat mysterious system which ultimately determines the presidency. It all came down to Florida, a state with one of the most interesting demographic mixes in the country.

Parts of Florida are highly urban, and parts are extremely rural. Parts are mainly white, mainly black, or mainly Latino. Some sections have a high youth population; others have a concentration of senior citizens. But the most important factor in determining the virtual electoral deadlock in Florida is money. Out of all the states in America, Florida comes the closest to giving the same amount of money to the federal government as it gets back.

Why does that matter? The best way to tell a Red state from a Blue state is not its location in the country but how much federal tax residents pay versus how much they get back from the federal government. People in the Red states tend to believe in smaller government; people in the Blue states tend to support (prudent) government spending. You would think, then, that Red Staters are pissed because they pay more than their share of taxes to the federal government. In fact, the exact opposite is true. Blue Staters pay more taxes to the federal government than their states get back in return. As one person on the conservative Free Republic website put it, decrying the Blue States, "We have those who work vs lazy slobs. We have morality vs immorality. Representative republic vs tyrantical [sic] communism." Given that the Red Staters are sucking up federal dollars, who exactly is immoral?[1]

Rural farm subsidies and pork barrel public work projects give the Red States a distinct fiscal advantage. But the myth that the Blue States are "takers" and the Red States are "givers" is one of the most pernicious and persistent in politics. By playing the "taker" card, conservative politicians have been able to cut back on popular programs including preschoolers' Head Start. The programs that serve Red Staters are rarely subjected to such scrutiny. The Blue States either have a bad political strategy or extremely bad P.R.

Or perhaps it's that the Blue Staters are perceived as "other," and the Red Staters are perceived as "we." Blue States are more urban and have a higher concentration of immigrants and people of color. Red States tend to be more rural, more white, and less first-generation immigrant. The fight over Red and Blue states, in this sense, is not just about taxes or ideology. It's about who is perceived as a "real" American.

A 2004 O'Leary/Zogby poll on American values described the Red and Blue State divide this way: "the Blue States have fewer Republicans, 55-69 year olds (the most conservative age cohort), rural dwellers, conservatives, Born-Again Christians, daily or weekly attendees at a place of worship, local sports fans, gun owners, investors, military veterans, and married voters. All of these differences portend a harder sell for Republican candidates. On the other hand, the Red States have fewer younger voters, single voters, college graduates, liberals, Catholics and Jews, union members, and non-prayers. In short, the two regions think and vote differently because they are different."[2]

By focusing on factors like religion, the Zogby report reinforces the electorate's split over social conservatism (for example, being against legalized abortion) versus social liberalism (for example, being for the hot button social issue of 2004, same-sex marriage). But "conservatism" and "liberalism" are complicated and often fuzzy labels in American politics. Social conservatives can be fiscal liberals—for example, Midwestern union members who support labor protection but decry abortion rights. Social liberals can be fiscal conservatives—for example, suburban "office park dads" who support gun control and also support tax cuts. The Red and Blue divide is not just a case of conservatism versus liberalism. It's also a study in how, over the past forty years, many voters have chosen politicians based on social issues rather than their economic interests. This has helped produce an increasingly bitter partisan politics. A 2004 study by the Pew Research Center for the People and the Press found that "Republicans and Democrats have become more intense in their political beliefs."[3] Adherents of the two parties are split on issues ranging from military/security policy to abortion, differences that have often deepened in the past four to ten years.

The map of Republican and Democratic states used to be very different, and showed how Americans voted based on economic issues. Before the New Deal, the Blue States were generally southern; the Red States, northern. But as the New Deal began attracting poor, working-class, immigrant and black voters to the Democratic Party, it dominated both North and South. Then, as the battle over civil rights heated up, more white Southerners turned to the Republican Party, favoring their conservative social values over their fiscally liberal, working-class economic interests. The South hasn't been prime territory for Democrats since. Carter and Clinton, both Democratic Southerners, were able to take more of that region by highlighting economic themes. But Gore, also a Southerner, did not fare well. Thus today's Blue/Red divide is largely a coastal/southern-central split.[4]

Today's political landscape is the result of a forty-year movement by social and fiscal conservatives to claim political power and reshape intellectual debate. One of the main funders of this movement is billionaire Richard Mellon Scaife, who gave $2.3 million to the *American Spectator* magazine to find any scandalous material possible on President Bill Clinton. In total, Scaife and his family's charities have given over $300 million to conservative media, think-tanks, and organizations.[5] And it's paid off. Fiscal conservatives have wooed the strong voting bloc of social conservatives, particularly evangelical Christians, in order to win elections—even though fiscal and social conservatives don't necessarily have that much in common. As (fiscal) conservative strategist Grover Norquist, head of Americans for Tax Reform, gloated in a 2001 interview, "I don't want to abolish government. I simply want to reduce it to the size where I can drag it into the bathroom and drown it in the bathtub."[6] Remember, however, that the Red States gain more from government than the Blue States. To the extent that the Democrats can reclaim an advantage in national politics, they will have to point out that Red Staters have as much or more to gain from reforming the federal government's faulty economic policies than Blue Staters. In other words, Democratic success relies on uniting fiscal liberals and social liberals, who may have divergent views and alliances, in the way that conservatives have united their fiscal and social believers.

Or to put it bluntly, a smart politician would say, "Screw (social) liberal and conservative labels. Those of you who support abortion rights may never agree with people who don't. But both of you have common economic interests, and neither of you are being served by government today. I'm going to change that. I'm speaking to you as a populist, someone who can deliver real healthcare and education and jobs growth and make sure that work in America pays." Of course, the politician—Democrat, Republican or third-party— would have to mean it, or risk alienating voters further.

The only recent presidential candidate who's come close to being a real populist is Chris Rock, playing a D.C. alderman-turned-unlikely-candidate in the 2003 comedy *Head of State*. The candidate's big speech comes as he ignores his handlers' advice and decides to speak truth to power to a Chicago crowd:

> How many of you workin' two jobs just to be broke? Let me hear you say "That ain't right!" . . . How many schools have old books but they have brand new metal detectors? Now, that ain't right! . . . How many of you workin' in cities you can't afford to live in? Cleaning up hotels you can't afford to stay in? We got nurses working in hospitals they can't afford to be sick in. . . . That ain't RIGHT![7]

The fact that it's laughable that a politician could run on a populist platform . . . well, that ain't right.

Sure, the ideological differences between Americans make true populism a risky proposition, but I'd wager that the prospect of losing big corporate political contributions inspires just as much fear. America needs enterprising politicians who are willing to acknowledge the ideological differences dividing America, but not give in to them; people who put serving citizens ahead of serving campaign contributors. These politicians could unite unlikely political constituencies, and reach many of the hundred million missing voters.

Partisan Nation, Dirty Politics

Many Americans don't trust the government because they don't feel they can change it. Three-quarters of Americans believe politicians quickly lose

touch with their constituents, and only 40 percent believe that "most elected officials care what people like me think."[8] The number of Americans who
identify as Republican has been rising; the number who identify as
Democrats, dropping. You would think that the Democrats would see dis-
satisfaction with the political system as an opportunity to reach new voters.
But the structural nature of politics—how expensive it is and how hard it is
to run a campaign—plus a healthy dollop of fear seem to prevent the
Democrats from making bold moves.

In fact, even though America is increasingly divided along partisan lines,
there isn't as much competition between Democrats and Republicans as
you'd think. Our system tends to concentrate power in the hands of those
who already have it: incumbents. *Spoiling for a Fight* author Micah Sifry points
out that 99 percent of U.S. House of Representatives incumbents won re-
election in 1998, and 98 percent won in 2000. Many ran without any
major-party opposition, and most incumbents handily beat their opponents
at fundraising. States Sifry:

> How has our country achieved such stunning stability? Are
> Americans so happy with politics as usual? Or is something
> else at work? Only rarely, as in the state of Louisiana, where
> the top eight Democratic and Republican officeholders
> recently made a public pact to not campaign against each
> other, do the two parties let voters in on their dirty little secret.
> The truth is, the major two parties don't like competition, and
> they'll do many things, even avoid attacking each other's turf,
> to keep themselves comfortable and unchallenged.[9]

In other words, instead of us having much choice about whether or not we
re-elect politicians, they often have virtual jobs-for-life. (After all, Strom
Thurmond was re-elected even when he was so decrepit and disoriented that
he couldn't cast a vote without help.) One of the United States' biggest crit-
icisms of the Soviet Union was that a one-party state couldn't serve the needs
of its people. Well, folks, in some ways, much of America has become a one-
party state.

On the other hand, when the two parties really decide to rumble, it's like
Godzilla versus Mothra—many, many people get trampled during an indis-

criminate show of force. The nastiness, duplicity, and disregard for the needs of citizens further endanger Americans' faith in our political system. Take, for example, the tortured birth of the controversial Homeland Security Act and the corporate reform Sarbanes-Oxley bill. Through deft political maneuvering, Republicans were able to divert attention from scandals over 9/11 and corporate corruption, screw Democratic candidates, and threaten the job protections of ordinary working Americans—all in one fell swoop.

Shortly after the terrorist attacks of September 11, 2001, Senator Joseph Lieberman proposed a Homeland Security Agency to coordinate the antiterrorist work of several government agencies.[10] Some critics worried that creating a new agency of this type could compromise individual privacy rights. But the president, who might have been expected to support the bill, actually opposed it.[11]

Flash forward to the summer of 2002. FBI Special Agent Coleen M. Rowley went public with shattering allegations. Did her agency ignore leads that could have helped prevent the terrorist attacks of September 11? Her memo to the FBI director read in part:

> I feel at this point that I have to put my concerns in writing concerning the important topic of the FBI's response to evidence of terrorist activity in the United States prior to September 11th. . . . I have deep concerns that a delicate and subtle shading/skewing of facts by you and others at the highest levels of FBI management has occurred and is occurring. . . .

At the heart of Rowley's memo is the case of Zacarias Moussaoui. The French citizen of Moroccan descent was arrested a month before the attacks on an immigration violation. He'd been training to fly planes—but not land them—at a Minnesota flight school, and concerned instructors contacted the FBI. French officials had a long record on Moussaoui, who had trained with al Qaeda in Afghanistan.

Local FBI agents wanted to search Moussaoui's computer, but top brass denied the request. In Rowley's words:

> [T]he agents in Minneapolis who were closest to the action and in the best position to gauge the situation locally, did fully appreciate the terrorist risk/danger posed by Moussaoui and his possible co-conspirators even prior to September 11th. . . . .[T]he FBI Supervisory Special Agent (SSA) who was the one most involved in the Moussaoui matter . . . seemed to have been consistently, almost deliberately thwarting the Minneapolis FBI agents' efforts.

Then, to add insult to injury, after 9/11 Rowley watched the FBI's director, Robert Mueller, defend the agency's handling of events. States Rowley:

> In the day or two following September 11th, you, Director Mueller, made the statement to the effect that if the FBI had only had any advance warning of the attacks, we (meaning the FBI), may have been able to take some action to prevent the tragedy. . . . I and others in the Minneapolis Office, immediately sought to reach your office . . . so that your public statements could be accordingly modified. When such statements from you and other FBI officials continued, we thought that somehow you had not received the message and we made further efforts. Finally when similar comments were made weeks later . . . we faced the sad realization that the remarks indicated someone, possibly with your approval, had decided to circle the wagons at FBIHQ in an apparent effort to protect the FBI from embarrassment and the relevant FBI officials from scrutiny.[12]

At considerable risk to her own career, Rowley ensured that the FBI *would* be scrutinized. Rowley pointed out that the agents at FBI headquarters who missed the chance to track Moussaui were never reprimanded for their inaction and stayed on in key positions after September 11. *Time* magazine made this a cover story, and it was front-page news across the nation.

In June, Rowley was scheduled to testify in front of a Senate panel. The very same day, the Bush administration announced their support for the Homeland Security Act. Some in the media even called it the president's plan.[13] The administration timed the announcement to shift the focus from Rowley's testimony on 9/11 to the president's support for Homeland Security. And it worked: newspapers made Rowley coverage a secondary story, and some television networks interrupted Rowley's testimony to go to the Homeland Security Department announcement.[14] (Of course, in spring 2004, the incredible revelations of the 9/11 Commission put the Bush administration in the hot seat again.)

The tactic worked; for the moment, 9/11 was last week's news. But the Republicans didn't stop there. The two parties had one major difference in the homeland security bill: labor laws. The Republican version of the bill removed civil service protections from employees moving from other federal agencies to the Homeland Security Department, a move widely interpreted as union busting. "It was completely gratuitous," says law professor Peter P. Swire of Ohio State University. "If the central challenge was homeland security, then getting it passed and into operation was the priority. Changing a century's worth of civil service laws was a choice that Bush and [presidential strategist Karl] Rove made. Compared to the overall importance of responding to terrorism, you think this would be a third-tier issue. But Rove made it a first tier issue."

In the weeks leading up to Congress's August recess, Senator Lieberman tried to compromise with the Republicans. They wouldn't. In order to preserve labor laws, Democrats repeatedly voted against a version of the bill that would have removed civil service protections from workers.

Meanwhile, another hot piece of legislation, the Sarbanes-Oxley bill on corporate reform, was also facing passage. The impetus: the failed multibillion dollar energy company Enron. When Enron went bankrupt, so did thousands of employees. Executives including Bush's friend Ken Lay, however, were able to sell millions of dollars in stock before it crashed. Enron gave $1.4 million to the president's 2000 campaign. In turn, Bush rewarded the company by fighting proposed California price controls. (Remember California's energy crisis?) Enron also participated in a secret meeting with Vice President Dick Cheney to help craft the administration's energy policy. The fight to require the release of notes from that meeting went to the Supreme Court, who referred it back to a lower court.

Republicans steadfastly opposed the Sarbanes-Oxley bill. Then, on June 25, telecommunications company and Bush donor WorldCom discovered "improper accounting" of $3.8 billion and planned to cut 17,000 jobs. In testimony before a congressional committee, the former CEO, Bernard Ebbers, said he had done nothing wrong. (In 2004, Ebbers was indicted on fraud and conspiracy charges. His deputy agreed to testify against him. And WorldCom's total fraud has now reached an astonishing $11 billion, enough to pay each of the 17,000 laid-off workers a tidy sum of nearly $650,000 apiece.)[15]

WorldCom put the fear into Republicans who intended to defend corporations from stricter regulation. So, presto, the Republicans gave the Democrats nearly everything they wanted on Sarbanes-Oxley. It passed before Congress's August recess. But the Homeland Security bill, with its anti-labor provisions, still was up for debate. Congressmen and senators went back to their home districts with Homeland Security undecided.

So what became the big issue in the November 2002 midterm elections? The refusal of Democrats to support the Homeland Security Act, which they had in fact sponsored. "It's clear that the Republicans didn't want to settle that issue in July when they could have," says Swire. "They wanted an issue for the election. And they also decided they didn't want corporate reform debated in the fall."

During the 2002 midterm elections, in a tight race, Republican challenger Saxby Chambliss ran an astounding advertisement against his opponent, Georgia senator Max Cleland. Cleland was a first-term senator who had lost an arm and both legs in Vietnam. He was also a co-author of the Homeland Security Act. Chambliss, on the other hand, used the excuse of a trick knee to keep from going to Vietnam.

One Chambliss television advertisement pictured Osama bin Laden, Saddam Hussein, and Max Cleland. "As America faces terrorists and extremist dictators, Max Cleland runs television ads claiming he has the courage to lead. He says he supports President Bush at every opportunity, but that's not the truth. Since July, Max Cleland voted against President Bush's vital homeland security efforts eleven times!"

Cleland lost his re-election bid. Even prominent Republicans, including Senator John McCain, decried the advertisement. But voters still rewarded Chambliss for his mixture of lies and false patriotism. If Americans won't hold a politician accountable for an advertisement this manipulative, then what will we hold our officials accountable for? The Republicans' success in turning the Homeland Security Act into a weapon against Democrats shows just how nasty and dishonest politics has become. It is no surprise that so many Americans are utterly turned off.

The Democrats' Chances in 2004

The presidential election is a series of winner-take-all statewide contests. To win in 2004, the Democrats will either have to capture southern and central swing voters who can tip Red States into Blue States, or entice new voters to the polls. (Both would be nice.) Democratic pollster Mark Penn found that only 31 percent of Americans identified as Democrats, down from 49 percent in 1958. (Only 30 percent of Americans identify as Republicans, but Republicans vote at higher rates than Democrats.) "Exciting the Democratic base alone will not bring enough voters into the Democratic fold," said Penn. He recommended going after "office park dads," the more fiscally conservative husbands of suburban "soccer moms."[16] But the Republican-lite themes that appeal to "office park dads" probably won't attract many nonvoters, many of whom are struggling economically. Democrats may have to make a tough choice: become more like Republicans to capture swing voters, or take a risk and become more populist to attract new voters and nonvoters.

What would it mean for the Democrats to return to the populist politics they espoused during the New Deal and Great Society eras? For one, they would have to convince working- and middle-class Americans, not just poor ones, that economic reform will benefit them. You don't have to be poor to struggle economically. You just need to be in a position where your financial needs overwhelm your ability to meet them, and that includes much of the working, middle, and even upper middle classes. The Democrats have traditionally been the party of choice for working-class voters, but recently that support has eroded. Many voters, including young working-class voters without strong partisan affiliations, see Democrats as the party of financial losers and Republicans as the party of financial winners. As author David Brooks put it in an op-ed for the *New York Times*:

> Why don't people vote their own self-interest? Every few years the
> Republicans propose a tax cut, and every few years the Democrats
> pull out their income distribution charts to show how much of

the benefits of the Republican plan go to the richest 1 percent of Americans or thereabouts. And yet every few years a Republican plan wends its way through the legislative process and, with some trims and amendments, passes. . . .

People vote their aspirations.

The most telling polling result from the 2000 election was from a Time magazine survey that asked people if they are in the top 1 percent of earners. Nineteen percent of Americans say they are in the richest 1 percent and a further 20 percent expect to be someday. So right away you have 39 percent of Americans who thought that when Mr. Gore savaged a plan that favored the top 1 percent, he was taking a direct shot at them.[17]

True. Give people a choice between feeling like they have futures and feeling like they're failures, and they'll pick the future any time. And it's no use telling people that they're stupid, that their dreams of hitting the earnings lottery are unrealistic. We're talking about the American Dream here. Hope springs eternal.

The fact is most Americans will never hit the 1 percent jackpot. But the Democrats haven't figured out how to break the news to us. Instead they, like the Republicans, play to our get-rich-quick hopes in order to win votes.

There is an alternative: building a bridge between the interests of middle- and upper-middle-class Americans and those of poor and working-class Americans. Because the fact of the matter is, those groups of Americans have more in common with each other than they do with the (largely Republican) One Percent. They share a sense of anxiety about the country's future and how they'll earn a living. They also share common interests on many political issues.

One example is Social Security, implemented in 1935. Middle- and upper-middle-class Americans rely on Social Security to help fund their retirement. (You better believe that rich folks cash their checks, too!) Today, without Social Security benefits, nearly half of American seniors would live in poverty.[18] Nonetheless, in February 2004, Federal Reserve Chairman Alan Greenspan suggested cutting Social Security benefits, but keeping the Bush administration's tax cuts for the rich.

Middle- and upper-middle-class Americans also share a need for real education reform. Because school funds are linked to property taxes, poor Americans tend to attend the nation's worst schools. But middle- and upper-middle-class Americans are increasingly overextending their budgets to try to live in wealthier school districts. In *The Two-Income Trap: Why Middle-Class Mothers & Fathers Are Going Broke*, Elizabeth Warren and Amelia Warren Tyagi paint a picture of middle-class families stretched to the financial breaking point. Why? Many of them get the most expensive mortgages that they can, ones that they can't afford if one of two working parents loses a job or takes a pay cut. They do it for the sake of their kids' educations, but they're taking a terrible risk. Four times as many families are declaring bankruptcy today as they did twenty-five years ago. Parents with young children are the most likely to go bankrupt, and 90 percent of Americans in bankruptcy are middle class.

With real education reform, these families could live in neighborhoods they can afford without putting their children's education at risk. Instead, cued by our consumer culture, they try to individually buy their way out of the problem rather than advocating for systemic change. But for the families depicted in *The Two-Income Trap*, it's just not working.

The lesson of *The Two-Income Trap* applies to issues ranging from healthcare to national defense. When I moderated the second Democratic Presidential Debate in Baltimore in September 2003, I asked a variety of people if they had questions for the candidates. I couldn't ask every question I received, but the suggested issues included:

> Being self-employed, I pay my entire health insurance premium out of my own pocket—and my premiums have doubled in the last three years. If this continues, I will be unable to afford health insurance at all by the end of the decade. How do you propose to make health care affordable for those of us who are not insured through employers?
>
> —From a freelance writer in San Francisco

> I work in a teaching hospital here in Oregon. We serve the poorest and the people who are either entirely uninsured or insured by the welfare medical insurance plan put in place by the state. I just received word that one hundred of my cowork-

ers will be laid off in six weeks. A company based in Germany
will take over their positions, and will now be answering the
complicated medical insurance problems of Oregon's poor
with the aid of its software and telephone support staff. The
support staff is itself outsourced by this German company to
India. . . . It saves the companies money in healthcare, salaries,
and benefits, but it also means that they put hundreds of workers out of jobs here, in favor of near slave-labor from third
world nations. How do you plan to address this issue?

—A healthcare professional in Oregon•

Both of the last two OB-GYN practices I used have closed
because their malpractice insurance premiums more than doubled in the last year. Hospitals in Pennsylvania and Arizona have
discontinued their obstetrics services, making women have to
travel many miles to give birth. And many doctors in Florida are
considering avoiding services with high legal risks (such as mam-
mogram reading), according to the Tampa Tribune. New York,
PA, AZ, Delaware, Mississippi, Nevada, New Jersey, North
Carolina, Ohio, Oregon, South Carolina, Texas, Washington
and West Virginia have been among the hardest hit states. In a
recent Harris Interactive poll, 76% of the 300 physicians sur-
veyed felt that concern about malpractice suits was hurting their
ability to provide quality care, and 94% felt that extra tests, refer-
rals and procedures resulting from their fear of liability contributed in a significant way to health care costs. How will you
deal with this?

—A writer and mother in New York

Nearly 44 million Americans, or 15 percent of the population, don't have
health insurance. During the economic downturn of George W. Bush's presidency, millions lost their insurance because they lost their jobs. At the same
time, many state Medicaid programs are so squeezed by cuts that they are dropping adults from their coverage. The biggest new group of uninsured in 2003
was among households earning $25,000 to $49,999 a year. Next came households earning $75,000 or more. Seventy-five thousand dollars is four times

the federal poverty level for a family of four.[19] In other words, the healthcare crisis among the middle- and upper-middle-class is rapidly approaching that of the poor.

National defense is seen as a Republican issue. President Bush calls himself the "war president." But who gets hit the hardest when we go to war? Today, wealthy, powerful men commission the war America fights, but the members of the military come from poor, working-class, and middle-class backgrounds. Even in the military, they get nickeled and dimed, just like so many American workers. In 2003, the Bush administration tried to cut the "imminent danger" pay for the men and women fighting in Iraq and cut spending on veterans' hospitals. It refused to buy Kevlar body armor for 40,000 active-duty troops in Iraq. And in its absolute cheapest move, it began to charge injured GIs eight dollars a day for food while they were in a Georgia military hospital. (They stopped after protests.)[20]

Upper-middle-class and wealthy Americans are less likely to serve. But the $87-billion-and-counting war in Iraq is also decimating the funds available for education, healthcare, Social Security, and jobs. Both directly and indirectly, middle-class issues are tied to national security. If this country can't make better decisions about when to use our military, neither our soldiers nor U.S. civilians will be safe.

The Democrats need to run on this not-so-radical idea: what's good for poor and working-class Americans is good for the middle- and upper-middle-class too. What's touted as good for wealthy Americans—in particular, tax cuts—will not solve most of the problems facing America's middle class. By building a bridge between the issues of the poor and working class, and those of the middle and upper middle class, Democrats will be able to bring more nonvoters to the polls.

In our current two-party system, however, middle-class voters are the bird in the hand, and poor and working-class voters are the two in the bush. In order to win over poor and working-class nonvoters, politicians will have to demonstrate that they mean business when it comes to economic reform: in other words, that they can be trusted to follow through on campaign promises. But few politicians, Democratic or Republican, want to risk the bird in the hand. They may not do so until the advocates for lower-voting populations organize themselves and demand representation.

5. Pop and Politics

Risks. They're what anyone seeking to get new voters to the polls will have to take. The old methods of mobilizing voters aren't working anymore, especially for younger Americans.

In his book *Bowling Alone: The Collapse and Revival of American Community*, Harvard professor Robert D. Putnam charts the decline of "social capital," the invisible bonds between Americans. In the past twenty-five years, Americans have become 33 percent less likely to have dinner as a family, 45 percent less likely to have friends over, and 58 percent less likely to attend club meetings. We are at least 25 percent less likely to attend church. And, yes, we are a quarter less likely to vote. For economic and lifestyle reasons, more of us end up uprooting our lives and moving to different communities. In fact, 20 percent of Americans move *every* year. "For the first two-thirds of the twentieth century a powerful tide bore Americans into ever deeper engagement in the life of their communities," writes Putnam, "but a few decades ago—silently, without warning—that tide reversed and we were overtaken by a treacherous rip current. Without at first noticing, we have been pulled apart from one another and from our communities over the last third of the century."[1]

If that's the case (and there's plenty of evidence to support Putnam's theory) then what *does* hold Americans together? In our media-saturated society, pop culture has become a powerful link between us. We may not live in the same neighborhoods or have the same creed, color, or income, but virtually all Americans consume television and other media. More Americans have televisions than telephones.[2] Television celebrities are treated like American royalty (witness the insane amount of media coverage of the last season of *Friends*). And "reality television," in which not-so-average Americans get a shot at the big time, is a national obsession. In fact, Americans watch an average of four to five hours of television a day, even more for people of color and low-income families.[3] We also spend an average of two hours a day listening to the radio and an hour and a half each day online. All of this media consumption creates a web of cultural connections. It gives us a sense of who we are, who our peers are, and who we wish we could be. For example, my friends and I, some of the now thirtysomething members of "Generation X," tried to act and dress like the musicians we saw on shows like *Friday Night Videos* and early MTV.

MTV also spawned the popular Choose or Lose political series and has supported the nonprofit Rock the Vote. (Rock the Vote helped push though the Motor Voter registration act.) And other youth-oriented media outlets have dabbled or dived into politics as well, from *Vibe*, *Spin*, and *Rolling Stone* to in-school television network Channel One.

More recently, comedy shows have jumped on the political bandwagon. Leno, Letterman, Conan, and *Saturday Night Live* all regularly do political material. *The Daily Show with Jon Stewart* has made a franchise out of it. In one bit, Stewart had President George W. Bush debate "the one man we believe has the insight and the *cojones* to stand up to him . . . Texas governor and Presidential candidate, George W. Bush." Stewart proceeded to pair clips from Bush's presidency with clips from his campaign. For example:

> **Jon Stewart:** Mr. President, let me just get specific. Why are we in Iraq?
>
> **President Bush:** Well, umm . . . we will be changing the regime of Iraq . . . for the good of the Iraqi people.
>
> **Stewart:** Governor, then I'd like to hear your response on that.
>
> **Governor Bush:** If we're an arrogant nation, then they'll resent us. I think one way for us to end up being viewed as the Ugly American is to go around the world saying, "We do it this way, so should you."
>
> **Stewart:** Well, that's an excellent point. I don't think you can argue with that! Mr. President, so is the idea to just build a new country that we like better?

> **President Bush:** We will tear down the apparatus of ter-
> ror, and we will help build a new Iraq that is prosperous
> and free.

> **Governor Bush:** I don't think our troops ought to be
> used for what's called "nation building."

Programs like the *Daily Show* aren't just amusement to their viewers. A poll by the Pew Research Center for the People and the Press found that 21 percent of eight-een to twenty-nine-year-olds turned to comedy shows for political information. Only 23 percent turned to the network news. (That's down from 39 percent four years ago.)[4]

And then there's the link between celebrity and political organizing. Celebrities not only endorse a bevy of different charities, many of them took very public stands on the war in Iraq. Bruce Willis supported the war and offered a million-dollar reward for Saddam Hussein's capture, while the *West Wing*'s Martin Sheen, who plays the president of the United States, spoke at antiwar rallies. The wildly successful online activism portal MoveOn.org lever-aged the power of celebrity to launch Bush in 30 Seconds, a contest to get their audience to film thirty-second advertisements critiquing the president. Howard Stern declared that any guests on his show—yes, even the parade of chesty strippers—have to be registered to vote. And stars including Madonna and Sean "P. Diddy" Combs have made ads and headlined rallies encouraging young people to vote. (Of course, at the time neither was registered.)

All of the celebrity glitz and glitter cannot mask what most young Americans believe about politics: in addition to being mean-spirited and corrupt, it's dry and boring. If you happen to catch a session of Congress on CSPAN, you'll see a bunch of men, most of them white, and a smattering of women, all dressed like corporate executives. They seem to spend as much time debating obscure procedural points as focusing on the issues. Political junkies like me may be willing to put up with this tedium, but most people would probably rather get a root canal. Adding celebrities to the mix will definitely get young Americans' attention. But will they ultimately bring new voters to the polls? A new movement of hip hop–generation activists is try-ing to prove that they can—and that they can swing elections in the process.

Hip Hop Generation Activism

On a gray, rainy day in June 2003, several thousand young people gathered near New York's city hall. Onstage: rappers Sean "P. Diddy" Combs, Fat Joe, dead prez, and 50 Cent; singer Mariah Carey; actors Susan Sarandon and Tim Robbins; politicians Mark Green, Andrew Cuomo, and Alan Hevesi; and music impresarios Damon Dash and Russell Simmons, the latter of whom organized the event. The cause: repealing the Rockefeller Drug Laws, draconian statutes that paved the way for federal mandatory minimum sentences.

The rally was not only a case of strange bedfellows but a turning point in politics. Since the early days of hip hop, grassroots activists have used the music and culture to reach young people. Now, music icons are trying to help lead a voter-mobilization movement aimed at the hip hop generation. For example, the Rockefeller Drug Law event was co-sponsored by Russell Simmons's Hip-Hop Summit Action Network (HSAN), which announced a goal of registering 2 million new voters in 2004.

Hip hop politics tends to mix flash and substance. The most heartfelt speaker at the Rockefeller Drug Law event was not a celebrity but a mother of four, Elaine Bartlett, who was sentenced to twenty years to life for her first and only time transporting cocaine. "I spent sixteen years in jail, and I don't know a single [drug] kingpin," said Bartlett at the rally. (Bartlett has become a national symbol of the failed drug war. In March 2004, journalist Jennifer Gonnerman's book on Bartlett and the prison system, *Life on the Outside: The Prison Odyssey of Elaine Bartlett*, made the cover of the *New York Times Book Review*.) Still, most young people at the rally probably showed up to see 50 Cent, not Elaine Bartlett.

Other hip hop generation organizations have used the celebrity/activist formula as well. The Malcolm X Grassroots Movement hosts an annual Black August concert in New York for human rights and political prisoners. In 2003, artists including Erykah Badu, Talib Kweli, and dead prez performed. And author Kevin Powell, a celebrity in his own right, joined with cultural entrepreneur April Silver to host a series of community forums, Hip Hop Speaks!

What is Hip Hop, Anyway?

To some of us, hip hop is like air: so pervasive it's invisible. To others it's utterly foreign. At one political conference, I met an eighty-year-old white teacher who volunteered in prisons. He knew that his students listened to hip hop, but he didn't really know what it was and certainly didn't listen to it. As a thirty-four-year-old African-American, I can remember when hip hop didn't exist—just barely. By the time I was in second grade, the hot, sticky Baltimore summers pulsed with the new sounds of songs like "Planet Rock" and "Rapper's Delight." Adventurous, showy, and more than a little goofy, early hip hop turned the music world on its ear. Like many people my age, I can name a hip hop artist for every stage of my life, from the roller-rink jams by the Sugarhill Gang in elementary school through the crushworthy LL Cool J in junior high; from black power groups like Public Enemy in college to Tupac's ghetto philosophizing in my early working years. And like many others of my generation, I've been disappointed that hip hop's commercial success seems to have eclipsed its politics and sense of history.

Hip hop isn't just the pop rap we hear on the radio today. When I explain hip hop to people who don't know it (or even like it), I point out the artform's four elements: graffiti art, MCing (rapping), DJing (turntablism), and breakdancing. Hip hop began in New York City, a fusion of Jamaican-style "toasting" (or MCing) with urban American music, lyrical themes, and rhythms. Graffiti: think the colorful subway cars in New York in the '70s and '80s, and the graffiti mural art of today. Breakdancing or b-boying now influences everything from popular dance to Broadway musicals. And even though today's flash and glamour may eclipse content, hip hop has always been political. Given that it sprang from the creativity and disfranchisement of urban black and Latino youth, how could it not be? Or as Public Enemy frontman Chuck D put it, hip hop is "the black CNN."[5]

Hip hop is a multibillion dollar industry, a global phenomenon, a street-corner pastime, a cry for action, and one of the great inventions of the twentieth century. As rapper and actor Mos Def puts it in his song "Hip Hop":

> We went from picking cotton
> To chain gang line chopping
> To Be-Bopping
> To Hip-Hopping . . .

> Hip Hop will simply amaze you
> Craze you, pay you
> Do whatever you say do
> But, Black, it can't save you[6]

Well, it's saved—or at least enriched—some people. The rap and hip hop industry has produced a new cadre of multimillionaires, including Russell Simmons. It has taken a place alongside basketball as the ultimate ghetto-aspirational career. It has been both unfairly and fairly blamed for violence ranging from the post–Rodney King violence in Los Angeles to the deaths of Tupac Shakur and Biggie Smalls. Rap has spawned a new genre of bitch/ho lyrics and produced female megastars including Missy Elliott and Queen Latifah. It has gone from underground phenomenon to black pop culture to a multiracial and even global cultural juggernaut.

But is it a movement?

Yes, argues Bakari Kitwana, author of the seminal *Hip Hop Generation: Young Blacks and the Crisis of African American Culture* and one of the organizers of the June 2004 National Hip Hop Political Convention. (The convention occurred after this book was completed.) Kitwana sees hip hop activists as the rightful heirs of civil rights generation leadership. Civil rights leaders have "been fighting and they deserve to see something that builds on their work," he says. "This is the opportunity to see their dreams fulfilled." To Kitwana, the emerging hip hop political movement takes several forms:

1. Grassroots activism by groups including the Malcolm X Grassroots Movement, the Center for Young Women's Development, LISTEN, the Ella Baker Center for Human Rights, and the 21st Century Leadership Movement

2. An electoral politics component, including political action committees, think tanks, and hip hop generation politicians Kwame Kilpatrick (mayor of Detroit), Ras Baraka (Newark, New Jersey, deputy mayor), and Congressman Jesse Jackson, Jr. of Illinois.

3. A student activist movement of hip hop clubs that host campus lectures and forums.

4. The spoken word and underground hip hop movement.

"Hip hop, having been promoted with our collective image as a generation, has to give something back," says Kitwana. "The most effective way is to move hip hop into the arena of politics. The questions: who's the power broker and what's the agenda?"

Russell Simmons and his Hip-Hop Summit Action Network are indisputably the best-known and best-financed of the power brokers. Simmons founded the group in 2001 to help mediate the rap culture wars. It moved into voter registration in 2003. Simmons is a big personality in the vein of Donald Trump, with flash, dazzle, and ostentatious displays of wealth. (The show *MTV Cribs* toured his palatial home, which includes a separate bathroom in his wife's walk-in closet.) In a cover story, *Business Week* named Simmons "The CEO of Hip Hop."

Simmons's story parallels the rise of hip hop from urban artistry to international phenomenon. The forty-six-year-old has earned his millions several times over. Simmons started Def Jam Records in the early 1980s with rock promoter Rick Rubin. Their star act was none other than rappers Run-DMC, led by Simmons's younger brother Joey (Run). In 1985, Sony began to distribute Def Jam records, bringing them a much wider audience.

Simmons and Rubin sold Def Jam to Universal Music in 1999 for at least $100 million. Then Simmons launched a fashion label, Phat Farm, and a women's wear line, Baby Phat, run by his twenty-seven-year-old wife, former model Kimora Lee Simmons. In early 2004, Simmons sold Phat Fashions for $140 million. Now he's fielding the Def Comedy Jam series; Def Poetry Jam, which won a Tony award in 2003; an energy drink; and even a credit card. And finally there's that small matter of trying to overturn the Rockefeller Drug Laws and register 2 million voters.

In other words, Simmons is the man who branded hip hop. But can he sell politics to the hip hop generation?

"Hip hop has always been political," says Simmons. "People have to realize that not voting is voting." He also believes that musicians are the best messengers. The HSAN has begun hosting a series of forums across the country—

Houston, New York, Chicago—all of them featuring major artists and aiming for large crowds. It does voter registration through the summits and collects contact information—two-ways, cell phones, pagers, email—so that it can encourage newly registered youth to vote. "I am trying to reach everyone who is connected to hip hop," Simmons says, pointing out that people from their forties down through their teens identify with the music. "The real rainbow coalition is now. We got Asians, Latinos, and compassionate and poor whites who have been separated systematically. Eminem sponsored our hip hop conference in New York. There are hundreds of thousands of people in Detroit who look like him and think like us."

Simmons doesn't shy away from associating with controversial artists like Eminem or 50 Cent. He also went to bat for Ludacris, who was dropped by Pepsi after an outcry about the rapper's lyrics. Pepsi then agreed to a $3 million settlement that benefited groups like the HSAN. Some critics say that defending Ludacris's lyrics, rather than focusing on issues like violence and racism, is the wrong use of time and money. Simmons says that the controversy was a chance for young people to "win something."

The HSAN's political director, Yale-educated political scientist, professor, and writer Alexis McGill, acknowledges that bringing controversial stars to bat for voting is "a contradiction," but argues that the summit creates a space for conversation where contradictions can be reconciled. McGill calls the rise of hip hop activism "a perfect storm": a result of the botched election in Florida, the failure of the Bush administration to connect with young urban voters, the economy, and young Americans' desire "to be a part of a movement." She adds, "Russell probably would have just done summits, but people kept asking for more." Thus the HSAN is attempting to evolve into a true membership-based organization, a hub which connects with local organizers at the grassroots and major media partners to disseminate its message. "If we turn out a million people every Tuesday to buy a record," she says, "we can turn out twenty million on election day."

Simmons's organization is willing to do some unusual coalition building. Its voter registration efforts are a partnership with World Wrestling Entertainment, formerly the World Wrestling Federation. As the HSAN puts it in a press release, "If war, terrorism, and a recession aren't enough to persuade the under-30 crowd to vote, maybe hip-hop stars and wrestlers can do it."[7]

But some long-term activists are skeptical that star-power alone will bring young people to the polls. "Power brokers need to be people who didn't become activists yesterday," says Kitwana. "There needs to be collaboration between grassroots activists and members of the hip hop community." The National Hip Hop Political Convention aims to bring together delegates from across the nation, each of whom pledges to register at least fifty voters in their home districts. These delegates will construct a political platform and press politicians to deliver on it. Unlike the Hip-Hop Summit Action Network, whose leader is indisputably Simmons, the convention has a wider array of co-organizers. Convention organizer Baye Wilson believes that "One reason young people have turned off to electoral politics is that the issues do not resonate. This will bring up the issues that are most important to them: education, criminal justice, economic development."

How can hip hop connect citizens with the political process? On a very basic level, hip hop generation activists will have to turn a cultural affiliation into a political affiliation. Instead of "hip hop" equating to the kind of jeans you wear, the attitude you cop, or even the rhymes you spit, it will have to mean a way of thinking about the world and interacting with—and claiming—power. One of the most potent aspects of hip hop is its effortless shorthand, its way of transmitting a whole range of cultural signifiers at once. But hip hop's political platform is not as crisp or well-defined as its aesthetics. Given cynicism about politics and the lack of civic education in schools, many young Americans have only a rudimentary understanding of how the government works. Some don't want anything to do with politics. Nor do most members of the hip hop generation know how to band together as a voting bloc and leverage their collective power. Wilson and the other organizers of the convention hope to change that.

Instead of reaching citizens directly, the convention will focus on bringing together activist-leaders who are already invested in their communities, particularly in key battleground states. "Five hundred people could come out and go back and organize in five hundred communities. That would be phenomenal," says Wilson. "Or we could have thirty-thousand people come and just see artists and that would be disappointing." He hopes to model the convention on the 1972 National Black Political Convention. Thousands of African-Americans, ranging from Julian Bond to Barbara Jordan to Minister Louis Farrakhan, gathered in Gary, Indiana, to set a political agenda for the black community. They announced goals ranging from a national healthcare system to home rule for the District of Columbia. And although most of those goals have not yet been met, the Gary convention provided a launching pad for the election of black officials.

Most hip hop generation activists, including the convention's organizers, are African-American. But they see their constituency as multiracial, even global. "With hip hop you have in some ways Martin Luther King's idea of cross-cultural engagement. [And] if we're effective with hip hop as a multi-cultural movement, older white people will be less afraid," says Kitwana, whose latest book is *Why White Kids Love Hip Hop*. "On a real fundamental level I believe hip hop is the voice of oppressed people," says April Silver, president of the lecture agency Akila Worksongs and co-founder of the Hip Hop Speaks! series. "And being oppressed is a universal craziness. It's not just here in New York City or the United States. The universality of hip hop is the fight for freedom and self-expression."

But, to return to the central question, does that make a movement? A movement has to have clear, well-defined goals that are broad enough to inspire large groups of people but not vague. They also have to have institutional infrastructure, like membership organizations.

"I don't see a cohesive movement," says Yvonne Bynoe, the president of Urban Think Tank and the author of *Stand & Deliver: Political Activism, Leadership, and Hip Hop Culture*. "Some people say there are too many issues on the table, we're never going to have that [cohesive movement like the civil rights movement] again. Other people say we possibly do need something along the lines of an NAACP or SCLC for our generation. I would advocate a national structure with autonomous local entities."

One organization attempting precisely that strategy is the League of Independent Voters, a progressive political mobilization project targeting the young and disaffected. The League, which has a partner voter-education organization, the League of Young Voters, hosts small brunches that bring politics into a comfortable space. These brunches and other events are publicized online. "Our online network is a Friendster or Tribe type network," says co-founder Adrienne Maree Brown, referring to "six-degrees-of separation" web networks that link like-minded people. Online networking became a hallmark of former Vermont governor Howard Dean's campaign for president, as well as the activism of MoveOn.org.

The league is printing progressive voter guides and has published a book, *How to Get Stupid White Men Out of Office*. "We're focused on 2004 but also on the long term," says Brown. "We have a fifty-year plan. Next year, our organizing will pull people together from across the country and [get] them to organize in blocs instead of being alone."

Independent Voters, High Stakes

The league's choice of the word "independent" is strategic. Younger voters of all races are more likely to see themselves as independents than older voters. A study of fifteen- to twenty-five-year-olds commissioned by the Center for Democracy and Citizenship found that a quarter of youth considered themselves independent, and fifteen percent do not know what party they identify with.[8] These independents come from all races:

Latino youth:
31% Democrat, 25% independent, 24% Republican, 21% don't know

Black youth:
43% Democrat, 23% independent, 16% Republican, 19% don't know

White youth:
30% Democrat, 25% independent, 31% Republican, 14% don't know

But "independent" is not the same as "swing voter." In a two-party system, many registered "independents" reject both major parties.

David Bositis of the Joint Center for Political and Economic Studies finds the voting patterns of young independents "troubling," and says it's a particular dilemma for communities of color. The African-American population is significantly younger than the white population, with a median age of thirty versus thirty-nine for whites. The Latino population is even younger, with a median age of twenty-six.[9] The more young voters in a population, the more "independent" voters there are. The more "independent" voters, the less likely they are to be mobilized to vote. "Voter registration is not the issue," says Bositis. "The issue is getting people to vote. . . . What has happened in the past in terms of the hip hop generation is that they've just not voted at all."

And what *will* motivate the hip hop generation to vote? Personality, says Bositis. "Clinton was a personality who attracted the hip hop generation and younger African-Americans generally," he states. "The right personality is not going to be one of the current [2004] crop of presidential candidates. It's going to be somebody who has a rapport and a connection and members of the hip hop generation say, 'Hey, this person is cool.'" Bositis believes that entertainment personalities and other public figures can motivate young voters, but they have to spark real interest. Traditional civil-rights issues and organizations don't necessarily resonate with the hip hop generation. "People like [President Lyndon B.] Johnson and Martin Luther King are as far in the past for this generation as George Washington," he says.

So is a popular entertainment figure like Simmons the right person to lead the hip hop political movement? "The goals of a Russell Simmons are going to be hugely different from the goals of someone who is not a multi-millionaire. That's just real," says Akila Worksongs' Silver. "Russell has done a great job of using his power and influence towards educating people. But he's also working to protect his empire." For Silver, the issue is how well people work together. "Are people in their corners doing different things? Yeah—and that's not always bad," she says. What hurts is infighting. "There's enough oppression for all of us" to fight, Silver says.

But before hip hop–generation activists can fight oppression, they have to battle internal misogyny. Silver, as a prominent female entrepreneur who started hosting hip hop forums when she was a student at Howard University, has seen enough to last her a lifetime. "I've been confronted by sexism," she says. "It's a huge challenge. Here I am a strong advocate for a culture that hates women. I have continued to be the advocate I have because I believe there is something more powerful in hip hop than the sexism. And I don't let men get away with dumb shit."

Other activists point out that the misogyny in hip hop has deep roots. Jeff Johnson, former youth director for the NAACP and CEO of Speaking Truth to Power, says misogyny has been learned from older generations, even from the church. "There are some places where woman still cannot be in the pulpit," he says. "Hip hop is the child of that generation's culture." Concludes National Hip Hop Convention organizer James Bernard, who helped found seminal hip hop magazines *XXL* and the *Source*, "We have to take hip hop back."

Many organizers believe that taking hip hop back from misogynist rappers and exploitative corporations has to go hand-in-hand with developing a viable political culture. "I remember a time when there wasn't a hip hop," says Bernard, who is also an adept fundraiser for the new movement. "People I'm speaking to now, they don't remember that. They don't remember a time when the music used to be more diverse and well-rounded."

In fact, much commercial hip hop these days is uninspired if not outright destructive. Rapper Busta Rhymes made a hit of a de facto liquor commercial with "Pass the Courvoisier." Eminem, the first white rapper with street cred, was embraced by the mainstream media in ways that equally controversial black rappers never were. The original (hardcore) version of his breakthrough song "My Name Is" contains lyrics about "raping lesbians, while they screamin' at me: 'Let's just be friends!'" And in his hit song "P.I.M.P.," rapper 50 Cent rhymes:

> I'm bout my money you see, girl you can holla at me
> If you fucking with me, I'm a P-I-M-P
> Not what you see on TV, no Cadillac, no greasy
> Head full of hair, bitch I'm a P-I-M-P[10]

Of course, many of these songs are accompanied by the obligatory soft porn–style video shoot, full of gyrating black female asses and preening men. "When hip hop became pop music, it became lowest-common-denominator," says Bernard. "Any artist who didn't sell three million records was a failure. . . . [But hip hop is still] very vibrant, very grassroots as a culture. It's important for us to define for ourselves what this culture means to us." Despite the way that so much mainstream rap has sold the generation's experiences for false gold, the hip hop soundtrack is a parallel to lived experiences. Or as Dilated Peoples rhymes: "My lyrics take care of me/they therapy/get shit off my chest."[11]

If hip hop generation activists have a say in the matter, the artform and the politics will grow and flourish together. But how much can hip hop generation activism succeed if the two major parties are resistant to new voices and voters?

6. The Future of Political Parties

A group of Americans is fed up with the government. The country is in a depression; they are suffering economically. Neither the Democrats nor the Republicans are addressing their issues. They join together with like minds to form a political party. That political party wins congressional seats, governorships, and the majority in several state legislatures. Emboldened by that win, they plan to run a candidate for the White House.

A fantasy? No. This was the Populist movement of the late nineteenth century. What they accomplished—and why they disappeared—shapes America's political landscape to this day.

Just as we have forgotten how recently many Americans didn't have the right to vote, we treat our two-party system as if it's the way things have always been and should always be. But in the late 1800s, third parties flourished. Then they were targeted for extinction. How and why is a fascinating tale of the way political parties grab and hold power. Or as political consultant Bill Hillsman puts it in his book *Run the Other Way: Fixing the Two-Party System, One Campaign at a Time*:

> As much as I love Aaron Sorkin's televised portrayal of politics, *The West Wing*, it presents an unrealistic, idealized picture of our government. The reality is much closer to *The Sopranos*—escapades in raw ambition, with professional political hit men operating in the shadows and out of the public's view to maintain a vise-like grip on political power and to eliminate any threats to the two political parties' profitable business territories.[1]

Hillsman should know. He advised campaigns for mavericks ranging from Democratic Senator Paul Wellstone of Minnesota to the politically independent wrestler-turned-governor Jesse Ventura, also of Minnesota, to Ralph Nader, Green Party candidate in 2000. Each of these candidates, including the late Wellstone, whose political positions were more progressive than his party's leadership, faced uphill battles as a direct result of the consolidation of power by the Democrats and Republicans.

Of Hillsman's star candidates, only one lost his bid for office: Ralph Nader. Nader is one of the most reviled figures in current politics. Many people (including me) believe he let his ego trump common sense when he decided to run for the presidency again in 2004. In 2000, he ran on the ticket of an established third party, and many people voted for him in an effort to get federal matching funds for the Greens. (The Green Party would have had to win 5 percent of the vote to get federal funds; they only won 3 percent of the vote.) This time around, it's impossible to argue (as Nader did and does) that there's little difference between George W. Bush and his Democratic opponent. And Nader is running as an independent *sans* party, meaning that even on the implausible chance that he wins 5 percent, it will not further the third-party cause.

But I'm getting ahead of myself. Candidacies like Nader's demonstrate that Americans want alternatives to the two major parties. A quarter of Americans say they have voted for an independent or third-party political candidate in at least one election.[2] In fact, in the past quarter of a century, a series of independent and third party presidential candidates have gotten a significant number of votes.

It's 1980. President Jimmy Carter is running against California governor Ronald Reagan. Reagan, a fiscal and social conservative, beats out ten-term congressman John Anderson of Illinois for the Republican nomination. So Anderson, a moderate with a trademark shock of white hair, decides to run as the nominee of the National Unity Movement. At one point, 20 percent of voters support Anderson, but he gets shut out of the debates. Reagan wins by a landslide over Carter, who's been buffeted by a bad economy and the Iran hostage crisis. Anderson ultimately wins 6.6 percent of the popular vote, but carries no states and wins no electoral votes.

In 1992, billionaire Ross Perot runs as an independent with the backing of his United We Stand America organization. His competitors: President George Bush and Arkansas governor Bill Clinton. Perot gets to speak at the debates. He doesn't win any electoral votes, but he gets a whopping 18.9 percent of the popular vote. (Perot also runs a less successful campaign in 1996 with the Reform Party, which later splinters into warring factions.) Clinton wins his first term in office.

Then, in 2000, consumer advocate Ralph Nader runs on the Green Party ticket. His opponents: Vice President Al Gore and Texas governor George W. Bush, plus Reform Party candidate Patrick Buchanan. Nader doesn't get into the debates. He receives 2.7 percent of the vote nationwide, not enough to qualify the Greens for federal matching funds. Gore wins the popular vote, and Bush takes the White House. Many analysts blame Nader for kiboshing Gore's chances.

Now, in 2004, President George W. Bush will face not only the Democratic nominee (at the time of this book's completion, Massachusetts senator John Kerry) but Ralph Nader again, this time running as an independent.

The question: will America's nonvoters care about any of these candidates?

David Bositis of the Joint Center for Political and Economic Studies pointed to politicians' personalities as a huge factor in getting people to the polls. None of the 2004 candidates seems likely to make nonvoters watch the debates instead of reality TV. So, scratch that: what *else* will get nonvoters to the polls? Two factors stand out: whether parties and politicians actively court them, and whether voters have a long-term view of political participation. In order to get more from government, people have to vote just to prove they exist. Then politicians will court them, and finally—hopefully— they will be better served. This equation relies on voters advocating for themselves and not waiting around for the parties to take notice. Instead, citizens have to serve notice on political parties that are ignoring them, something that's beginning to happen.

Take one of the big political "givens": the loyalty of African-Americans to the Democratic Party. In an August 2003 front page story, the *New York Times* explored the rocky relationship between younger African-Americans and the Democrats. The article cited Sylvester Smith, a twenty-seven-year-old African-American. He's a registered Democrat and also a policy advisor to Arkansas's Republican governor. "I have a Frederick Douglass philosophy," said Smith. "I believe African-Americans have no permanent friends and no permanent enemies, only permanent interests."[3] The Republican Party has largely chalked African-American voters up as a lost cause. (For example, when Jeb Bush first ran for governor of Florida, a reporter asked what he would do for African-Americans. He said, "Probably nothing.") Even politically independent African-Americans aren't voting Republican—

yet. But many are thinking about it. "This is a crossroads for African-Americans in the Democratic Party," says strategist Donna Brazile.

Advocates are trying to teach new voters to work the system. Take a groundbreaking 2000 outreach effort by a group called the Democracy Compact. Founder Matt Brown, now Rhode Island secretary of state, told young nonvoters that politicians would not represent them until they became a proven voting bloc. But the Democracy Compact didn't try to talk to nonvoters directly: they used peer-to-peer communication. The nonpartisan organization recruited young "Democracy Captains" and trained them to explain why each vote counts. Each captain pledged to recruit twenty nonvoters and make sure they went to the polls. In the 2000 election, 55,000 new voters turned out in Rhode Island, and youth turnout rose by 41 percent.[4] Now the Democracy Compact has become a national organization, Vote for America.

Even the best of these efforts can't overcome one factor: potential voters who loathe their choice of candidates. Many nonvoters, especially young ones, are looking for politicians that they don't have to compromise to support, people who speak their language and reflect their needs. Getting the two parties to fight over their vote is a start. Giving them a chance to vote for viable third parties as well could truly transform the political landscape.

More than a Two-Party Democracy?

America is one of the few democracies across the world with a winner-take-all two-party system. Most Western-style governments, including Germany, Spain, Japan, Israel, and Australia, use proportional representation. Instead of each race resulting in one winner from one party, major and minor parties get seats in the legislative body (like our House and Senate) in proportion to the number of votes they get. The chief executive is usually the leader of the party with the most votes, and in many nations, two parties can form a coalition government. Germany currently has a coalition government composed of the Social-Democratic Party of Germany (center-left) and the Greens.

The American system tends to make third-party votes seem like a waste of time or "spoilers." Author Micah Sifry describes America's democracy as a duopoly:

> A duopoly is defined as a market with just two sellers. Picture a beach with just two ice cream stands selling essentially similar products. While the vendors may start out anywhere, eventually they will locate right next to each other in the middle of the beach where they will each be closest to half the bathers. In such a setting, as long as they can lock out any other competition, they can jointly act to raise their prices, lower the quality of their ice cream, even take a vacation at the same time. As long as this is the only beach to swim at, the bathers will be stuck. (If, however, more ice cream trucks break in, this produces a wide scattering of positions.)[5]

In other words, in cases where politicians have no serious opposition, they don't provide real alternatives. This erodes public trust and depresses voting.

Things weren't always this way. In the elections of 1876, 1888, and 1896, nearly 80 percent of eligible voters went to the polls. The Democrats and Republicans worked hard to reach voters, and series of third parties reached out to new constituencies. These third parties tended to focus on the needs of farmers, who were being squeezed by low crop prices and high transportation prices by the railroads. An increasing number went bankrupt and became sharecroppers. Spurred by outrage, these farmers formed a series of political clubs called Alliances. The Alliances then became the People's or Populist Party. They wanted to branch out from serving only farmers to dealing with the labor concerns of urban workers. In 1890, the Populists won Senate and Congressional seats, three governorships, and the majority of seven state legislatures.

In 1896 the Populists joined with Democrats to support William Jennings Bryan. (The two parties actually ran two tickets with separate vice presidential candidates.) Frances Fox Piven and Richard A. Cloward write: "The Democratic-Populist challenge was alarming, even horrifying—and to wealthy Democrats as well as Republicans. Accordingly, corporate interests mobilized and poured unprecedented sums into Republican coffers for the McKinley campaign. . . ."[6] Bryan lost decisively to William McKinley and his big money donors, and the Populists were absorbed by the Democrats.

Before 1896, the two major parties battled each other in many states. After 1896, Democrats tended to control the South and Republicans the

North, making a two-party system into a virtual one-party system favoring incumbents. Voting reforms weakened the ability of parties to reach poor and working-class voters, and states instituted requirements like literacy tests. Both the Democrats and the Republicans became more conservative. As a result of all these factors, between 1896 and 1920 voter turnout declined from 79 to 49 percent.[7]

Why didn't another third party emerge to replace the Populists and make the two major parties work harder for votes? States felt so threatened by the Populists that they actually changed the laws to make third-party voting more politically risky.

The Populists were able to win so many seats in part because they used a strategy of "fusion." In fusion, two or more parties (usually a third party and a major party) nominate the same candidate for office. Voters then have the choice of voting for a major party candidate, but registering their overall support for the platform and goals of a third party. Politicians can track how many of their votes came from third-party voters, and they know these voters will hold them accountable for their positions. Or as Elizabeth A. Hodges writes in *Z Magazine*, "If Candidate Johnson wins an election by ten percent, and ten percent of her votes came from people voting on the minor party's line, Candidate Johnson must be accountable to the minor party to win re-election."[8] In some ways, fusion parties also act like a "Good Housekeeping Seal of Approval." Voters who trust their minor party's leadership will trust a major-party candidate who's endorsed.

Now the bad news. Between 1896 and the 1920s, all but ten states blocked the ability of parties to run candidates in conjunction with each other. This meant that more and more often, a third-party vote was just a protest vote. These protests have included strong conservative movements as well as liberal ones. During the civil rights era, two segregationist candidates carried a significant number of presidential votes. In 1948, Strom Thurmond ran on the States' Rights ticket and got 2.4 percent of the vote nationally, reaching double-digits in parts of the South. And in 1968, George Wallace ran as the candidate of the American Independent Party and got 13.5 percent of the vote.

Then, in 1996, a third party named the New Party filed an objection to Minnesota's anti-fusion law. (They wanted to run a Democratic candidate as one of their nominees.) The New Party won in state court. Minnesota's election officials appealed to the Supreme Court. Well-known Harvard Law professor Lawrence Tribe was counsel for the New Party. But by a 6-3 decision, the Supreme Court ruled that the state law blocking fusion parties could stand.[9]

In 1998, however, the New Party helped to found the Working Families Party (WFP) of New York, one of the states that permits fusion. Currently, the WFP is running a major campaign to raise the state's minimum wage from $5.15 an hour to $7.10 per hour. A bill has already passed the State Assembly, and is awaiting passage from the State Senate.

The Working Families party attracts voters from liberal New York City neighborhoods like Park Slope, Brooklyn, as well as citizens from working-class upstate towns. The WFP's Bill Lipton describes their voter outreach as "sitting on a three-legged stool"

> First, we have a really good track record of turning out occasional voter and nonvoters, especially in local elections. We do a lot of targeted voter registration.
>
> Second, we go after working-class union voters—Reagan Democrat types. In Suffolk County, Congressman Tim Bishop [who ran as a Democrat/Working Families Party candidate], beat Felix Grucci [who ran on the Republican, Independence, Conservative, and Right to Life lines]. Grucci was the only Republican incumbent to lose in country. . . .
>
> Third, [we attract] progressive [and normally Democratic] voters. We basically get forty percent of the vote in Park Slope and the Upper West Side.

In all, about 15 percent of the votes cast in New York are on the Working Families' line. In general, the party endorses major-party candidates, usually but not always Democrats. But this year, a Working Families' candidate, Letitia James, won a city council seat against a Democrat.

Fusion does not guarantee high voter turnout. Of the ten states that still permit fusion, half have above-average voter turnout; half have below-average turnout, including New York. But fusion does seem to provide the leverage needed to push through ground-breaking legislation. In New

York, for example, several Republicans are sponsoring the move to raise the minimum wage.

Even in states that don't have fusion, third parties are finding ways to reach new voters. In San Francisco's 2003 mayoral runoff, for example, a Green Party candidate, Matt Gonzales, narrowly lost to Democrat Gavin Newsom. Third parties have made their biggest strides in local races and small community positions. In the 2000 elections, writes Sifry,

> Greens won thirty-two races, swelling their presence in local politics to eighty officeholders spread over twenty-one states. Several Progressive Party state legislators were returned to office in Vermont, while their gubernatorial candidate drew a respectable 10 percent of the vote and participated in all the statewide debates. In Minnesota, Jesse Ventura's Independence Party showed that it had legs, with nearly two dozen candidates for the state legislature getting respectable chunks of the vote, and one congressional contender reaching 20 percent in a three-way race. The New Party continued to rack up its victories in a half-dozen cities, while a newly created effort based on its model, the Working Families Party of New York, emerged as a fresh force in state politics.[10]

The WFP is hoping to expand to more states, including Connecticut, Massachusetts, and New Jersey. In some cases, the party hopes to change anti-fusion laws through ballot initiatives or in the legislature. Either process will require time, money, and energy.

Third parties have generally failed to attract large numbers of voters of color, including the emerging hip hop generation political movement. The broad cohort of hip hop generation voters is looking for real representation. The third party movement is looking for new constituents and fresh ideas. Will these two movements connect?

Yes, say urban third party advocates, who are beginning to reach out to new constituencies like working-class African-Americans. In April 2004, a group of African-Americans hosted a forum called "Why We Joined the Green Party" in an Oakland church hall. The room was filled not just with

African-Americans but local citizens of all races, some of them party members and activists, others distinctly skeptical.

Three party advocates, Donna Warren, Henry Clark, and Wilson Riles, told listeners why they'd joined the Greens. "I'm talking to my Black brothers and sisters. Go back to your communities and tell them the infrastructure is already in place if we want to have a voice," said Warren, a former Green Party candidate for California's Lieutenant Governor. "Join the Green Party. They will not do what the Democrats do to Black people. They [Democrats] want our votes but not our voice."

The other two speakers echoed similar themes: a sense of frustration with the major parties and a sense that they could make real changes through a third party. Henry Clark, long-time environmental activist with the West County Toxics Coalition in Richmond, California, tries to hold local oil refineries accountable for pollution. Appearing in a pinstriped suit with a red tie and matching pocket square, he looked like a mainstream politician himself—but spoke passionately about winning a spot on North Richmond's governing party as a Green. The Republicans and Democrats didn't hold the refineries accountable, he claimed. Third party activists did.

Clark also didn't hesitate to criticize the Bush administration. "Bush talks about building schools and hospitals in Iraq and Afghanistan," he said. "Well, [the local hospital] is scheduled to close on July 31. Schools are being cut back. And I'm supposed to be happy about them building schools in Iraq and Afghanistan? Charity begins at home."

The third speaker, Wilson Riles, had a long track record of working with the Democrats, first as an aide to Congressman Ron Dellums and the Alameda County Board of Supervisors, and then as an Oakland City Council member. As a mayoral candidate, he even challenged Oakland mayor Jerry Brown in a runoff. But recently, Riles joined the Green Party. "One of the hallmarks of insanity is doing the same thing and expecting a different outcome," he told the crowd. "Hopefully I'm not insane any more. I've joined the Green Party," he said to laughs and claps. He spoke forcefully about the times African-American voices have been muted by the Democratic Party, as when Rev. Jesse Jackson brought new voters of all races to the fold with his presidential race but wasn't given a voice in the party.

All three of the candidates tried to convince the audience that the Green Party's platform jibed with African-American interests. The Greens are the only party to support reparations for slavery, they said. The Greens favor education, not incarceration. And Riles spoke about changing California laws that have undermined public financing for schools and services, like Proposition 13. He favors reforming the law so that corporations, whose share of the tax burden has shrunk, pay their share.

You'd think that reform of the criminal justice system would be an easy win for the Green Party with African-Americans. But this produced the biggest controversy of the night. During the question and answer period, a coiffed and poised woman raised her hand. LaDonna Williams said that she and her six children had "been through it, homelessness, you name it." She believed in instilling in her children a strong sense of discipline—and disagreed with the idea of eliminating California's "three strikes" law, which gives long sentences to anyone who commits three felonies. Oakland's seen more than its share of addiction and drug-related crime, especially related to crack cocaine. Even though Williams agreed that the sentences are unfair, she was afraid that reducing the "three strikes" penalties would remove a deterrent to drug use and crime. "I tell my kids they are accountable for their actions," she emphasized.

The Green Party's Warren replied that she understood drugs: her thirty-one-year-old son, a crack addict, had been murdered. "I want people to be accountable," Warren said, "but accountable to the truth. What keeps people away from drugs? Good schools, jobs, having an opportunity to succeed in this society. There's no options in our community," she said. Then she added, "I held my child accountable, but he got addicted to crack cocaine, and he's dead."

Riles emphasized that even if "three strikes" were eliminated or reformed, people would still go to jail for their crimes. Then Warren pointed out some of the excess of the system. For example, over four thousand Californians got sentences as high as twenty-five-to-life for petty theft or, in another case, taking a motor vehicle test for someone else. "The state pays $30,000 per year per prisoner. That's coming out of your schools." But LaDonna Williams wasn't convinced. "I have to go with that tough love," she said, shaking her head. "Something has to be in that place to deter them, whether it's an ass-whupping" or the three-strikes law.

Finally another person in the audience stepped in. The tall young man had a tousled afro and a quiet but authoritative voice. "There isn't going to be a strategy for sentencing youth that prevents crime," he said. "We're focused on jail and that has never worked in America. If you look at the rest of the world, you see they know that." Instead, the government should focus on preventing crime by providing educational and job opportunities.

His name was Andrew Williams, and he told me he'd joined the Green Party right before the 2000 election, as he turned eighteen years old. "Bush was, well, Bush, and I wasn't feeling Gore," he said. Williams wanted to join a party he believed in, and he chose the Greens. Voting third-party doesn't run in his family. He laughed when I asked if his parents had prompted his choice. "No," he said, "I fight with my family about politics all the time."

I followed up with LaDonna Williams and Andrew Williams (no relation) after the meeting. They're both black. They're both savvy and politically aware. And they each have very different takes on what American politics means to them.

For LaDonna Williams, deciding to vote in the 2004 election was not an easy choice. As a Jehovah's Witness, LaDonna's faith advocates against voting. "The answer to our problems lies with God," she says. And when God decides, "we're going to see world peace." "But until then, you have to live life." For LaDonna, given the current political situation, that means choosing to vote. She is particularly troubled by America under the Bush administration. "I think President Bush is doing such a horrendous job," she says. "He just outright lies and the people support it. And going to war. . . . You want to protect our freedom of speech and the rights we have, but does that mean we violate everyone else's rights?"

"We talk about the weapons of mass destruction," LaDonna continues. "If you look over in Livermore [a nuclear weapons research facility in California], they've stored this radioactive stuff and they're trying to expand it more so they can build more bombs. We're the ones having the weapons of mass destruction here. It's so hypocritical."

LaDonna's politics are socially conservative and fiscally liberal. She wants a politics that reflects "family values," secures the finances of working Americans, has a strong and fair criminal justice program, and delivers educational opportunity. She's hammered the importance of education home to her children, who range in age from twenty-five to just four. When her twenty-two-year-old was recruited to play baseball out of high school, she urged him to go to college. He's still hoping to play pro ball, but he's also finishing up a degree in environmental engineering.

So why did she show up at a Green Party meeting? "I'm not pleased with the Democratic Party," LaDonna says. "They really went out of their way to hush up Al Sharpton. With the debates, they really attempted to hush him up and Carol Moseley Braun. I think that was very disrespectful. If the Democratic Party is going to take it to the next level, they need to put a black person on a presidential or vice presidential position." But she doesn't believe just anyone should get the slot. She's holding out for a black leader with strong morals and good ideas. In the meantime, she likes Kerry, "more than [she liked] Dean, and definitely more than Bush." She still hasn't decided who she'll vote for in 2004, but it probably won't be a Green Party candidate; she wasn't impressed with the answers she got on criminal justice at the community forum.

Andrew Williams, on the other hand, is committed to the Green Party as a vehicle for political change. It's just one part of his larger view of how to make change happen. When I reached him by telephone, he was in the middle of a "Stop Clear Channel" hip hop tour with musicians from an organization he founded, the Collectiv (www.collectiv.com). The Oakland-based organization aims to connect like-minded musicians and activists, empowering the hip hop community through education and entrepreneurship. Their campaign against the entertainment industry giant, which owns over twelve hundred radio stations plus music venues and television stations, centers on the way they've cut out local radio programming, blocked independent music promoters, and even retaliated against top-selling bands by not playing their songs when the bands did promotions with other stations.[11] Clear Channel has made news as part of the ongoing debate over the Federal Communications Commission and media ownership rules. And for organizations like Andrew's, focusing on the politics of music is a great way to get young voters engaged.

At the age of twenty-two, Andrew already has a finely tuned political sensibility and a willingness to commit his own time and energy for social change. The urban politics major at San Francisco State can expound on everything from pacifism versus revolution to Latin American politics. Being well-read and -reasoned, Andrew is struck by contradictions not only in national politics, but his own politics. He believes in voting but doesn't

(given the 2000 election) believe that every vote counts. He is going to conduct a voter registration drive, but he admits he may not be that successful at
convincing people to vote. "I have a hard time arguing with my friends when
they say, dude, [voting's] a joke."

Yet Andrew is committed to voting as a way to "say your piece" and get a
piece of the political action. He compares the way politicians target voters to
the way advertisers and corporations target consumers. Companies spend a
lot of money convincing people who already buy products to switch their
brand loyalty. Politicians spend a lot of money convincing people who
already vote to vote for them. As Andrew says bluntly, "If you didn't vote last
time, [politicians] don't give a fuck what you want."

Andrew votes Green because he sees both major parties as beholden to
the same corporate interests. "There will always be a minority that have a
vested interest and try to protect that interest," he says, "And there's always
going to be a majority that fight against that interest." The problem is that
that majority is fragmented, including many of the Americans who don't
vote. For the record, Andrew is convinced that "most Democrats are Greens
waiting for the Green Party to get to the point where they can make that
decision [i.e., vote Green] and not make it feel reckless." He believes that by
voting for a third party now, he paves the way for more Americans to take
them seriously. "God willing," he says, "I'm going to be living through a lot
of elections. I don't want to make a decision [with my vote] that won't make
long-term change." Still, he understands the position of older members of
his family, who see a critical need to vote Democratic now, to, for example,
ensure a more progressive Supreme Court. The most important thing is to
make a choice on election day. "If nobody voted, it would be terrible," he
says. "The cats who are doing what they're doing would be able to say, see,
you wanted it that way. I need to say my piece. I need to be able to say fuck
that: that's not what I wanted."

LaDonna Williams and Andrew Williams reflect both the opportunities
and hurdles for third parties wanting to reach new constituencies. LaDonna
Williams is reflective of the social conservatism of many working-class
African-Americans, which doesn't mesh easily with some more liberal third-
party politics. That she showed up to a community forum like this one is a
heartening reminder that Americans are still looking for new ways to participate in our democracy. Andrew Williams highlights the changing face of

politics and the possibility that the growing hip hop generation activist movement and the third-party movement could join forces. All across America, individuals like LaDonna Williams and Andrew Williams are exercising raw will, transforming the nation's calcified political system into something that serves them and their communities better. If more people took a similar hands-on attitude towards politics, the question would not be whether our system will change for the better, but how soon.

Selected Essays

Campaigns, Voting, and
Down and Dirty Politics

George W. Bush, One-Term President

January 29, 2003

GWB is going down. History books will mark both Bush presidencies as one-term tenures marked by war in the Middle East and crushing financial instability. There's the hard evidence: his poll numbers have been sinking (just like employment figures) and corner men like Gen. Norman Schwarzkopf are saying we need more proof if we even *think* about going into Iraq.

But for me the "Oh, damn, he's toast" moment came during a phone call with a long time friend and former roommate. Elaine is a total *Sex and the City*–style fashion plate who would rather read *Lucky* than *Week in Review*. She's also a recovering Young Republican. But she called me frothing about Bush's plan to give special tax breaks to people who buy SUVs. "I've got to volunteer for the Democrats," she sputtered. "Tell me what to do!!"

I lifted the phone from my ear. *Who had replaced my power-shopping friend with a political activist?* I thought. If Bush has pissed off the silent majority, people who are more comfortable voting nightly with their remotes than during elections, he is really in deep doo doo. Alas, the Democrats have all the charisma of cartoon chump Dudley Do-Right, but there's nobody else on Capitol Hill to cut us from the tracks as the war train rushes in.

In his State of the Union address, President Bush laced his hard-right policy agenda with a couple of compassionate conservatisms, like a modest plan for AIDS relief in Africa. Of course this is the same administration that cut international family planning and condom distribution. The president took Americans' silent grief over 9/11 as a policy mandate. But there is no mandate for war, or tax cuts for the rich, or ending abortion or most other Bush-era initiatives. Voters in the center are waking up and realizing they've been had.

What do I mean by "had"? Let me break out one example—the link between the drumbeat for war and oil profiteering.

Vice President Dick Cheney received a $34 million severance package from Halliburton, the company he headed between Bush regimes. During his time at Halliburton, Cheney brokered $73 million in oil equipment contracts through subsidiaries with Iraq. Yes, that Iraq, the one he fought for

Bush *pére* and the one he's angling to fight again. Sounds like a protection racket to me. *I know we blew you guys up a little bit, but, y'know, we can fix it. For a price.*

A war in Iraq will open an incredible oil and natural gas supply, 30 percent of the world's total, to Western companies. And President Bush has made himself into the foremost advocate for American oil interests. He ran a failing oil company called Arbusto (Bush in Spanish) but through family connections parlayed it into stock in a larger company and eventually a sweetheart investment in the Texas Rangers.

As a governor he proposed tax protection for oil producers and got $50 million in campaign donations from oil and energy companies during the 2000 race. In addition to the buildup around Iraq, the government has recently expanded our involvement in the civil war in Colombia in order to protect a pipeline for Occidental Petroleum.

In the words of Secretary of State Colin Powell, "We thought a $98 million investment in Colombian brigades to help protect this pipeline is a wise one and a prudent one." And in the words of columnist Ariana Huffington, "Oxy will never give taxpayers free gas in exchange for our pipeline protection subsidy. Instead, we'll pay for it three times over: on tax day, at the gas pump, and, finally, when the flag-draped coffins start being shipped home."

And here's the doozy my friend got worked up about. The new Bush tax cut proposal would give business owners who buy huge-ass SUVs a 50 percent increase in an already generous deduction. It means people who don't need them will be financially stupid if they don't buy them.

For example, someone who bought a fully loaded Hummer (perfect for your local florist shop!) could deduct $87,000. By contrast, if the same business bought a car, the owner could only deduct $7,660 in the first year. In his State of the Union speech, the president proposed "$1.2 billion in research funding so that America can lead the world in developing clean, hydrogen-powered automobiles." Hydrogen engines will end our dependence on foreign oil, but only if the government stops rewarding people for buying gas guzzlers first.

The prospect of body bags for oil will alienate swing voters. So will the administration's looming battle against affirmative action, which may erode their attempts to reach Latino voters, and what the *New York Times* describes as a war on women—not just against abortion, but also family planning, condoms, and sex education. Then there's that pesky problem of the economy: we can't blame 9/11 forever, and we certainly aren't going to solve the problems facing working- and middle-class families by giving tax cuts to the rich.

Bush eked out a victory by convincing just enough women, Americans of color, and working families that he was on their side. But his attempts to appease his religious right and corporate donors are so blatant, it'll be impossible for him to play the same aw-shucks, just-folks role next time around.

Aw, shucks. Bye bye.

Dreaming a New America: Peaceful Regime Change in 2004

March 20, 2003

Our dreams are the North Star by which we navigate. In hard times, they should get bigger rather than smaller. I think of the first enslaved Africans in America standing on auction blocks, someone's dirty thumb checking their teeth as if they were horses. They dreamed of freedom, and passed that dream to children and children's children until some modicum of freedom was achieved.

Today we face another freedom struggle. It's time to retake, and remake, American democracy.

There are no inalienable rights and no self-evident truths. We live in a time when our government erodes civil rights daily, not just those of black and brown Americans, immigrant or poor Americans, but all Americans. We live with relentless Orwellian doublespeak. President Bush argued that the war on Iraq would promote "liberty and peace." A classified State Department report said it would increase Middle Eastern anti-Americanism, and that certainly seems to be the case.

All of this is being done in the name of patriotism. But in the words of Benjamin Franklin, one of the few Founding Fathers who owned slaves but freed them, "They that can give up essential liberty to obtain a little temporary safety deserve neither liberty nor safety." Instead of feeling comforted by America's military posturing, many of us feel neither safe nor free.

The financial costs of the government's actions are staggering. The 1991 Gulf War cost $61 billion. The recent invasion of Iraq will likely cost $100 billion. That just buys the military campaign, not the peacekeeping and "nation-building," which will cost just as much or more. Meanwhile, we are embroiled in a series of wars at home that could make America a shell of itself.

Take the War on Education. In January, the Republican-led Senate passed a spending bill that cut $29 million from after-school programs, $13 million from programs for abused children, and $61 million from child care programs. To put this in context, a single Tomahawk cruise missile can cost up to a million dollars.

The lack of federal support for schools is having deep ramifications. A veteran Oakland, Calif., schoolteacher wrote me: "The district sent out letters to 1,000 teachers as notice of possible layoffs, San Francisco sent out almost 800. California is a disaster and George wants to go to war."

It's not just California. Portland, Oregon, has had to shorten its school year by five weeks because of a budget shortfall. The state of Oklahoma cut education funds by over $100 million in 2001–2002, leading to thousands of staff cuts each of the past two years. In Baltimore, where members of my family teach, there is lead in the schools' drinking water and so few substitutes that when a teacher gets sick, students are split between other classes.

In the face of this, I dream. I dream an America that is a democracy and not a kleptocracy, where we bail out the schools before the airlines.

I dream technology that increases our freedoms rather than curtailing our liberties. The merging of private and public databases for Soviet-style spying on citizens is now doing the latter.

I dream that every single American votes and we collectively decide our future.

I know a lot of people share my dreams. How do we make them real?

The best hope is to awaken the sleepers, the 100 million Americans who do not vote in presidential elections. How can anyone claim to know the will of the people when half of Americans have given up on politics? After the debacle of the 2000 elections, more may abstain in 2004.

The antiwar movement provided a blueprint for mapping constituencies, some new or long dormant, who can collaboratively restore democracy. It would be a shame if the National Council of Churches and American Muslims, the hip hop activists and the suburban antiwar moms lived through this war, then never met on common ground again. We must find a way of convening Americans with an interest in peaceful regime change at home— what we call an election—and make plans for 2004.

I mentioned slavery not simply because it illustrates the power of dreams, but also because it demonstrates the ways in which our struggles are linked. America has always suffered from a crisis of belief in mutual advancement. This country has always tolerated exploitation in the name of personal gain, whether of slaves, immigrants, or Enron employees. Our fear that we will move from being temporarily secure to suddenly exploited keeps us silent on some of the most important issues of our time. The opposite is also true. My belief that improving my life does not require diminishing yours lifts my spirits. Hope is contagious.

Our struggles are not the same, but they are linked. Whether we are worried about the economy, education, privacy or civil liberties, we have a vested interest in working together. We must devote the coming months to building connections between grassroots coalitions, building independent media, holding politicians accountable for their actions (like the White House's secret meetings with energy companies), and entering our concerns into the policy debates. And we must increase participation in one of the most simple and critical aspects of democracy, voting. If we join together, to quote President George W. Bush, "The tyrant will soon be gone. The day of . . . liberation is near."

Talkin' Loud, Saying Nothing

September 12, 2003

Last Tuesday, I had the privilege of moderating the second Democratic presidential hopefuls' debate. I hustled through questions on Iraq and the economy so that I could get to my own pet query: "What is your favorite song?"

Music is a Gen X Rorshach test. In the same way that a Slayer fan probably wouldn't date an Englebert Humperdinck lover, a White Stripes fan might not vote for a politician who just adored John Philip Sousa. But getting a frank answer out of the candidates proved even harder with this question than it was on foreign policy.

**

Ambassador Carol Moseley Braun: Des'Ree, "Gotta Be"
Pandering: 3
Originality: 7
Subtext: I am Black Woman, Hear Me Roar

The ambassador, first in the lineup, looked startled and barked out the answer. Des'Ree's hit self-help ditty is a safe choice. Or maybe it's just a commentary on Moseley Braun's middle-of-the-pack candidacy: "Some may have more cash than you, Others take a different view/My, oh, my . . ."

**

Rev. Al Sharpton: James Brown, "Talking Loud, Saying Nothing"
Pandering: 5
Originality: 9
Subtext: None

It's all about the hair. Rev. Sharpton, who's married to one of Brown's former backup singers, couldn't have picked anyone else if he tried. The Reverend introduced his answer by saying it was "James Brown's song on the Republican Party."

***

Senator John Edwards: John Cougar Mellencamp, "Small Town"
Pandering: 7
Originality: 4
Subtext: I am not a trial lawyer, I am not a trial lawyer. Repeat.

Edwards hemmed and hawed to stall for time, then pulled out this crowd-pleaser. Yes, it's a great song. And yes, you did grow up the son of a mill-worker. But the number of years you were a highly paid lawyer should have eased your class-disenfranchisement, so don't go spoutin' that "Small Town" stuff around here.

***

Senator John Kerry: Bruce Springsteen, "No Surrender"
Pandering: 7
Originality: 7
Subtext: I'm rough and tough and bad enough to be your commander in chief, even though I look like a Harvard psych professor.

You're already doing a good job looking presidential, senator. You should have tried harder to seem fun.

***

Governor Howard Dean: Wyclef Jean, "Jaspora (Diaspora)"
Pandering: 4
Originality: 10
Subtext: So what if there's no black folks in my state? You know I got soul.

Dean was quizzed on how he could govern a multi-ethnic country when his state is 97 percent white. Under the circumstances, picking a black musician is an obvious play. Picking former Fugee Wyclef, and a song that is all Haitian Creole at that, is not.

***

Senator Joe Lieberman: Fleetwood Mac, "Don't Stop Thinking About
    Tomorrow"
Pandering: 10
Originality: 0
Subtext: Yay! This question was in my talking points!

Frank Sinatra, "My Way"
Pandering: 8
Originality: 0
Subtext: Ditto

Lieberman introduced his answers by saying, "Like a good politician, I'm
going to take two." Would that be two chances to pander? Clinton completely and utterly sucked the juice out of the feel-good Fleetwood Mac tune. And
Sinatra? "My Way?" Bzzt—try again.

***

Congressman Dennis Kucinich: John Lennon, "Imagine"
Pandering: 5
Originality: 6
Subtext: I am Jimmy Carter

"Imagine a new America," said Kucinich, a dyed-in-the-wool liberal who
favors a single-payer healthcare system. The song still pulls heartstrings. But
in a political context it somehow recalls the thirty-ninth president—not in
his current Nobel Prize days, but the era of oil lines, recessions, and an
earnest man who had lust in his heart.

***

Congressman Dick Gephardt: Bruce Springsteen, "Born in the USA"
Pandering: 10
Originality: 0
Subtext: I am trying way too hard.

Okay, it is an excellent rock-out tune. But it would have worked better if
Gephardt had a clue that it's a protest song about veterans. ("Sent me off
to a foreign land/To go and kill the yellow man.") Only one who could
have called this with any grace is Kerry, and thankfully he declined.

***

Senator Bob Graham: Jimmy Buffett, "Changes in Latitudes, Changes In
    Attitudes"
Pandering: 2
Originality: 7
Subtext: I've spent too much time in the sun

"We're going to change some attitudes and latitudes," said the senator, who
apparently keeps an exacting diary of his daily dealings. Tuesday, September
9, 9:35 PM. Kicked ass at the debate. One step closer to mission accomplished: putting a Parrothead in the Oval Office.

Leave No Flygirl Behind

December 9, 2003

The only thing worse than having a marvelous booty call, only to find the person you're waking up next to is a Republican, is finding out that one of your best friends so loathes the political system that she has not voted and will not vote.

I had one of those shocks the other day. Keisha (name changed to protect the guilty) is not your average Jenny on the block. She is multilingual, has traveled extensively and lived abroad, and pulls down a six-figure salary. She's a compulsive reader and knowledge-seeker. And as a thirtysomething African-American, Keisha is also part of a demographic whose political disappearing act should worry Democrats and anyone who cares about democracy.

Keisha's reasons for not voting are simple. She hates most of the candidates. "I vote," she says, "with my money."

It should go without saying that "voting" for Gucci or Wal-Mart is not quite the same as voting for Bush or Sharpton or Dean. But the construct of American consumerism—what writer Steve Waldman calls "the tyranny of choice"—does give people a sense that they hold decision-making power. Politics, too often, seems to give us none. Many younger Americans see politics as a distasteful opportunity to make a series of wrong choices. As long as that is the case—as long as the choice is the lesser of two evils—then younger voters will continue to sit out the game.

The key to reinvigorating younger voters, and the untapped 100 million nonvoters, is to find an aspirational, inspirational language for political change. The Republicans have been very adept at creating a clear narrative of power and self-determination that appeals not only to the people they serve (the rich), but to anyone seeking to better themselves. Thus the trend of the "NASCAR Dad," a demographic whose economic interests should go clearly Democratic but whose voting patterns are stubbornly Republican. Right now, at least, the Republicans are better storytellers.

Better, livelier, and more hopeful storytelling on the left and from Democrats is key to this election. Front-runner Howard Dean has been adept at attacking the Bush administration, but less able to paint vivid word-pictures of the nation he hopes to create. This kind of red-meat politicking appeals to party faithful and young Internet volunteers, but it may not bring many of the 100 million nonvoters back into the fold. Messaging need not be an either-or dilemma. The candidates can continue to legitimately point out the failures of the current administration while honing their vision of a post-Bush America.

What would that vision consist of? Democrats have to reclaim the language of opportunity, enhanced by a solid grasp of social justice. The concept that a rising tide lifts all boats needs to be updated for the more acquisitive hip hop generation, who want immediate rewards for the fruits of their labor. The Democratic Party must be the party of strivers who are opportunistic but not parasitic, people who believe their own personal gain will not be enhanced by the misery of others. Right now some voters feel they have to choose between personal opportunity and social justice. A spot-on narrative will demonstrate that social justice—including no more no-bid contracts for fat cats, more educational opportunity, halting the growth of the prison-industrial complex, and better jobs creation—benefits those seeking economic gain. Call it "Leave No Flygirl Behind."

Targeting the hip hop generation, people like Keisha, with these messages is critical. The average age of white Americans is thirty-nine. The average age of black Americans is thirty. Younger Americans are less likely to vote than older Americans. Black voters are 90-plus percent Democratic Party faithful. The party has taken the black vote for granted, but as time passes, unless messaging is on point, the flow of black support will dwindle. The hip hop generation is, of course, multiracial. Across ethnic lines, they are disgruntled with the lack of political storytelling that appeals to them.

It's not too late to find the language of inspiration. And it certainly isn't too early to start.

The Young Volunteer But Don't Vote

June 4, 2000

The young woman in the African dress stood a bit stiffly before a thousand young peers and a smattering of Silicon Valley CEOs. As a refugee from the civil war in Liberia, she explained simply, little was more precious to her than democracy. It was just one of the many moving moments at the annual convention of City Year, an organization that leads a thousand seventeen- to twenty-four-year-olds in service across America. As a board member of the organization, which was the model for the AmeriCorps national service program, I've seen these diverse teens and twentysomethings endure low pay and cramped housing in order to run afterschool programs, aid the elderly, and rebuild community centers. This is patriotic stuff, a valuable part of knitting together the fabric of this country. But in five years, this was the first time I'd heard a corps member mention democracy explicitly. It seems to be a tough concept for even young idealists to warmly embrace.

Only a third of eligible eighteen- to twenty-four-year-olds voted in the 1996 presidential election, though this year's highly publicized race could boost participation. Still, there's a powerful culture of suspicion to overcome. Research by the National Association of Secretaries of State shows that young voters feel they are being ignored by Washington fat cats more obsessed with winning campaign contributions. Political advertising isn't often targeted at young adults, and reliable senior voters get far more attention than their grandkids. Voter participation numbers are even worse among young African-Americans and Latinos, who see only a handful of nonwhites in bodies like the U.S. Senate and see our government uphold bad policy like mandatory minimum drug sentences. When young Americans reject voting, it's not as much out of blind apathy as a legitimate sense they're being ignored or even harmed. The good news is that they're finding their own way to be civic minded.

This generation has a deep and abiding faith in their own ability to change America one community at a time. According to Volunteers of America, 32 percent of this country's volunteers are young Americans, and 72 percent of UCLA freshman had volunteered in the past year, a ten percent rise over the past decade. Individuals like City Year alum Taj Mustapha go one step further and start their own organizations. The poised twenty-seven- year-old turned her Stanford thesis on homelessness into At the Crossroads, an award-winning program for homeless San Francisco teens. "When I started out, I didn't know what I was doing," Mustapha told City Year members at a forum on social entrepreneurship. "If I did know what it would take, I might not have done it." That leap of faith is critical; some of our most innovative organizations, like Teach for America, were birthed by young idealists. But the image of young Americans as slackers and service as some sort of luxury persists.

National service has only slowly gained a firmer footing in Congress, although the 100,000 young Americans who have served in the past five years help build low-income houses with Habitat for Humanity and run programs like a mobile preschool in Reno, Nevada. But even this year, a House appropriations subcommittee voted to defund the entire AmeriCorps program, a quick thumb in the eye of the man who spearheaded the program, President Clinton. Lawmakers quickly replaced the money, but it's exactly the kind of partisan wrangling that turns young people off of politics to begin with.

At City Year's conference, one young member asked Li Lu, who helped lead the pro-democracy students at Tiananmen Square, why young people don't vote. "Democracy is like oxygen," he said. "When you have it, you don't really notice it. But when you don't, you can't live without it." He's right in more ways than one. Democracy is not only vital but often seems invisible. If we want more young Americans to vote, we have to make democracy visible to them, and give them a reason to show up at the polls. With a combination of words and deeds, lawmakers must legislate for the needs of this generation—not just national service but criminal justice reform, education and job training—and then broadcast a message about their efforts and successes. This generation's desire to serve connects them to the concept of democracy in action, but it will remain just a concept if they don't show up at the ballot box.

Redefining Patriotism

October 20, 2000

As we rushed along the highway to pick up the cake for my grandma's eight-
ieth birthday party, my mom started to recite one of the poems she learned
as a child. Maybe it's one of those generational things. I grew up with phon-
ics and set theory. Mom learned to memorize Langston Hughes,
Shakespeare, and patriotic poems like the one she pulled out of her hat this
time, "The Ballad of Barbara Fritchie."

> Up from the meadows rich with corn,
> Clear in the cool September morn,
> The clustered spires of Frederick stand
> Green-walled by the hills of Maryland.

The poem is set in our home state, as Confederate General Stonewall
Jackson rode past "the clustered spires of Frederick." A ninety-year-old
woman named Barbara Fritchie stonewalled him, preventing him from
shooting down the union flag. Even though she had recited this poem for me
many times before, Mom always chants the good parts with plenty of drama.

> "Shoot if you must this old grey head,
> But spare your country's flag," she said.
> A shade of sadness, a blush of shame,
> Over the face of the leader came . . .
> "Who touches a hair on yon gray head
> Dies like a dog! March on!" he said.

The fact that my mother can recite this poem with such gusto amazes me.
(I can't remember where I put my keys, let alone quote poetry.) This poem in
particular—this poem about our region of the country, the Civil War, and
standing up for what you believe in—seems hopelessly romantic and outdated.
For all of my willingness to criticize this country, I still believe in it. But this

type of ardent patriotism rings false to most people in my generation. The question is why.

Is it just a question of attitude? Have we watched too much MTV and too many hip car commercials to admit we love America? I don't think so. The questions are far deeper and more substantial. We can't stop being critical of our nation, mired in a campaign finance morass of both parties' making, often churlish about its international obligations (remember that billion we owe the U.N.?), even ungenerous towards its own children, a third of whom experience poverty and hunger each year. There's a fine line between critical and ungrateful, and youth tread it often.

Perhaps we simply need to re-invest in patriotism on our own terms. Maybe we should think of civic engagement, participation not only in voting but other social institutions, as the active expression of patriotism. I was lucky enough to get to hear Harvard sociologist Robert Putnam talk about the theories in his book *Bowling Alone*, which include the idea that this generation may need to create new civic institutions that we find meaningful. Putnam charts the decline of "social capital," a decline of interaction between Americans, whether in neighborhood organizations or simply families eating together. But the thousands of young Americans who are swelling the ranks of the national service movement may help to reverse this decline, not only filling the needs of America's communities but reinvigorating belief in a larger sense of national community.

Of course, we aren't an isolated nation, and most younger Americans view global culture as a desirable and growing part of their lives. It's telling that this generation has embraced Ralph Nader and dismissed Pat Buchanan's increasingly irrelevant mumblings about putting troops on the border to stop illegal immigration and maintaining an "America first foreign policy." Immigration never comes without complications—didn't when the Italians came, or the Irish, or the Jews. This generation doesn't expect things to be easy, but most people I talk to want real help with real issues, whether it's figuring out how to diminish the downside of economic competition between blacks and Mexicans in South Central or how to further the anti-sweatshop movement on college campuses. And by the way, while we ponder these deep thoughts, we can do it over takeout burritos or jerk chicken or thaw some of those frozen edamame from the supermarket.

Encouraging civic engagement must be one part of the new patriotism; a realistic sense of our diversity certainly has to be another. However we find ways to be proud of our country in the twenty-first century, they must be new ways to fit a changing America. This country is worthy of poetry, perhaps words yet to be written.

On Felons Reclaiming the Right to Vote, Clinton Speaks Loudly But Late

January 21, 2001

When Americans gathered to celebrate the life of Rev. Dr. Martin Luther King, Jr., on his national holiday, the litany of hopes and prayers turned not only familiar themes about the content of our character, but renewed calls for stronger voting rights. In Brooklyn, New York, Myrlie Evers-Williams, the former head of the NAACP and widow of slain activist Medgar Evers decried the wrongful purge of Florida voters on the grounds that they were felons. Senator Hillary Rodham Clinton took the same stage to echo her husband's call for a new, controversial policy: that all felons who have served their time be allowed to vote once more.

Smart sentiment; late timing. America's policy on felons and voting is one big racially charged jumble. Now, during the primaries, when an editor at the hip hop magazine the *Source* asked Bill Bradley and Al Gore whether all felons should eventually regain their voting rights, Bradley said yes while Gore hemmed and hawed. It's a bit ironic, then, that Clinton is only now championing the policy change. Had the Clinton/Gore administration sought to remedy the situation during its two terms, the vice president would likely have won the presidency.

Here's the situation across the nation. Most states allow felons to vote once they have served their time (and four actually allow them to vote from prison). But ten, mostly Southern states with large African-American populations, disenfranchise felons permanently. Many of these states, including Florida, passed their ban on felons voting shortly after the Civil War and added a series of more minor offenses to the felony list to boot. Today in Florida, nearly one-third of black men cannot vote because of this ban.

President Clinton brought Congress an entire policy proposal on race, which included eliminating racial profiling and improving access to healthcare. But the call to restore felons' voting rights is probably the most controversial item on the list. Most politicians are too afraid of getting painted as criminal-coddling liberals to speak out against the way race plays into criminal justice enforcement. White Americans often go free for offenses that get black Americans hard time. According to federal statistics and out-going "drug czar" Barry McCaffrey, twice as many whites in raw numbers as blacks use crack; yet fully 90 percent of those incarcerated for crack cocaine possession or sales under federal law are black.

This type of discrepancy in prosecution and sentencing also leads to a gap in participation at the polls. Today, African-Americans are five times as like-ly as whites to be disenfranchised under felony voter laws. And if someone permanently lacks the right to vote, they become even more disconnected from the society they live in and the government with which they interact.

In addition to pondering the question of felons voting, we should keep track of what happens as the U.S. Commission on Civil Rights looks into Florida's problems, including the disfranchisement of nonfelons. Voters mistakenly listed as felons, including one county elections chief, testified before the commission during a series of hearings in the state's capital. One local pastor had to threaten to bring a lawyer to the polls before being allowed to vote. A Republican-led Texas firm helped purge the Florida rolls of felons and ended up excluding eight thousand voters who never commit-ted any crimes.

A lot of the recent election commentary has treated the question of voter abuses in black communities as if a bunch of Chicken Littles were running around with their heads snapping in the breeze. But it's worth remember-ing that it was just forty years ago that Fannie Lou Hamer, a Mississippi sharecropper, found out that she had the right to vote, and then was beaten and lost her job because she tried to exercise it. That was 1962, not 1862. We took a tremendous leap, especially in the following ten years, but are we really smug enough to think our democracy is perfect? And if it isn't, are we willing to look beyond the superficial questions of dimpled chads? If so, creating some standard for returning the franchise to people who have served their time should be a cornerstone of election reform.

Bush 100: Grading on a Curve

May 1, 2001

There hasn't been such a frenzy of measuring without a yardstick since the British converted to the metric system. I'm talking about the Bush hundred days phenomenon, where much of the press corps seems lulled by the Mr. Malaprop charm campaign. The contemporary political press is like a dog without teeth, determined to catch the postman and gnaw on his pants legs with moist and softened gums. Not everyone is willing to wallpaper over the deep political fissures in our society, however. On CNN, Susan Page of *USA Today* graded Bush an "incomplete" on leadership, since a poll by the network and her paper showed that 25 percent of Americans still do not view him as the legitimate president of the United States.

Now, just imagine an alternate scenario for the first hundred days. Imagine if George W. Bush had stepped out on inauguration day and said. "My fellow Americans, I know my number one agenda was tax cuts. But American democracy has just been shaken to its foundations. Our number one priority in this administration will be the reform of our electoral process, so the confusion and errors that plagued our system will never happen again!"

Woulda put kind of a different spin on things, huh?

The party line from Florida Secretary of State Katherine Harris is that no one was disenfranchised, no one turned away from the polls. At this point abuses are still being uncovered, and staking that claim is like calling fried chicken that's just started browning on the outside done. Many residents fought their way through different government bureaucracies before they could vote, and the United States Commission on Civil Rights states: "The evidence may ultimately support findings of prohibited discrimination." In Florida, the names of felons and nonfelons were sloppily cross-matched, despite warnings that this would muck-up qualified voters. Nonetheless, the process—under the watch of firms that contributed to the Bush campaign—went ahead. Most of those erroneously cross-matched as felons were African-American. And, by the way, Bush has not put any funds for election reform in his budget.

What he has done is shattered his image, for those who held it, as a right-moderate. Moderate voters, especially pro-choice women, who took the debates at face value were in for a real shock when Bush began to craft his public policy. While maintaining the demeanor of a political naïf, Bush immediately revoked funds to international organizations that provided abortion services as part of family planning, and then began a series of anti-environmental moves culminating with the media frenzy over arsenic. (In truth, CO_2 emissions are a far bigger issue.) He directly broke a campaign promise to reduce emissions, a reflection of his desire to please business allies.

What Bush has accomplished in one hundred days is to make a billion-plus dollar tax cut a reality. Americans were feeling more prosperous during the campaign, and we still did not want a tax cut. Americans wanted money spent on schools and roads and healthcare. In other words, Americans wanted *government*—a body of people and institutions that provides services that we cannot provide for ourselves.

It's unpopular these days to talk about wanting government. So George W. Bush, a wealthy man whose campaign was spectacularly financed by other wealthy people, wrapped himself in a mantle of populism.He promised less government and a return of money to "the people." But wealthy backers benefitted the most. Despite all the talk of populism, it's a lot easier for the rich to opt out of government than the working and middle classes. Public hospitals don't serve the rich. Eighty percent of children go to public schools; a disproportionate slice of the twenty percent who don't are wealthy. In the first hundred days, Bush has favored Americans of mega-means over the rest of us. We still rely on the institutions of government—and we still drink the tap water, too.

What About the Kids?

May 21, 2001

We are leaving the children behind.

During the 2000 presidential campaign, Governor George W. Bush said "we will leave no child behind" so often that one expected to see little ones following him down the street as if he were the Pied Piper. But that mantra is a trademark of the Children's Defense Fund (CDF), a private nonprofit that has been working to end child poverty for nearly three decades.

"Mr. Bush has used our slogan and we want to tell him what it means," says CDF chair Marian Wright Edelman, who this week is launching Act to Leave No Child Behind on Capitol Hill with Senator Chris Dodd (D-Conn.) and Congressman George Miller (D-Calif.). The omnibus bill presents a laundry list of the top issues affecting children in America, from gun violence to the 11 million uninsured children in the United States, along with proposed legislative remedies for each. Top on the agenda: a plan to channel the current tax-cut mania in support of working families.

"How can we say our first big act is to give a tax cut when children are hungry, homeless, left at home alone without adequate childcare?" Edelman asks. While the proposed tax package doubles the per-child credit to $1000, it is not refundable to the many working families who pay payroll taxes but don't earn enough to owe federal taxes come April 15. The majority of the Bush cut goes to wealthy families for whom an extra $500 or $1000 might provide a much-needed vacation but won't make or break a family's decision to pay for healthcare. Without making the per-child credit refundable, says Edelman, "sixteen million families and children will be left behind." The CDF estimates that a refundable tax credit alone would provide the extra edge needed to lift 2 million children out of poverty.

Over 12 million American children live in what the U.S. Census defines as poverty, an income of below $13,290 for a family of three. Three-quarters of these children live in homes where at least one person works, a number that has risen since the implementation of "welfare reform." And families who technically qualify as poor are just the tip of the iceberg. In her new book *Nickel and Dimed: On (Not) Getting By in America*, Barbara Ehrenreich sets out on a stunning journey to see what low-wage work in America is, how it pays, and how low-wage workers must live. For Ehrenreich, who worked at jobs ranging from a Wal-Mart clerk to a housecleaner, simple survival often meant working two jobs, seven days a week, and living in residence hotels with only a hot plate on which to cook.

Plenty of hardworking American families consist of a mother and father, or often just a mother, working long hours for $5 or $6 per hour. Those with young children are hit doubly hard, by the childcare crunch as well as the money crunch. At different points in my childhood, my mother worked higher-paying night shifts (which studies show to be both physically and neurologically taxing) or two jobs simultaneously in order to support our family. She had a graduate degree, which helped her find good work, and we had an extended family that could contribute to childcare. Many families have neither, and until the dot-com crash, the economic boom seemed to anaesthetize us to the issues facing working poor families.

Are we still numb? Edelman doesn't think so, or more important, she believes we can warm to the politics of child-focused change. "It is really time for a movement," she says. "I believe it will start with women. We're motivating people to come to Washington to say take care of children first."

Georgie, Ya No Blow Up the World, Nuh?

October 2002

In a radio interview this week, musician and activist Harry Belafonte challenged the secretary of state—who like he is of Jamaican origin—saying, "In the days of slavery, there were those slaves who lived on the plantation and [there] were those slaves that lived in the house. You got the privilege of living in the house if you served the master . . . exactly the way the master intended to have you serve him. Colin Powell's committed to come into the house of the master. When Colin Powell dares to suggest something other than what the master wants to hear, he will be turned back out to pasture."

In that "I coulda been a contender" way, Powell was once viewed as presidential material. Now he's fighting for his political life. Everything he says, Bush says nuh uh, from condoms to caution on Iraq. So why would Powell settle for being the Bush administration's whuppin' boy when he's not going to get the keys to the kingdom? Well, maybe he thinks he's kept George W. Bush from doing worse than he's already done. Maybe it's not about movin' on up. It's about keeping the kid out of trouble.

A friend of mine moved to New York and said, "Why do all these black women have white kids?" (Honestly!) She was looking at all the women, mainly Jamaicans and other Caribbean immigrants, pushing upper-middle-class princes and princesses around in their prams. So, maybe Colin Powell isn't a house Negro. He's a Beltway nanny, sent to keep a tight leash on the commander in chief. Just imagine an average day:

Georgie (picking up the red phone): Hallo?

Powell: Georgie! Georgie! I told ya nuh pick up that phone! That's Daddy's phone!

Georgie: Daddy said I could play.

Powell: That phone is not for play. Go play with the other phone.

Georgie: I like the red phone. Things go boom.

Powell: I told you Georgie. No boom.

Georgie (screaming): I want boom! I want boom!

Powell (taking off apron): George, there's a legal process for declaring war. First, the powers to declare war are given only to the U.S. Congress and cannot be delegated to any other branches of government. Follow me here. After German submarines, the little boats under the water, sank American ships in 1917, President Woodrow Wilson asked Congress to pass a resolution authorizing troops for World War I. And after Pearl Harbor, okay that's the zoom zoom airplanes, President Franklin Delano Roosevelt asked Congress for troops for World War II, in 1941. You have to ask Congress for power *after* things go boom. No "preemptive strike" crap.

Georgie (considering): Things go boom now!!!!

Sound of door opening. Vice President Cheney walks into Oval Office. Powell straps on apron. Georgie puts down phone.

Cheney: How's he been?

Powell: A perfect angel. A perfect angel.

The Schmoozing of Church and State

May 21, 2001

Would you like a little Jesus with your justice? More important, would you like prayer to be a part of the office ritual at the Justice Department?

Let's rewind things a little, past the confirmation of ultraconservative John Ashcroft for attorney general, to the beginning of President George W. Bush's term.

When the president announced his plan to open a Faith-based Charity office in the White House, seventy-nine-year-old UPI correspondent Helen Thomas had a couple of questions.

"Mr. President, why do you refuse to respect the wall between the church and state?" Thomas asked. "And you know that the mixing of religion and government for centuries has led to slaughter. I mean, the very fact that our country has stood in good stead by having the separation—why do you break it down?"

Bush looked annoyed, answering, "Helen, I strongly respect the separation of church and state—" And Thomas broke in to say, "Well, you wouldn't have a religious office in the White House if you did."

We are a nation which manages to churn out a seemingly endless slew of World War II documentaries and Greatest Generation books without really taking a step back to consider what the conflict was about. One reason: a group of people looked at another and thought that because of their faith, they deserved to be exterminated. Doubtless, most Americans who went over to fight in that war didn't do it to save the Jews. They did it because they were patriotic Americans, bound to do as they were told, bound to uphold the freedoms of American society.

One of the freedoms we enjoy (and boy, it's hard to be preachy where every other televangelist takes a fall for adultery) is to choose your own faith, if any. Those of us who are Christians are lucky. We get to kneel, pray, hang tinsel and sing along to Nat King Cole on a regular day off from work. We don't have to explain Ramadan or Rosh Hashanah to our bosses.

It'd be hard to be a nonbeliever in Ashcroft's office. Every morning, he does a Bible reading, followed by a discussion or prayer. Attendance is optional, but I'd be surprised if folks in the office aren't keeping count. Barry Lynn, executive director of Americans United for Separation of Church and State, stated, "Justice Department employees who do not participate may feel their job advancement is hindered. . . . Whenever a superior orchestrates a religious event, the people who work for him feel pressure to participate in order to advance their careers." And the reverse is true. As one Jewish friend of mine at a television network said about her boss, "If he had a daily Talmudic meeting every day, don't you think I'd be there every day to get face time?"

In the end, this whole prayer meeting thing isn't about God. It's a little club, a place where certain members of the We Are Righter Than You group can get together, murmur a few words, and exert power. If prayer were really the goal, why not do it on personal time, the way most of us pray?

No, this is junior high school all over again, the insies and the outsies. And like most of the wrangling in junior high, it's just not fair.

Watergate.com

February 3, 2004

When I was young and stupid—say, three years ago—I dated a guy heretofore known as the Control Freak. One day I noticed he'd left his e-mail account open. I felt a powerful urge to see if he'd treated his ex-girlfriend the way he treated me. I found out that he had.

Three things happened. One, I confessed. (I'm Catholic. I can't help it.) Two, I never read his e-mail again. And finally, despite my apologies, he lorded my indiscretion over me until we mercifully broke up. I can't say I blame him. Like many people who grew up in the computer era, I consider private e-mail a sacrosanct space, more like a diary than a daykeeper. Invading someone's e-mail is like sitting on that person's bed and flipping through his or her journals.

Which brings us to the curious case of Republicans infiltrating Democratic e-correspondence. Private, or supposedly private, Democratic memos were leaked to conservative media outlets the *Washington Times,* the *Wall Street Journal*, and possibly radio and television host Sean Hannity. At issue is a computer system that allowed Republican staffers to read Democratic memos and correspondence without a password. Some of these staffers argued that they told the Democrats about the security breach in the summer of 2002. Others believe mum was the word before November 2003. In any case, the Republicans had more than a year of unfettered access to Democratic documents before this scandal became public.

And what a year it was. At issue is a series of Democratic strategy memos on controversial judicial appointments. A year ago, columnist Bob Novak detailed Democratic strategy for blocking conservative nominees to the federal bench. The descriptions in his column, including the Democratic characterization of blocked nominee Miguel Estrada as a "stealth right-wing zealot" who was "especially dangerous, because . . . he is a Latino" were straight from the pilfered electronic files. In some accounts of the case, the content of the memos has become as much of an issue as the spying itself.

In a press conference, Senate Judiciary Committee Chairman Orrin Hatch admitted that an investigation by federal prosecutors "revealed at least one current member of the Judiciary Committee staff had improperly accessed at least some of the documents referenced in the media reports and which have been posted on the Internet."

The staffer, Manuel Miranda, first went on paid administrative leave and then resigned. Reached by the *Boston Globe*, which broke the story, Miranda said, "There appears to have been no hacking, no stealing, and no violation of any Senate rule. Stealing assumes a property right and there is no property right to a government document. . . . These documents are not covered under the Senate disclosure rule because they are not official business and, to the extent they were disclosed, they were disclosed inadvertently by negligent [Democratic] staff."

Nice try. Lee Tien, senior staff attorney for the Electronic Frontier Foundation, notes, "Each time the Republicans accessed the Democrats' files without authorization, they at a minimum violated the federal Computer Fraud and Abuse Act, 18 USC Sec.1030(a)(2)." That statute includes anyone who "intentionally accesses a computer without authorization or exceeds authorized access, and thereby obtains 3; information from any department or agency of the United States."

Tien also rejects the reports that focus on the content of Democratic memos versus their theft. In describing this crime, he says, "It's pretty sleazy to blame the victim when you're the one exploiting the weakness in the first place. Good computer security is hard. Poor computer security is extremely common. . . . I don't believe in double standards, so maybe we should think of all the companies and governments who have been hacked in the past few years because of poor security."

And what about the disputed Republican argument that they told Democrats about the problem a year ago? "It's as if they're saying 'I told you the lock on your back door was broken—if you didn't fix it, I should be able to walk right into your house and take what I want,'" says computer-privacy expert Mike Godwin, senior technology counsel at Public Knowledge.

It's been hard for this story to get much play in a time filled with talk of weapons of mass destruction (or the lack thereof), Democratic primaries, and presidential budget recommendations. But the continuing investigation could turn this case of file spying into a full-on electronic Watergate.

Senate Sergeant at Arms William Pickle is now turning over backup tapes of the Judiciary Committee computer to the Capitol police. This prompted a group of Republicans on the Judiciary Committee, including Saxby Chambliss of Georgia and Lindsey Graham of South Carolina, to complain that the investigation could compromise their own e-privacy. "We strongly object to allowing anyone to read backup tapes or other electronic media from the Judiciary Committee server, the Exchange server or otherwise breach the privacy of our electronic files and communications," they wrote in a letter to Pickle. So far, their concerns have taken a back seat to the needs of the investigation.

In the end, Republican gains from scanning the memos may be far out-weighed by disclosures from the spying case. After all, those who live by the sword—or the mouse click—can die by it as well.

War and Terror

Can a Video Country Grasp Real Violence?

November 4, 2002

This is what terror feels like. A year ago, after 9/11, we asked why they hated us. Today we ask why we hate ourselves.

On October 28, a student at the University of Arizona shot and killed three professors and then killed himself. Robert S. Flores happens to be a Gulf War veteran, like John Allen Muhammad, the alleged Beltway sniper, and like executed Oklahoma City bomber Timothy McVeigh.

In interviews shortly before his death, McVeigh, speaking of Iraq, said, "What right did I have to come over to this person's country and kill him? How did he ever transgress against me?" He also said he became personally disillusioned with the opportunities he received after failing a test to join the Special Forces. By the age of twenty-four, McVeigh was honorably discharged, disgruntled, and dangerous.

Why did they do it? Flores is dead, and Muhammad isn't talking. At least one columnist has tried to blame Muhammad's spree on hip hop. And while I'd hesitate to blame the military for producing these three killers, we should at least ask if their anger had any commonality. This whole country seems to be on the verge of a nervous breakdown, tracking terror-sprees on television and watching friends and family lose jobs. But few people with free-floating anxiety turn toward murderous rage, or have the skills and weapons to act it out.

For Gulf War veterans, today's talk of war must seem like an unwanted flashback. Anna Quindlen's compilation of columns from the *New York Times* contains articles about the war buildup in 1990 that could have been written today. Military recruiters visit housing projects and farm-town high schools, not college-prep academies. Nineteen-year-olds who thought they'd entered something akin to a military jobs program ended up being sent, to their surprise, into combat.

In a theater recently, I saw an advertisement showing recruits climbing a virtual mountain of good deeds—helping feed poor people in other countries, planting the flag, doing everything but killing. That is a part of the job that no one wants to talk about.

And it raises a question: did Flores, Muhammad, and McVeigh bring the war home with them?

We can't stomach what our veterans have seen. At the start of the "war on terror" last year, some newspapers refused to put pictures of dead Afghan civilians in their pages to avoid upsetting readers. Indeed. And how did the images upset the soldiers who saw the carnage? Whether veterans participated in actual combat or not, they surely knew what was going on at the front, on the burning roads. Even in our violence-saturated culture, we gloss over the true face of death. Unlike some European networks, our television media show extended, almost reverent shots of bombs dropping, but not the dead bodies that bombing produces.

It's a soldier's job to kill without feeling. These rogue veterans, did they feel when they killed? Can we who sit and watch at home even feel anymore? On CNN, a witness to one of the Beltway shootings said, "It was like a video game."

A Japanese child psychologist once told me, "I feel sorry for children today. All they have is virtual emotions." Life equals video game. Death equals game over. Restart. Press play.

We wish.

***

After this article ran on Alternet.org, a Gulf War veteran from Virginia wrote me a detailed letter about the aftereffects of combat. He offered a series of resources that helped him and might help other Gulf War (and Iraq) veterans:

1. The VA's Vet Centers offer free psychological counseling. Call 1-800-827-1000 to find the nearest center.

2. Seek community in spirituality and faith.

3. Be aware that having served in combat will change you, and try to allow yourself time to accept and deal with the changes.

4. Seek to end unnecessary combat. One resource: Veterans for Common Sense (http://www.veteransfor-commonsense.org).

He ended his letter: "We have a moral responsibility to let the public know what war really means and to prevent it. To honor our responsibility to those living in freedom is to honor our fallen comrades. . . . The larger question looms on the horizon for ourselves and our posterity: 'Can we break the cycle of violence?' The answer must be a firm yes because there is no other option."

Cowboys, Caution, and Courage

February 16, 2003

In a floor speech delivered Wednesday, February 12, Senator Robert Byrd (D-W. Va.) questioned why the Senate was so "ominously, dreadfully silent" about debating a war that could change America's moral standing in the world.

"The doctrine of preemption—the idea that the United States or any other nation can legitimately attack a nation that is not imminently threatening but may be threatening in the future—is a radical new twist on the traditional idea of self defense," Sen. Byrd said. "It appears to be in contravention of international law and the UN Charter. And it is being tested at a time of world-wide terrorism, making many countries around the globe wonder if they will soon be on our—or some other nation's—hit list."

President George W. Bush has taken the cowboy imagery that flows from John Wayne to *Lethal Weapon* and repurposed it in public policy. The lone gunman may work against international terrorists in *Die Hard*. But the American people do not support the government fighting terrorism alone, in ways that make us more isolated and vulnerable and arouse opposition from the international community.

Even the cowboy ethos rejects fights that are, as every five-year-old on the playground would put it, just not fair. Most Americans think that going into Iraq when the nation isn't a direct threat is just plain stupid. A new *New York Times*/CBS News poll found that 59 percent of Americans favor delaying plans for war while the U.N. continues inspections. An even higher number, 63 percent, said America should not go to war without the support of our allies.

This marks a clear division between the rhetoric of the administration, which has claimed it speaks on behalf of the American people, and the will of the people itself. Despite pervasive terror warnings, Americans are more concerned about the economy than they are about Iraq. "The economy" is shorthand for quality of life: children who need help learning, parents who need jobs, communities that need improved relations with police. With our deficits, there's little money to allocate. Dealing with these issues will require at least as much strength from our government as fighting terror.

Why has it taken so long to unearth the feelings of the general public? The media, notably chastised for ignoring early antiwar protests, hasn't looked for responses that challenge the war effort. War is flashy, brilliant, and bright. It plays well on television. In fact, most of the networks have already invested hundreds of thousands, if not millions of dollars, in overseas staffing and infrastructure to cover the war-that-might-be. If it doesn't happen, it'll be a financial loss.

According to the *International Herald Tribune*, CNN has allocated $30 to $35 million for coverage of a new Iraq war. The big three networks could spend more. Financially, war is a double-edged sword for television outlets, which build their reputations and viewer bases but often lose ad dollars in the short run.

In the words of Mark Twain, "It is curious that physical courage should be so common in the world and moral courage so rare." Right now, Americans are displaying the courage to challenge their own government's recklessness. War on Iraq has been reported as a done deal, but the emergence of a thoughtful response to this historic challenge is just building. It's not too late for our government and our media to follow the citizens' lead.

Fighting Our Fathers' Wars

March 27, 2003

One of the biggest ideological battles of all time has been between the concept of free will and the concept of predestination, or walking the path that God or our fathers have set for us. Iraq is no exception.

Last September, President George W. Bush blurted out his most controversial justification for attacking Iraq and Saddam Hussein. "After all," the President said, "this is the guy who tried to kill my dad." Many politicians said this was a Bush vendetta. No doubt, but maybe it's deeper.

"The more insight one gains into the unintentional and unconscious manipulation of children by their parents, the fewer illusions one has about the possibility of changing the world." That's a snippet from Alice Miller's seminal book, *Prisoners of Childhood*.

Miller focuses on narcissism, a psychological disorder in adults she feels has gotten a bad name. The Oxford Dictionary calls narcissism, "a mental state in which there is self-worship and an excessive interest in one's own perfection"—or, as we say with friends, being stuck on yourself. But Miller argues that narcissism is a valuable stage in a child's development. Children are born thinking they are the center of the world. Disabusing them of this notion too early, especially by giving them a mission to fulfill, can turn them into emotional clones of their parents.

So Bush the First decided to enter Iraq. He failed to get Saddam. Meanwhile, he raised his three sons to navigate the intertwining rivers of money and politics. Neil and George bought and sold companies. George and Jeb went into politics. They had big shoes to fill. By all mainstream standards, they succeeded, especially George.

If your father is president, it's pretty hard to dismiss his ideas and his choice of battles. It's even harder to walk away from fighting those battles yourself. Alice Miller argues that kids of overachievers unconsciously follow their parents' patterns. We all want to be immortal, and having children— then browbeating them into thinking what we think—is the easiest way to achieve that.

But what if kids don't follow the script? For George W. Bush, rebelling may have meant not only rejecting his father but rejecting God and country as well. Miller hints that challenging our powerful parents is the psychological equivalent of death. The war on Iraq, like most others, gave us the superficial choice between loyalty to our lineage and rebellion against the ones we love. If we love our families, yet we question what America has become, where do we go?

I won't pretend to know what George W. Bush thinks, but I do know many people who are torn between the false dichotomy of patriotism and intellectual freedom. This loop of conflicting thoughts forms the suburban cul-de-sac of American identity. *I love America. I criticize its methods. I love America. I hate America. I love, I hate. I can't understand.*

So we retreat. Countries are our parents, telling us who we are and what we can do. America the father, come back from war, shows us with his body he is weary but tells us to march on.

Miller's texts, and many others, allow us to create political change through our personal interactions. Do we always have to be right? Can we tolerate new ideas and thoughts? We will never end wars if we can't imagine evolving, in our own small battles, from combatant to diplomat. The feeling that we're conscripted soldiers in wars we didn't choose—Israeli/Palestinian, Christian/Muslim, black/white, rich/poor—constricts our options and diminishes our humanity. The way we treat each other is not just a sideline but an essential part of evolution.

In *The Pianist*, starring Oscar-winner Adrien Brody, an artist survives genocide in wartime Poland. In the end, a Nazi soldier provides him with the substance for survival, an indication that even the clearest conflicts provide surprising glimpses of humanity. It's a terrible thing to be torn between duty to country and love of humanity. Perhaps that's the essential tragedy of war. Most wars today are a continuation of sectarian violence that began before we were born. *The Trojan Women*, a fifteen-hundred-year-old play, graces theaters around the world now because it mirrors our own time. The crux is the story of a hero tasked with slaying a child who could grow up to fight his nation. The language eerily echoes 9/11. You smell the smoke of charred bodies, feel the ash settle on your shoulders.

Our memory of pain is both individual and institutional. We are our fathers' and mothers' children. But if we don't see the possibility of forging our own path toward peace—the possibility of sharing our inner selves with people we fear—we're lost.

Working-Class Women as War Heroes

April 4, 2003

Private Jessica Lynch is a hero, the kind who in her hopefully long life will never escape her youthful fame. The baby-faced nineteen-year-old reportedly fought off Iraqis in an ambush, endured broken bones, gunshot and stab wounds, and went eight days without food. This movie played in real time has all the elements that make fast-paced war flicks like *Behind Enemy Lines* box-office magic. Her face, frozen with what must have been shock, pain, and relief during her rescue, is already one of the most haunting images of the war.

Lynch is linked in more ways than one to Shoshana N. Johnson, a thirty-year-old mother from El Paso, Texas. Johnson, who left her two-year-old daughter with her parents when she deployed, joined the army to get training to be a chef. She ended up one of the first American prisoners of war in Iraq. Lynch—well, she wanted to be a kindergarten teacher.

How did a chef-in-training and a future teacher end up toting guns in the desert? Both of these female war heroes come from hometowns fighting their own battles, economic ones. Lynch comes from the you-can't-make-this-stuff-up town of Palestine, in Wirt County, a farm community in western West Virginia of 5,900 people, 99 percent of them white. Wirt has a 15 percent unemployment rate; 20 percent live below the poverty line; the average income per person is $14,000.

El Paso County is huge by comparison—nearly 700,000 people—but no more prosperous. Seventy-eight percent of El Pasoans are Latino, and twenty-four percent live below the poverty line. The border city, hit hard by the impact of NAFTA, has a per capita income of just $13,000.

The folks in Wirt and El Paso are separated by half a country, but they have a lot in common. In both places, the economy has collapsed. The military is probably one of the best games in town. Jessica Lynch's family says she joined to get an education, something she probably couldn't have gotten otherwise. Now that she's a hero, a group of colleges have stepped forward to offer her a scholarship.

Wouldn't it be great if people like Lynch and Johnson didn't have to go to war to get a job or an education? At the same time that Americans are protesting against the war, thousands this week protested in favor of affirmative action, which faces its latest Supreme Court challenge. Working-class women and African-Americans like Lynch and Johnson will be among those to lose if affirmative action is ended. But affirmative action, as useful as it is, only gives a fraction of Americans the chance they deserve. Schools in working-class neighborhoods are becoming more like truly impoverished ones. In other words, they've become places where too many bright students lose hope.

Yale graduate and notably lackluster student George W. Bush got the benefits of an affirmative action program called "legacy admission," i.e., preference for the kids of alums (particularly the rich ones). For all his hawkishness, Bush went AWOL from his National Guard duty during the Vietnam War, 1972–1973. His father was a war hero. But these days rich men (and women) don't fight.

That's left to the working class. A *New York Times* article titled "Military Mirrors Working-Class America" notes, "With minorities over-represented and the wealthy and the underclass essentially absent, with political conservatism ascendant in the officer corps and Northeasterners fading from the ranks, America's 1.4 million-strong military seems to resemble the makeup of a two-year commuter or trade school outside Birmingham or Biloxi far more than that of a ghetto or barrio or four-year university in Boston."

Don't get me wrong—I'm not saying money's the only reason people join the military. A lot of enlistees are following their dreams of serving their country. Others, like a twenty-seven-year-old interviewed in the *Times* article, like to blow things up (though not necessarily people). And some, like a friend of mine who spent ages seventeen through twenty in the military, think it's a great way to grow up and find your mission in life.

There are a few other options for young Americans seeking a way to give to their country, earn money for college, and get skills—in particular, the service corps like City Year and AmeriCorps. In these programs, young Americans the same age as Lynch can spend a year or two giving back to a local community—working on buildings, serving the elderly, even helping teach kindergarten. With school budgets being slashed, there's plenty of need and plenty of room for young recruits to lend a hand.

But these programs are still modest compared to the size and stability of the military. Before the motto an "Army of One," the Navy boasted the slogan, "It's Not Just a Job, It's an Adventure." Some people just want a job. What they get is far more uncertain.

More Like The Matrix Every Day

April 24, 2003

I was in a restaurant in New York the other day and the waitress said, "We can't catch a break: the war, the economy . . . the weather."

New Yorkers are usually a little tougher than this but the city has lost 200,000 jobs in the past two years. And snow in April? Damn.

There is one bright spot on the horizon. Everywhere I go, people are counting the days till the new *Matrix* comes out. The first movie was a surprise hit. But *Matrix Reloaded* and *Matrix Revolutions*, scheduled for May and November releases respectively, are already cult phenomena.

They're also all too real.

Every morning I walk past a scene straight out of *The Matrix*. Remember those cops, the ones on the roof, with the helicopter? Full riot gear, dorky helmet . . . yeah, them. They're on Wall Street just off of Broadway, guarding the New York Stock Exchange. Every morning I walk down Wall Street to work, I expect Keanu and Carrie-Ann to jump out in their nouveau bondage gear, tha-thwacking the riot cops on the head and using up a zillion rounds of ammo.

But these cops are the good guys, not the bad guys. I think. Seeing men with enormous guns rarely makes me feel safe. I guess they'll protect the brokers from the random crazy with a Saturday Night Special, but from an attacker with anthrax or a hijacked plane—nah. Meanwhile, it makes me profoundly aware that I'm living in a war zone. I don't know if I'm an observer, hostage, or combatant.

It's hard to imagine the endgame for a post-terror America. Will we one day decide that we don't need assault rifles on our streets? Or does it seem like street-corner surveillance cameras and office buildings fingerprinting employees (which I will soon have to undergo) are a part of the New World Order that's here to stay?

I turn to my Oracle—*The Matrix*. Not only stylish and sophisticated, *The Matrix* says quite a lot about our barely veiled rage against the modern state. It takes leaps a movie set in contemporary times would never get away with.

In *The Matrix*, the state is the enemy, not protector. One of the climactic scenes takes place in a sterile glass-and-steel office tower whose clones clutter financial districts around America. Keanu Reeves's Neo, staging a daring rescue of guru Morpheus (Lawrence Fishburne), first guns down the uniformed guards by the metal detector. The he blows the place up from the inside out, setting off a powerful bomb in the elevator shaft.

The symbol of America's power explodes, here, from the inside out, not from the outside in as with the September 11 attacks. Maybe I'm reading too much into this, but let me ride for a bit. How many movies have you seen where the massive office tower—the place in which the American worker is symbolically trapped—explodes in a shower of steel and glass? From *Die Hard* to *Spiderman*, the impregnable fortresses of commerce seem to be the first to go. Take the Westin Bonaventure, a monstrous set of mirrored-glass cylinders plopped in Downtown L.A. On weekends, there are a few homeless people on the streets, which are otherwise nearly empty of both foot and car traffic. In the hotel's auto lobby, you can see posters of all the movies in which the building exploded or threatened to.

Watching the business world literally explode seems to be one of the top American fantasies. It's a nice distraction from watching the actual implosion of the American economy. Frankly, I feel less scared in the theatre.

Operation FUBAR

September 2, 2003

In Iraq last week, the United States launched Operation Jimmy Hoffa with a raid in Khalis, north of Baghdad. Members of a crime ring were apprehended. But like the body of the former teamster leader, the weapons of mass destruction used to justify war cannot be found.

I'd like to propose a name for the next massive raid: Operation FUBAR. This is a military acronym for F*ed Up Beyond All Recognition, a phrase which certainly seems to fit our failed empire building exercise in the desert.

But how, Farai—you might say—can you argue we went to Iraq to feather our own nest? I think I got the idea from Paul Bremer III, the U.S. Envoy to Iraq. In a telling interview with NPR's Juan Williams, Bremer made the case for spending billions more of U.S. money in Iraq. "Even if we succeed in getting our oil revenues back to normal," Bremer said, that won't pay for the cost of our military presence. "When you say 'our,' you mean Iraqi" oil revenues, Williams interjected. "Yeah," said Bremer, without much enthusiasm.

Let's face it: From afar, Iraq looked like a cash cow, a place that could provide an additional base for U.S. operations plus a steady stream of black gold. Now the black gold has become a quagmire devouring U.S. and Iraqi lives and U.S. dollars.

Next week, the Congressional Budget Office will forecast the federal budget deficit for the next year. According to a new report in the *New York Times*, the forecast will likely be over half a trillion dollars, even larger than previous White House estimates. Of course, those White House estimates didn't include the cost of a protracted war in Iraq, a war estimated to cost nearly $5 billion per month. "There will be no retreat," says the president. But there may be no victory, politically or economically, either.

What are the upsides of this FUBAR situation? Perhaps Americans will learn to let go of one of the most persistent myths in U.S. politics: Republicans stand for good economic governance.

The median family income and GDP grew more under President Clinton than President Reagan. Fiscal management under Bush I inspired the Democratic attack line, "It's the economy, stupid." And Bush II is turning out to be even worse than Bush I.

In a persuasive article, writer David Brooks argued that Americans vote for Republicans rather than Democrats because Republicans speak to the aspiration to be rich. Nobody wants to be told that you're poor and you're going to suffer. Nobody wants to hear that taxes will rise because of the profit-taking that occurred in a past presidency. This presents the Democrats with a critical challenge: how to preach the politics of rebuilding without offering only austerity. (We Americans have never been good at austerity.) After a bruising four years, Americans going to the ballot box in 2004 will be looking for hope. We hope that the economy will recover, that the FUBAR war will end, that no more terrorist attacks will hit our shores.

There are ways to blend realism and inspiration. By re-aligning our political priorities, we can end the slow destruction of the public school system, provide decent healthcare for working Americans who can't afford it, and make sure that our strong military is also a smart military. If that isn't cause to wave the flag, I don't know what is.

American Jihad

October 21, 2003

There are several battles going on simultaneously in Iraq. One is to secure the country against lawlessness and terrorism. Another is to dole out the spoils of the oil resources. Third is to secure victory for George W. Bush in the 2004 elections. And yet another is to win a public relations offensive, convincing the world that this was a just war in the first place.

In that last campaign, mark one for America in the "skirmish lost" column.

Recently NBC News broadcast footage of Army Lieutenant. General William Boykin, a deputy undersecretary of defense, equating our campaigns in the Middle East to a religious war. Among his arguments: that Islam is "a spiritual enemy." "He's called the principality of darkness. The enemy is a guy called Satan," out to destroy America "because we're a Christian nation."

For bonus points, Boykin also pegged God (not the Supreme Court) as the deciding factor in the 2000 elections. "Why is this man [President Bush] in the White House?" he said. "The majority of Americans did not vote for him. Why is he there? And I tell you this morning that he's in the White House because God put him there for a time such as this."

Who does it serve to antagonize not Islamic terrorists, who need no further incentive for their deeds, but the rest of the members of the world's fastest growing religion? If any Islamic cleric or politician were to make similar statements about Christianity in a public forum, you can bet our government would decry their hate speech.

Therefore the most troubling aspect of the Boykin incident is not his words, but the Bush administration's reaction to his attacks. Defense Secretary Donald Rumsfeld called Boykin "an officer that has an outstanding record in the United States Armed Forces." He then defended the Lt. General's statements on free speech grounds, saying, "We're a free people."

A free speech defense has great appeal. But this administration, which has relentlessly criticized those who speak out against the Iraq war and occupation, seems to have a very selective view of its uses. (Remember former White House spokesman Ari Fleischer admonishing Bill Maher of *Politically*

Incorrect and "all Americans that they need to watch what they say, watch what they do"?)

Much has been made of the evangelical Christianity of President Bush. He has tried to blend his courting of evangelical voters with attempts to extend an olive branch to a growing political force, Arab-Americans. But the president and his administration cannot have it both ways. They cannot restrict the meaning of "true American" to "Christian-American" and also purport to believe in a pluralistic society. And they cannot allow the military to promote the idea of an American Jihad—a religious war—while claiming to fight a religion-neutral War on Terrorism as well.

The issue of religion in American identity will be one of the linchpins around which the 2004 election turns. In 2004, the Supreme Court heard a case in which a father, who was an atheist, asked the phrase "one nation under God" be removed from the Pledge of Allegiance. "Under God" wasn't originally in the Pledge recited in schools across America; it was added during the Red Scare of the 1950s. The case was dismissed on a technicality, meaning the phrase stays in—for now. More liberal members of the court voted to dismiss the case, while three of the more conservative members voted to reject it on its merits. Some observers questioned whether the liberal justices were sparing Democratic politicians from having to leap to "under God"'s defense while running for re-election. On a much deeper level, the Red State/Blue State faultline corresponds nicely with states in which evangelical or fundamentalist beliefs pervade (Red) versus states with a healthy, if hard-won, sense of religious pluralism (Blue).

In our own nation and abroad, we cannot take lightly the threat of religious warmongering. The administration must recognize the speech of Lt. Gen. Boykin and any others like him for what it really is: a threat to national security and American democracy as well.

The Age of Uncertainty

November 6, 2003

It seems like half of my friends are unemployed and the other half are stuck in jobs that don't match them, like ill-fitting suits. Maybe it has something to do with our age. Most of us are in our mid-thirties, too old to work happily for peanuts at some crap-ass job, too young to stay put for a pension. (They still have those, don't they?)

We are desperate for change, desperate for guidance and vision and prospects and improvement. There's only one problem. We want the same amelioration in political life as we seek personally.

Why is that a problem? To state the obvious, if sobering, truth: what's good for America seems good for President Bush. If the war in Iraq is contained, it increases the president's chances of re-election. If the economy blossoms rather than withers, the same is true. America is fundamentally a conservative country: conservative in the sense of conserving energy and reserving harsh judgment. Voting out a sitting president, even one with such an egregious track record on issues from the economy to the environment, strikes many Americans as somewhere between impossible and undesirable.

Progressives/left/liberals/you-name-it must move beyond the politics of opposition, where what's bad for America is good for the president's foes. We cannot rely on America's fortunes continuing to tank—the up-tick in the economy proves that. There has to be a way to encourage and enjoy any improvement in America's fortunes while still building a base for change.

What if? That simple statement is one of the most powerful in the human imagination and in politics as well. If the left and America are to do well simultaneously, we must "what if" our way into a new vision of progress.

What if the president had listened to his own father, who wrote in his 1998 memoir *A World Transformed*:

> Trying to eliminate Saddam . . . would have incurred incalculable human and political costs. Apprehending him was probably impossible. . . . We would have been forced to occupy Baghdad and, in effect, rule Iraq. . . . There was no

viable "exit strategy" we could see, violating another of our principles. Furthermore, we had been self-consciously trying to set a pattern for handling aggression in the post-Cold War world. Going in and occupying Iraq, thus unilaterally exceeding the United Nations' mandate, would have destroyed the precedent of international response to aggression that we hoped to establish. Had we gone the invasion route, the United States could conceivably still be an occupying power in a bitterly hostile land.

What if we could take back the hundreds of U.S. military and thousands of Iraqi civilian deaths, plus billions of U.S. dollars we have expended thus far on a war which has, as President George Bush the First wrote, "no viable 'exit strategy'"? How powerful would America be then? How much global good will would we still have if we had not defied the international community? How much safer would we be if Muslim countries still perceived us as victims of an unwarranted attack who, nonetheless, were willing to work in conjunction with others, rather than unilaterally, to fight terrorism?

What if we had taken the over $100 billion we will spend on the Iraq war and applied that money to America's failing schools, or to the healthcare conundrum, or to shoring up Social Security? For working Americans my age, healthcare is the most critical of these issues. People who work as full-time "permalancers," getting no benefits, must either pay exorbitant amounts of money out of pocket or hope, without insurance, not to get sick or get hit by a bus.

As the National Academy of Sciences stated in a report, "The health care delivery system is incapable of meeting the present, let alone the future, needs of the American people. . . . The cost of private health insurance is increasing at an annual rate in excess of 12 percent. Individuals are paying more out of pocket and receiving fewer benefits. One in seven Americans is uninsured, and the number of uninsured is on the rise."

What if this were no longer an issue? What if we had fought and won the war to keep America healthy instead of becoming embroiled in an international quagmire?

This is only one example of the road not taken, the good America could have leveraged in the past three years. What's good for America is good for the president only if we forget what could have been. America could have been, as it was in the 1990s, promising and prosperous. No, nothing would or will be the same after the attacks of September 11. But the choices our government has made along the way have only led us deeper into the age of uncertainty, and further from the path of security.

Sex, Drugs, and Hip Hop

Secrets and Cries

August 6, 2003

"What if one woman told the truth about her life? The world would split apart." When she wrote those words, poet Muriel Rukeyser must have been envisioning Tricia Rose's new book *Longing to Tell: Black Women Talk About Sexuality and Intimacy* (Farrar, Straus & Giroux), in which a chorus of women rip stereotypes of black female sexuality to shreds.

There's Sarita, who begins her story, "Ever since I was born, my life has been one big drama." Her father, an American-born Muslim, had two wives. Now she struggles to balance her hard-earned feminism with her love for her family. AIDS activist Linda Rae recounts her physical and sexual abuse at the hands of her family, and the turning points that made her a symbol of hope for others. Cocoa has tried playing Miss Perfect and failed. "I don't think that society understands black women's sexuality," she says. "They go to a light-skinned woman with long hair and say this is pretty, and when they see the dark-skinned lady, they say this is the nurturing type. . . . Or if they show a dark-skinned woman in a sexual light, she's poor, she's loud talking, she's not intelligent. . . . I know it has an impact on my little niece. . . . She watches BET and MTV."

Taking a page from Studs Turkel's oral history playbook, author Tricia Rose lets the women speak for themselves in natural language. This makes for the fastest four-hundred-page read of the summer. Rose, now a professor of American Studies at the University of California, Santa Cruz, came to prominence with the seminal book *Black Noise: Rap Music and Culture in Contemporary America*. In this book, the theory appears only in small cameos. The stories take the fore.

Each of her subject's lives is so impossibly complex that together they defy stereotypes—precisely the point. But certain common experiences emerge. Many of the women have been sexually exploited, either as children, adults, or both. Most who have not been raped fear it. One of the deepest myths of Western society is that our values prevent this exploitation. Or as Dr. Judith Herman puts it in her book *Trauma and Recovery*, "Women like to believe that they have greater freedom and higher status than they do in reality. A woman is especially vulnerable to rape when acting as though she were free—that is, when she is not observing conventional restrictions on dress, physical mobility, and social initiative."

Those words echo a story I heard from a black American reporter in South Africa. Before the fall of apartheid, he was accompanying a local man through a township. The man said, "My brother, you walk as if you are free." In In other words, lie low, change your gait.

In this sense, Rose's book bridges the gap between narratives of (white) women and black (men). Just as white male is the default position in American society, the female is assumed to be white, and the black assumed to be male. Rose's book is a classic example of law professor Kimberle Crenshaw's theory of intersectionality, which considers multiple identities at once. In one description, intersectionality puts the black woman at a literal crossroads. If she got hit by a bus, it could be racism, or sexism, or both. A black woman harassed by black men, then fetishized by white men, has just been hit by two buses.

Add to that heterosexism. Some of Rose's subjects are lesbians. Others, many others, have had one-time or ongoing sexual experiences with women. Says Pam, "I'm very shy, but I'm politically a lesbian. I've been an out lesbian on campus since I've been there. . . . I've had really good sexual relations, I think. I expect my partners to be attentive and ask me what I want, and to try new things."

Despite the struggles, there is still both good sex and good love in this world. As Anondra says, "Sex with love is on a whole other level. It's not just physical. It's emotional. It's mental. It's sensual." Sex + love is a basic human longing. Along with uncovering pain and shame, *Longing to Tell* reveals that this dream still comes true.

The Real Drug Litmus Test

December 22, 1999

During the 1992 presidential race, William Jefferson Clinton reluctantly admitted to trying marijuana. Today, cocaine is the drug under debate in the 2000 campaign. The question is, did George W. Bush inhale?

After months of telling reporters he wouldn't "play that game" and admit or deny using cocaine, the leading Republican contender has given a series of contorted non-answers. When asked about drug use six years ago, while running for governor, Bush said, "What I did as a kid? I don't think it's relevant." In early August, reporters from the *New York Daily News* asked all twelve Republican and Democratic presidential contenders if they ever used cocaine. Eleven said they had not, while Bush, who has answered questions about youthful drinking and applauded his own marital fidelity, declined to answer the question. Under successive waves of questioning, he stated that rumors of cocaine use were "ridiculous and absurd"; implied that he had not used cocaine in the past seven years; and later implied that he had not used cocaine from 1974 on. Reporters continue to barrage the leading Republican contender with the question of whether he has ever used cocaine; he still refuses to answer.

We shouldn't be surprised that the drug litmus test in this election concerns cocaine. There has already been a fundamental shift in how Americans view "softer" drugs like marijuana. Vice president and presidential candidate Al Gore admits to having tried marijuana, as have other national politicians including Newt Gingrich. While no candidate brags about marijuana use, it is no longer a bar to higher office. Cocaine, however, is a very different drug. Use is a felony. Addiction is a severe risk. Any candidate who admits to using cocaine will face tough questions about his or her fitness for office.

But while the press is quizzing Governor Bush about cocaine, we are missing a much larger issue. Ultimately, the former drug use of a candidate may be far less important his or her stance on drug policy. Governor Bush, for example, supports a Texas law to make it a felony to possess less than a gram of cocaine. That would add to the already harsh federal "mandatory minimum" sentences on drugs. America's prisons routinely parole violent criminals while nonviolent drug users serve out their full terms.

We must ask some serious questions of our presidential candidates. Will they support reforms of mandatory minimum sentencing? Will they support measures like the Racial Justice Act, which would end the federal penalties which give crack users (mostly black) a felony record while letting those with an equal amount of powder cocaine (mostly white) off with a misdemeanor? Will they compel law enforcement to arrest the white users who drive into the inner-city to buy drugs as well as the black and brown pushers who sell them? Will a rich white cocaine user have the same chances of arrest and prosecution as a poor black user? Or, to put it another way, will a poor, black addict get the same chance at rehabilitation and redemption as a rich, white addict quietly shuttled into a private facility?

The reality is that America often finds only the drugs it is looking for—the drugs used by poor and working-class Americans rather than the indulgences of the middle-class and rich. Seventy-eight million Americans have used drugs. Young African-Americans in the inner cities, where police routinely stop and frisk people who look "suspicious," are likely to be caught if they possess drugs. White Americans in the relative privacy of the suburbs or on college campuses can use with much less risk of being apprehended. Both groups have committed a crime; only a few are targeted to do the time.

Over the years, the prosecution of only a select subsection of drug users—mostly the poor, the black, and the brown—has curtailed the life-choices of a generation of Americans. Virtually every job application in America contains the question, "Are you a convicted felon?" Those who answer yes range from cold-blooded killers to teenagers who made the foolish decision to earn money by dealing drugs on the streets. A person convicted of felony drug possession will always bear the mark: often unable to vote, unable to qualify for most jobs that pay enough to support his or her family. And of course, incarceration in America's prisons helps turn some of these nonviolent offenders into hardened criminals by the time they leave.

Only a handful of politicians have had the courage to question the efficacy of the War on Drugs. Baltimore mayor Kurt Schmoke saw his chances for a run at the Senate evaporate when he proposed decriminalizing drugs. New Mexico governor Gary E. Johnson, who is forthright about his use of both marijuana and cocaine in college, suggests research on the same. Decriminalizing drugs is risky and controversial, but at the very least Americans must demand better: federally funded drug treatment and prevention, not simply incarceration. Changing how America deals with drug use requires strength of character and leadership. We must ask all of our presidential contenders if they can stand up to the political pressure and call for reform of America's deeply flawed War on Drugs.

Casualties of the War on Drugs

April 24, 2001

"It's a matter of balance," said White House press secretary Ari Fleischer, speaking of how to weigh the deaths of two members of a missionary family against those saved by the War on Drugs. But the details of the Peruvian incident, and its timing, are exposing just how unbalanced our strategies in the War on Drugs have become.

What happened in Peru? The U.S. government and local officials are still debating details, but CIA employees spotted a plane carrying a missionary family and a pilot and alerted the Peruvian military of their suspicions the flight may have been carrying drugs. The Peruvian air force did not make radio contact with the plane before shooting it down. The surviving family says the plane was strafed by gunfire, killing Veronica Bowers and her seven-month-old daughter. Supporters of military-style intervention credit these tactics with helping to decrease coca production by two-thirds. But supply in America remains abundant; production has simply moved to other parts of the region, including Colombia.

Just as we supported military intervention in Peru, we are pushing forward in Colombia as well. The U.S. Congress recently passed a $1.3 billion "Plan Colombia" to destroy coca farms and seize land held by guerrillas. Under Plan Colombia, we could strengthen the Colombian military's ties to right-wing militias connected to drug trafficking and massacres of civilians. Farmers charge that anti-cocoa chemical deforestation harms family food crops as well.

Days before the Summit of the Americas began in Quebec, a group of Latin American leaders requested that the United States rethink the military-style enterprise, which some U.S. analysts believe could plunge us into an unwinnable Vietnam-style conflict. The Latin American leaders, including Guatemalan Nobel Laureate Rigoberta Menchu and former Colombian Foreign Minister Rodrigo Pardo, asked that aid to Colombia target economic development, which would undercut one leg of the drug trade. They also noted, "We believe the United States has a legitimate interest in reducing the damage done by illegal drug use. But we are gravely concerned that current policy will cause more harm than good in Colombia and the region at large—while having little or no effect on the drug problems of the consumer countries."

By "consumer countries," they mean nations like the United States whose citizens consume billions of dollars worth of cocaine. While the U.S. government is prepared to spend billions on interdiction, we consistently underfund drug treatment. Today, a record 2 million Americans are in prison, a quarter for nonviolent drug crimes. That fact alone is having a ripple effect through America's towns, families, and economies, even adding to controversies over voting rights.

It must seem appealing to imagine that we can fight the drug war safely on other people's turf, far from our own streets. In addition to Plan Colombia, the Bush administration is pushing another $900 million for counternarcotics programs in the Andes, including Peru. But there is no way to avoid America's role in supply and demand and the human costs of fighting a militarized "war" against drugs.

A Selective War on Drugs

May 1, 2001

In the finale of the hit show *The Sopranos*, angry mob bosses retaliate against a rogue youngster, Jackie Junior, by executing him near a housing project and letting the blame fall on black drug dealers. One Mafioso who's had drug problems of his own praises boss Tony for the way he handled the situation. On screen, and in real life, black dealers are a convenient scapegoat for America's much larger drug problem, the public face of a multiracial, multinational, multibillion dollar industry.

In fact, an analysis of government statistics by the organization Human Rights Watch last year revealed that in ten states from Maine to Illinois, black men are twenty-seven to fifty-seven times more likely to be locked up for committing exactly the same drug crimes as whites, though five times as many white Americans use drugs as blacks in raw numbers. This system, says the group's executive director Ken Roth, "corrodes the American ideal of equal justice for all."

While the focus of drug use in America is on street dealing and street crime, the bulk of dealing and consumption goes on quietly, in private settings far different from the urban street corners depicted on shows like *NYPD Blue* and *Law and Order*. The May issue of *Spin* magazine ran an article called "Confessions of a Pot Delivery Girl," in which an Ivy League graduate talked about her uneventful time at a high-end delivery service for Manhattan marijuana smokers. She stated, "I soon became convinced that virtually every person on the island of Manhattan smokes pot. I delivered to doctors, lawyers, professors, architects, housewives, and stockbrokers." And while seeing a young black man arrested by police, she added, "for a moment, I felt my heart race. But the feeling passed as I walked by them in my black leather mules and knee-length skirt, a confident felon, young and white and female, handily concealed from the scope of the law."

The delivery girl's tale reveals a fundamental truth about drug use in America. Recreational use of drugs, as well as addictive use, cuts across socioeconomic sectors. But enforcement falls only on a few, in part because of laws that actually reward drug kingpins for turning states' evidence on their low-level employees. The discrepancies between use and treatment and use and punishment are finally starting to hit some discordant notes with observant Americans and culture mavens. The hit movies *Traffic*, *Blow*, and *Requiem for a Dream* all turned popular attention to drugs at the same time that stars Robert Downey, Jr., and Daryl Strawberry were being arrested again and again.

The weekend of June 1 in Albuquerque, academics, activists, and high-level government officials, including the governor of New Mexico, are meeting to rethink the future of drug policy in America. The confab is funded in part by billionaire George Soros, who funds leading think tank the Lindesmith Center, Drug Policy Research Institute. Soros and two other financiers are also funding ballot initiatives in Florida, Ohio, and Michigan designed to send first and second time drug offenders to treatment instead of prison. A similar measure, Proposition 36, already passed in California.

America's War on Drugs has produced few successes and a number of high-profile failures, including the recent downing of the missionary plane in Peru. Throughout this decades-long "war," we have been willing to accept massive collateral damage in poor, black, and urban communities. Now, other Americans are feeling pressure as well. In some states, the prison industry has grown so rapidly that nineteen-year-olds are being recruited as guards for violent maximum-security facilities—the equivalent of sending teenagers into battlefields. Laws that once provided loopholes for the rich and famous are now snaring them as well, admittedly after they've been given second or third or even fourth chances.

And what have been the results? The rates of teenage drug use have recently nudged down slightly. But despite a focus on interdiction, the flow of drugs into the country continues unabated. Only half of America's addicts are receiving treatment, and many are on waiting lists stretching for months. Plan Colombia is a $1.3 billion military approach similar to that used in Peru. But when White House officials debated spending just $100 million of that on treatment last year, the suggestion was shot down by "Drug Czar" General Barry McCaffrey. Failing to deal with the cycle of addiction (and support harm reduction and needle exchange programs) has helped prolong the cycle of IV drug use and raise AIDS infection rates. In some cities, including Jersey City, New Jersey, one in fifty African Americans is HIV positive.

Ignoring the civil rights and public health implications of the War on Drugs is like examining the remains of Aloha Flight 243 and saying "Who cares if one of the flight attendants got sucked out the ceiling?" For now, the casualties have mainly been poor, black, and brown. That's changing. Will our policies change, too?

Avoiding the Rush to Gloat

October 5, 2003

I was going to write this snarky column on the allegations that Rush Limbaugh is a pill-popper (as well as just being dinged from ESPN for racism). Wasn't it just delicious that this malicious conservative firebrand, this master of condemnation, was living in a house of glass? Wasn't it just the comeuppance that he couldn't hack it without uppers and downers?

I only had one problem. I couldn't finish that piece.

It strikes me that this sad, angry man says more about the tragedy of America's emotional life than an attack piece could convey. Who is he, this standard-bearer for anger and hate, and why did he allegedly feel it necessary to douse his own flames with illicit painkillers?

Like conservative moralist William Bennett, who lost millions of dollars gambling, Rush Limbaugh may become a symbol of the moral hypocrisy of the hard right. These two men helped build the frenzy to impeach President Clinton on charges of lying to the public. But were they themselves living a public lie?

If the ongoing investigation proves that Limbaugh got his housekeeper to buy thousands of addictive OxyContin pills illegally, he will join Bennett as a symbol of right-wing moralists' deadly dual consciousness. Morality is for the little people and liberals. (Same thing.) Talking about welfare queens and poverty pimps, not to mention philandering presidents, excuses your own failings.

So why not, excuse the pun, rush to judgment? In the book *The Power of Now*, philosopher Eckhart Tolle speaks of a cycle of identification with the negative aspects of life that hurts the thinker as much as anyone around him or her. "To complain is always nonacceptance of what is," Tolle writes. "It invariably carries an unconscious negative charge. When you complain, you make yourself into a victim."

Conservative complaints about the poor, about liberals, about (Rush's term) "feminazis" are a veiled form of victimology—the very syndrome they decry. Beset by enemies of his own making, is it any wonder that Limbaugh could feel the need to turn to powerful drugs for relief?

But before we get too comfortable bashing Limbaugh, we should question the negativity in our own lives. Individuals on both sides of the political fence are prone to complaining, to victimology, more than problem solving or acceptance. Our collective anger also leads to a collective need to numb that anger—the multibillion dollar legal alcohol, television, and tobacco industries, as well as the illegal and illicit drug trade. This world is dangerous and beautiful, war-torn and peaceful, the site of both negative and positive changes. The more we can see the world for what it is, the better decisions we'll be able to make.

Would the vast majority of our political leadership have voted to give the president powers to invade Iraq if they had truly seen the world for what it was, not simply looked for a target? We must remember that Democrats as well as Republicans, left as well as right, voted to endorse this breach of the Constitution. Our need for revenge blinded us to the fact that our actions in Iraq truly had little to do with the hurts we suffered on September 11, 2001.

And now, as we seek to deal with the ramifications of the Iraq war, are we seeing the world as it is or looking for scapegoats? Are we willing to look clearly at the situation we face, or do we feel the need to escape? The more we focus on the blame game versus problem solving, the more likely we are to self-sabotage by seeking false relief. Most of us are a little closer to being Rush Limbaugh than we'd like to admit. If that thought isn't scary enough to cause us to evolve, I don't know what is.

The opposite of complaining is not silence. As Tolle writes, "When you speak out, you are in power. So change the situation by taking action or by speaking out if necessary or possible; leave the situation or accept it. All else is madness." Nor is acceptance the opposite of change. Acceptance of our situation allows us to see clearly and make change. If we can see the world as it is, and speak to the necessary and positive changes we need to implement, we can avoid the trap of victimology and make America the nation we dream.

Pipe Dreams and Promises

March 10, 2003

Last week I found out that someone I love very, very much was so addicted to drugs that he became homeless. It's the second time this has happened to me. I remember going five years ago to the wrecked apartment of a friend in the music industry. Clothes, garbage, and kitchenware were heaped across the floor. He was probably looking for an imaginary baggie of heroin that he thought he'd stashed in dirty jeans or the cookie jar. Some friends and I staged a mini-intervention and all but tied him to the seat of a plane to get him to rehab. He got clean, dirty, clean. He's still battling.

Now the streets have claimed another person I care about. He's also deeply creative, a musician. Troubled. Usually kind. It's heroin. Maybe cocaine. I worry and pray.

Why do some of the most creative people immolate on drugs? Everyday Kurt Cobains, they slip into the routines of addiction like an old, soft shoe. Maybe these dreamers are too bruised by today's harsh realities to face them head on.

Most folks I know who experiment (or more) with illicit drugs are no more screwed up than average. It's easy to call addicts weak and lazy. It's harder to look at the role drugs play in all our lives.

The spectrum of drug use in America is broad and deep. In 1998, Drug Czar Barry McCaffrey said alcohol caused the most drug violence. (Just watch *Cops*.) Five times as many Americans die from alcohol abuse as illicit/illegal drugs. The alcohol industry pays $2 billion a year to promote the consumption of beer, wine, and spirits. Increasingly, sweet malt beverages are snaring the 10 million underage drinkers.

Tobacco kills even more people. Switzerland's Addiction Research Institute notes that tobacco is the primary killer addiction worldwide and in America. In 2000, 4.9 million people across the world died from tobacco, 71 percent of drug-related deaths. The fact that it's legal dulls many of us—me included—into thinking that nicotine is different. But at least two of my friends, both incredible women, have been cycling on and off tobacco like junkies battling the urge to shoot up. It comes down to this: Legal drugs, the most lethal, are taxable. Illegal drugs are not.

America's drug laws are both draconian and racist. Even though white Americans consume the majority of illegal drugs, black and brown

Americans—a fraction of the population—are the majority of those convicted for drug crimes.

Sometimes, as in the infamous Tulia, Texas, cases, drugs are merely a
pretext for railroading African-Americans. Two weeks ago, *New York* magazine's cover featured Lucy Grealy. Undergoing reconstruction for facial
cancer, the author of *Autobiography of a Face* slipped from the bestseller lists into
heroin addiction. Eric Breindel, the conservative *New York Post* editorial page
editor who died from complications from his heroin addiction, has a scholarship named after him rather than a jail wing. This knowledge doesn't
change the fact that most of the people I see strung out on the streets—shuffling, nodding, hollow-eyed—look more like me than Grealy or Breindel.
Money lets you hide your problems, and race and money are Siamese twins.

Our government's response to drug use is to launch the new "Operation
Pipe Dreams." As we duct-tape our windows against bioterrorism, Attorney
General John Ashcroft has deployed twelve hundred federal agents to catch
businesses that encourage smoking up. Federal law bars the sale of products
targeted towards illegal drug use, including bongs and marijuana pipes. (Just
tell that to my nabe, the Village, head shop central.) So far, authorities have
charged at least fifty stores and Internet retailers with selling illegal drug paraphernalia.

Paraphernalia is not the problem. Junkies can smoke off a spoon, snort
coke from any reasonably flat surface, and what do you think most bodegas
sell cigarette papers for? Maybe the issue is motivation.

In the past, and for a few people today, drugs were, and are, part of
sacred rituals. Native American tribes have had to sue, repeatedly, to use the
psychotropic peyote cactus in centuries-old religious ceremonies. The
Council on Spiritual Practices has an entire crispy-dry Web site dedicated to
"entheogens," or psychoactive religious substances. Entheogens helped people tune in, not tune out. I guess way back if you were tuned out on the permanent, you'd be eaten by an animal, killed by a rival, or starve to death. But
I've seen some of the same shadows walking my streets for years.

Now most drug use is about escape rather than engagement. America,
the key consumer of drugs, blames the suppliers. According to the *Ecologist*
(UK), the United States is considering carpet-bombing coca-producing
Colombian regions with a killer fungus, Fusarium oxysporum. It kills coca,
the base of cocaine, but can also cause an infection in humans that is fatal in
70 percent of cases. We plan to drop it on small family farms, far from our
streets, whether or not they're growing goods we detest but pay for. And what
are we doing here, about our addictions? The federal government won't
increase funds for rehabilitation. Politicians are addicted to alcohol and

tobacco money. An investigation by Common Cause reveals the concessions the alcohol industry's $23 million in campaign contributions and PAC money from 1989 to 1999 bought.

We can't fight this by going outside. The only way we can balance the need for transcendence with the drive for survival is by going inside. We must push ourselves to be centered and strong; question what we seek from substances promising transcendence; and figure out what we're willing to offer in return. In this environment, that could include our freedom or our very lives.

What are our alternatives? Marijuana, judging by the furious debates between states and the federal government, will be sensibly legalized at least on the local level. But it's scary to envision a world where hard drugs are legalized and rehab continues to be underfunded and stigmatized. In America legalization, taken to a capitalist end-stage, is linked to marketing, sexism, and big corporate profits. What if we had "Pot Girls" and "Ecstasy Girls" just like "Bud Girls"?

The fear of that scenario is just one factor keeping us from moving forward. Talking to a suburban family with small kids, I described drug experimentation as a rite of passage for most people in their teens and twenties. They cocked their heads, remembering some long-ago bong hit, and said, "Ooh, we don't want to think about that."

We sure don't. And as long as we don't, we won't be able to discuss what our options are. Decriminalization of drugs, a policy which most European countries follow tacitly or explicitly, means that people can buy certain substances without fear of being arrested *and* without money going to the government treasury. In America, decriminalization has stalled in part because we can't imagine something being legal (or not-illegal) and also not taxable. We can't imagine substances being taxable but having money *really* go to prevention and rehab. We can't imagine acknowledging the need most people have to leave their skins for a minute, or building a world where more people have less reason to escape.

Organizations like the Drug Policy Alliance and publications like Alternet's Drug Reporter newsletter are trying to kickstart policy debate. Let's start talking. Let's start dreaming. Now.

The Rap on Censorship

July 31, 2001

Let me be the first to say it in the language of hip hop: I've been hating on Eminem for a long time.

Yeah, yeah, I know he's got skillz, but so do a lot of other guys whose rhyme dictionary begins with "bitch" and ends with "ho." Maybe it's the fact that I heard the original version of his album, including jokes about raping lesbians, before he cut a clean version and became a crossover hit. Rappers like Eminem made it harder and harder for women like me (who actually listen to the lyrics) to dance to the music we once loved, and many of us have abandoned ship for other music like soul or drum 'n' bass.

But when the FCC, led by Gen. Colin Powell's son Michael Powell, decided to battle the Real Slim Shady by fining Colorado's KKMG for playing an edited version of his song, I reluctantly have to stand up—not in his defense, but ours.

The call to make the airwaves safe for America's children sounds good, doesn't it? The problem is, the approach is all wrong.

First of all, it's a slippery slope.

Just look at who else has gotten caught in the FCC's net: one of the most effective critics within the hip hop movement. Sarah Jones is an actress, writer, and poet whose song "Your Revolution" has given young women a sense of personal freedom. In it, she sings lyrics like "The real revolution ain't about bootie size/The Versaces you buys/Or the Lexus you drives." It gets spicier, and more effective. For that, the FCC fined station KBOO in Portland $7,000 on May 14 of this year—for playing the song in 1999.

Frankly, hip hop was a lot less vulgar before it became a crossover hit in white households and a cash cow to record labels. When the music was an underground phenomenon, DJs and MCs produced party music and more political songs like the anti-cocaine track "White Lines" and KRS-One's black history lesson "You Must Learn." But how many white suburban kids want to listen to a black history lesson? The market quickly devolved into lowest-common-denominator blaxploitation, images of the "real" life on the streets that often bore no semblance to reality.

The reason teens listen to rap is probably twofold: one, to piss off their parents and, two, to find an authentic mode of expression in a world where everything seems shiny-happy-false. Yes, hip hop often presents a false mirror of the gritty and grimy, but censoring it will simply end an incomplete conversation about issues like drugs, sexuality, schools, and aspirations for the future, all of which come up in hip hop lyrics.

But how do you urge the conversation to go to a higher level when market forces are pushing it to a lowest common denominator? The record industry itself is finally beginning to take proactive steps with meetings like June's Hip Hop Summit, attended by moguls including Russell Simmons and artists including Queen Latifah, Sean "Puffy" Combs, and Talib Kweli. Nation of Islam leader Minister Louis Farrakhan, who has long set out to have a dialogue with the rap community, stated: "Society wants lyrics cleaned up but it (society) doesn't want to clean itself up." For their part, artists committed to bringing more positive content into hip hop without top-down censorship.

Led by a bipartisan group including former vice presidential candidate Senator Joe Lieberman, Congress seems set on proposing even more restrictions on pop culture content. But the best reason not to censor musicians like Eminiem is the same reason prohibition backfired—government repression increases demand. Those parental labeling stickers simply made f***ed-up lyrics sexier to teenagers. Efforts to take songs like Eminem's off the airwaves will create even more of an us-vs.-them mentality, leading people who don't support the lyrics but do support free speech to band with moneymakers in it for a quick buck. Meanwhile, a much better approach would be to turn down the rhetoric, discuss the actual issues behind the music, and make sure the Sarah Joneses of the world are as well known as the Eminems.

***

Update: In 2003, two years after Sarah Jones decided to fight the FCC's fine, the agency ruled that "Your Revolution" was *not* indecent.

The Real Rap Controversy:
Free Speech Flap Over a Muzzled Music

February 22, 2001

I watched the Grammys with a bunch of jaded New York music critics who discussed whether Elton 'n' Em would end the set with a smile, hug, or French kiss. The inevitable middle road was marketing, pure and simple. It was a good way for Sir Elton to put another trophy in his publicity case, and a godsend for "My Name Is." Grammy president Michael Greene's belabored "can't we all just get along" speech preceding the set made the stilted shebang about as convincing as John Ashcroft going over to Ronnie White's house for a barbecue. As the crowd stood afterward, I wondered if they knew what they were applauding.

Nonetheless, at least one of my viewing companions knew exactly why she was clapping. "He is," she gushed about Eminem, the Great White Hope of rap, "the next Elvis."

And you know what—she is right.

Just as Elvis (embraced by some for his prodigious talent; by others for his skin color) marked the end of the black dominance of rock 'n' roll, Eminem formally marks the transition of hip hop from a "black" medium to a neutered "pop" medium. Immediately, a lyric popped into my head from another rap group: a gifted and controversial collaborative that I doubt today's record companies would promote as heavily, nor today's Academy of Recording Arts and Sciences would defend so staunchly.

Elvis was a hero to most
But he never meant s—t to me you see
Straight up racist that sucker was
Simple and plain
Mother f—— him and John Wayne.

Those lines come straight from Public Enemy's "Fight the Power," which took over the airwaves in '89 as part of the soundtrack to Spike Lee's *Do the Right Thing*. A year later, the song was released on *Fear of a Black Planet*, an album that arguably marked the beginning of the end of rap's rise as political commentary.

Chuck D's clearly enunciated growl (much has been made of Eminem's clearly enunciated whine) sent shivers down the spines of suburban mothers who unspooled reels of tape and sent little Jimmy back to his room to listen to Rush instead. But the beats and rhymes had so entranced a generation of Americans that the music crossed color lines. But how could you mass-market the music of revolution to mainstream white America?

First point: take out the tough stuff and the black stuff. The controversies in rap lyrics used to be about issues that belonged on the front page of America's newspapers, like poverty and police brutality. But folks still wanted to be *down*, so many records substitute sexual controversy or blaxploitation instead.

A few years ago, P.E. (pre-Eminem), I visited white hip hop fans in a tiny Indiana town while interviewing teens for a book about race. In eighth grade, B.J. had gotten into rap while hanging out in multiracial L.A, but in Delphi he was the only hip hop fan for miles. By high school, the "wigger" craze was blanketing newspapers and television, and he was surrounded by kids who wore the fashions, listened to the beats, and didn't really care about the history.

Plus ça change, plus que la même chose. I lectured about racial demographics and the book at Georgia State University just this Monday. During the question and answer session, a student with a sleek brown bob said that though she looked white, she was racially mixed and shocked to hear some of her dorm-mates using the word "nigger" or calling black people "scary." Another student, who hung out with both blacks and whites, had to tell his white friends not to use the word "nigger" around him as they played cards.

I didn't have the presence to ask him what kind of music they were bumping as they shuffled, cut, and dealt, but I wouldn't be surprised if it was hip hop. Rap has become a universal soundtrack for teen and twentysomething life. Hip hop's Johnny-come-latelies, most of them white, can get into tales of (ha ha) raping their mother (it's just a joke) or putting mouthy women in their place. Don't get me wrong: there are some plenty of DWBs and DWSs (Down White Brothers and Sisters) out there, usually known as backpackers in hip hop lingo. But it's easier to swallow the ghetto-fried fantasy of the pimp or the baller than it is to get down with rapper Mos Def who reminds folks that "Chuck Berry is rock and roll . . ./You may dig on the Rolling Stones/But they ain't come up with that style on they own." The good news: when Mos performs, even when he chants "Black people unite, and let's all get down," you're likely to have a white person on one side, a Korean-American in front, and a couple of Carribean peeps nearby.

Today, while the larger issues of race in America's future still remain, most new fans only know hip hop as booty bump 'n' grind music and controversy as lyrics over locking someone in the trunk of a car. There are better things, bigger things, for us to argue about.

An Open Letter to Michael Jackson

November 26, 2003

You were my first. Back when the other kids were swaying to nursery rhymes, I wanted to rock with you. I had everything I needed—a portable stereo and an album of you singing with the Jackson Five. According to my mother, I would drag around my little stereo, and I would put you on, and I would dance. Nothing else in the world could have made me happier.

I remember you. Your lips were full and your nose was wide and your face was brown. This only rates mentioning because it is no longer true, so untrue, in fact, that sometimes I wonder if I imagined you as you once were. I'm sure at night, as a child, I dreamed of the boy with the afro who sang and spun on his heels like a miniature James Brown.

I wish that boy had become a man. That wish seemed reasonable all the way through *Off the Wall*, when your nose grew narrower and hair more lank, but you were still visibly black. With every subsequent album, your relationship to your original appearance grew fainter and fainter until you were no longer even an echo of yourself. But the further you fled from black masculinity, the more international crowds lionized you. Today you are grotesque.

And an alleged child molester—that too? If we can believe what we see in the camera lens, that this pale alien being (recently parodied in *Scary Movie 3*) was once cute little Michael, then we can believe anything. The danger for us is that we will judge you by your appearance. The danger for you is that you have set up a situation, with your reckless behavior around your own children and others', that we cannot help but judge.

In his book *The Hip Hop Generation*, Bakari Kitwana relentlessly outlines America's broken promise to black males. Mandatory minimum sentencing guidelines and unbalanced enforcement of drug laws have helped make prison a waystation or home for many more black men than white. In Los Angeles and Cincinnati, frustrated youth up-end their own neighborhoods to draw attention to police brutality. The global economy undermines the fortunes of lower-skilled workers, many of them African-Americans. The military, in many cases, remains the only way out.

This social warfare has hardened many black men, aiding and abetting the culture of hypermasculinity that permeates hip hop. It's hard to be a sister and be down with the bitch/ho lyrics, hard to be down with men who spout rhymes full of anti-female fury. Commercial hip hop may appeal to young women who can pretend that the men are calling out someone else, but to an older head like myself it sounds as if they are speaking my name. I cannot listen to it. I cannot dance.

But I long to take the floor with the same childish glee that I did when you and I were together. I desperately want you to be there for me, to reassure me that things aren't so bad that the primary options open to black men are hatred of black women or physical and mental disintegration. I would like to think that you, the shadow Michael who never had a chance to grow up, wouldn't treat me the way those other men do. But I'm the furthest thing from your mind.

In your absence, the absence of a Michael I can relate to, I have only questions. Why does America destroy and pervert black men? Were you squeezed between racism and perfectionism until your very soul compressed? And what about those without your millions of dollars? What options are left for them?

I feel—and I know it cannot be true, for I still breathe—that if you cannot exist, I cannot exist. If there is no room for a loving black masculinity in the world, I fear there is little room for the black feminine as well. You, Michael Jackson, are not all black men, and for that I am grateful. But your decline says more about America than we can bear to hear.

C.R.E.A.M.
(Cash Rules Everything Around Me)

Bush, Taxes, and the Recession Question

December 19, 2000

Even Bill Gates can't save us now.

When Microsoft lowered its earnings expectations for only the second time in its fourteen-year history, the markets dropped like stones, again. Some financial analysts started murmuring the "r" word in earnest: recession, recession, recession. The news came only three days after the Supreme Court ruling that closed out election 2000 and gave the nod to president-elect George W. Bush.

What a sense of timing.

Throughout the election saga, the financial markets did a little cha-cha. The market usually remained stable at best following court rulings for Vice President Al Gore. They often rose following good news for Bush, leading some conservative commentators to dub him a darling of the markets. Astoundingly enough, journalists and neutral analysts of the election began to pick up the refrain: a quick Gore concession would be good for the economy. Subtext: ballots be damned if the money be right.

Well, the Bush bounce didn't appear. Our economy doesn't run on charisma, and to be fair, both candidates often seemed to be trying to convince us that it did. But the difference is that Bush ran on and remains committed to a $1.3 trillion tax cut—one that will hurt our ability to mitigate the effects of economic slowdown. Whether or not we enter a full-blown recession, we certainly don't seem likely to enjoy the same kind of runaway growth of the Clinton/Gore years.

The dot-com craze overshadowed real technology gains. Now the bad money is leaving gaping holes in the markets. Companies that grew fast and generated nothing but hype are laying off employees, and like trees that fall in the forest, they're sometimes wiping out healthy little saplings in their wake. And what about the slowdown in sales of hardware? Economist Dr. Julianne Malveaux says, "People are not buying [new] computers. The sucker still prints, it still goes online." Microsoft's chief financial officer felt compelled to say, "The PC is far from dead." Gee, thanks for the vote of confidence.

Consumer debt may damage the economy far more. According to our financial statements, "I shop, therefore I am" is no longer just the Valley Girl Motto. One-eighth of households—and a third of those making $10,000 or less—spend more than 40 percent of their income on debt payments. That number has risen by 17 percent since just 1995. Personal bankruptcies and credit card delinquencies are at record highs. The minimum wage in America is far from a family's living wage. And while the Bush tax cut favors higher income households, the administration has not come out in favor of a rise in the minimum wage.

Finally, as the economy slows down, some of us will be hit harder than others. I was part of that generation who was told that for the first time, we would not earn more or live better than our parents. After us, a generation of college grads—bolstered by the dot-com boom—have gone on to earn previously unthinkable sums for graduating from respected schools. Now, the reversal: the layoffs at dot-coms, law firms, and the like. But college grads aren't going to be the hardest hit, even if they float a couple of notches down on the income ladder.

Among the structural changes in the American economy in the past eight years were the growth of what Newsweek called "the prison generation" and the end of the welfare entitlement system. On top of that, the black unemployment rate is consistently double that of the white unemployment rate, even in good times. Congresswoman Eleanor Holmes Norton (D-D.C.) notes that "The Clinton/Gore economy was so robust that black men getting out of jail could often get jobs and black women getting off of welfare could often find work. If that goes away, and we have a president who's into tax cuts, the first people who will suffer are black people." Concerns like these, not some slavish love of the Democrats, motivated the black community to vote for Gore.

If there is an economic downturn, and the most vulnerable citizens are once again jobless, how will we react? By demonizing the failed job-seekers? Or by tempering our taste for tax cuts and admitting it's still about the economy, stupid?

***

Update: President Bush pushed through not one but two multibillion dollar tax cuts. By March 2004, America had lost nearly three million jobs since Bush took office.

It's the Economy, Stupid

September 18, 2002

The only paper I read with regularity these days is the *Wall Street Journal*. Although its editorial writers are patently insane, the news and feature writers have recently dedicated themselves to thoughtful pieces on what should be the most important story of our day: the collapse of our economy.

Perhaps I mean the collapse of the *illusion* of our economy—a place of endless riches, where everyone's a winner. (Old America: Getting off the plane in Vegas. New America: getting on the plane back home, broke and jacked up.)

Take the September 10 edition of the *Journal*. On the far left of the page is a feature story on New London, Connecticut. This tired, slumping, working-class town invoked the government prerogative of eminent domain and razed the houses of elderly citizens so that drug company Pfizer could come in and build a new plant. The article by Lucette Lagnado details how the company was promised millions of dollars in tax breaks and incentives in exchange for building a $300 million research facility, conference center, and hotel. The project hasn't been completed because some empowered and pissed off residents have filed suit.

The completed part of the plant doesn't employ many folks from New London nor does it spill revenue over to local businesses. This is the downside of globalization: demolish locally, employ globally. Many conglomerates these days act like mercenary armies, bringing in the troops they need and asking little except food, shelter, and complete obedience from those who quarter them.

In the center of the same day's *Journal* is a story titled: "WorldCom Board Will Consider Rescinding Ebbers's Severance."

WorldCom, known to many of us as the company that swallowed MCI long distance, has been in the news for misplacing $7 billion and filing for bankruptcy. This story, by Susan Pullam, Jared Sandberg, and Deborah Soloman, details how the former CEO, Bernard J. Ebbers, got a whopper of a good-bye present: a $408 million loan at 2.3 percent interest, plus $1.5 million per year in lifetime salary.

Let me run that by you again: a man who was at the helm of a company that just up and lost $7 billion got a $408 million loan, plus $1.5 million in free cash each year. Let's pretend to spend that money for him:

$408 million is the equivalent of: 204,000 fancy laptops, enough to give one to roughly one in ten graduating high school seniors this year, or 2,000 new homes at their roughly $200,000 average price.

$1.5 million a year equals: 345 average yearly payments of TANF (the post-reform welfare); 100 students' full tuition, board, and fees at UCLA.

I hesitate to compare lost corporate cash to real world dollars. While we're more than happy to talk about "welfare queens" and "poverty pimps" (and yes, there are welfare cheats), we don't seem to hear the vast sucking sound of white-collar criminals hoovering out our economy. (Not to mention the estimated $12 billion in legal federal "corporate welfare.")

A quick note about welfare, which more people will need in the current downturn. Since "welfare reform," the number of child-only families receiving assistance has doubled across the nation, rising in New Jersey, for example, from 17 percent of the caseload to 33 percent. This means that parents with addictions, mental health disorders, or simply too few coping skills have left their children as wards of the state. Like most people, I have no idea where the money lost in Enron et al. really goes. But I'd love to see it spent on programs like childcare and drug rehab. Even for people of means, like Florida Gov. Jeb Bush's daughter, Noelle.

I will spare you my full rant on Jerry Springer and Eminem but let me simply say: white kids have figured out this country isn't rolling out the red carpet for them, the same way black and brown kids did years ago. The result is an often poorly articulated but justified rage against a country that manages to stock fifty types of snack products in every mini-mart but rarely generates a decent neighborhood public school.

America has found one very successful method for dealing with black rage: massive incarceration of people who were never trained nor expected to be a part of "mainstream" society, regardless of their potential. And in fact, incarceration of nonwhite Americans (often on drug crimes) is a growth industry that largely employs working-class whites and nonwhite Americans. But at a certain point, particularly in an economic downturn, the system begins feeding on itself. We will either have to jail undereducated white youth en masse, or we will have to try something radically different, like training working-class kids to think for themselves and not just take jobs but invent them.

Actually, a lot of white-collar Americans are feeling the need for a good solid job right around now. I've never had so many unemployed friends in my life; friends who, admittedly, are still holding out for something new and better, while running up their credit card bills to bridge the gap.

One problem is that the implicit contract between companies and workers seems very much broken. Today, no matter what the job level or contract, people are being fired seemingly at will, from downsized managers making six figures to the 17,000 employees of Consolidated Freightways, who were laid off via voicemail on Labor Day. Employees, in turn, find little reason to offer themselves as paragons of loyalty. No, they do not want to work unpaid overtime. Yes, they steal the pens and fax paper. Yes, they take two-hour lunches. Why? They're looking for another job.

In his two years in office, President George W. Bush has managed to mangle the economy, allow the guise of homeland security to demolish the guarantees of freedom inherent in the Bill of Rights, and get away with seeming—God knows how—presidential. At least to some of us. On trips abroad, the comments, even from conservatives, usually run something like, "Your President's an idiot, eh?" In fact, the conservatives (I'm thinking here specifically of a trip to Switzerland) are often more vitriolic, embarrassed, and abashed that someone with so little sense of governance speaks in their name.

There's good reason for President Bush to go on the warpath. After all, war is a traditional and often successful distraction from domestic woes, which we have in abundance. We also still have, in my humble opinion, the greatest country in the world. So I will wave my little flag for America, the country that I love, and note:

You can telephone the White House at (202) 456-1111. Wait out a short machine message and then a live operator will take your (hopefully concise) message for the president, along the lines of "I oppose" or "I support" the proposed war against Iraq. And, if you're really feeling your beans, you could mention the need to reconsider mandatory minimum drug sentencing laws, which his niece may soon be facing.

***

Update: Obviously America went to war, the economy is still tanking, and there's no time like the present to call the White House and register your opinions.

Follow the Money and the Documents

October 3, 2002

I spent Sunday brunch with a bunch of journalists, many of them on war patrol doing quickie documentaries on Saddam, for example. But one producer with a major media company spent the past week trying to get a member of the Bush cabinet to return her calls and those of her even better connected on-air reporter on an economic story.

"They just refuse," she said. "Worse, they won't refuse [outright]; they say they're too busy. Why should they spend their time answering the legitimate questions of a reporter? Why should they be accountable?"

One of the biggest underreported economic stories today (and boy is there competition) is the vice president's attempt to withhold records of his meetings with oil companies. For the first time ever, the General Accounting Office (auditors for Congress) is going to federal court to order the executive branch to turn over documents. The eighty-one-year-old agency wants to know which energy companies helped the Bush administration shape its policies. Yes, the energy companies were right there in the White House, all but holding the pen as policy was drafted. It's one thing to be friendly to business interests, another to walk out of the Oval Office and let them raid the till.

Cheney and other members of the Bush administration met with Enron executives six times last year. But that was just the beginning. In just four months during the dawn of the administration, February to May, Cheney and his economic task force met with hundreds of representatives from 150 corporations and trade associations. Then they set the administration's new energy policies, which included the plans to drill for oil in the Arctic National Wildlife Refuge and build hundreds of new electric plants. Now, despite a Congressional request for documents, they've been stonewalling for more than a year.

Both President Bush and Vice President Cheney have long records of allying themselves with oil interests, being rewarded in 2000 with campaign contributions, and in turn rewarding the companies with policies that will enrich them. Cheney, who polishes his image as a thinker and policymaker, is actually much more of a wheeler-dealer than Baby Bush. As the former CEO of Halliburton, a multibillion dollar oil and energy corporation, he once stated, "The good Lord didn't see fit to put oil and gas only where there are democratically elected regimes friendly to the United States."

At the time, Halliburton was brokering a deal with military dictators in Burma, who were using slave labor to build oil pipelines. One of the companies involved in the Burma deal was Unocal, which also courted the Taliban as a possible protector of its oil projects in Afghanistan. In addition, as CEO of Halliburton, Cheney—the secretary of defense during President Bush *père*'s war on Iraq—sold $24 million in oil-related construction services to the Iraqis. Money is inherently amoral. Oil is money.

Now, to add fuel to the fire, Cheney's former firm is embroiled in an Enron-style scandal. The Securities and Exchange Commission is investigating Halliburton for allegedly fudging its accounting numbers. Cheney has refused to answer questions about this issue as well.

There are dozens of political catchphrases that come to mind, particularly "It's not the crime, it's the cover-up." But Cheney's chicanery also reminds me of a song from Disney's animated film, *Lady and the Tramp*. Two devious felines sing, "We are Siamese if you please; we are Siamese if you don't please." The Bush administration is ruthless in flouting all public accountability and crafty in cloaking itself in the flag. It's a Siamese government, which presents the face of a grieving America to the public while continuing to cut backroom financial and political deals.

Right now, the White House is telling us to ignore the economic crisis at hand in the name of patriotism. At the same time, it refuses to admit its own complicity in the decline of our economy. When you feel the pinch in your wallet or pocketbook, think how Bush and Cheney have helped siphon out the American economy. Then contact the White House and Congress, and most important, vote your conscience and your future.

***

Update: In June 2004, the U.S. Supreme Court referred the Cheney energy case back to a lower court. Some observers saw it as a victory for Cheney; others, as a sign the White House was still in the hot seat.

The Revolution Must Be Monetized

April 17, 2003

I just finished my annual financial marathon. It starts in January, when I put the last bank statement into the huge plastic bin containing folders of different receipts. Over the next few weeks, I sort through these receipts and total them. I gather my 1099s and W2s, thin slips of paper that drift in from California, D.C., anywhere I could scrounge a dollar. Then I try to make sense of it all for the taxman. I can't. I hire someone to do it for me.

The last time I did my own taxes, maybe a decade ago, was back when I was employed only by a corporation. For years now, my income has come mainly from what I seek out myself, a mix of writing, lecturing, and consulting. Freelancing is always the best and worst of both worlds. Once you become your own boss, you usually realize just how lousy a manager you are.

Take Farai the Manager. Every year, FtM claims that she will move to a more efficient computerized accounting system. Every year, FtM tries it for a month or two, throws up her hands in disgust, and moves back to what FtE—Farai the Employee—calls shoebox accounting. (That big plastic bin used to be a humble cardboard shoebox.) Particularly in this political climate, where many people mask their feelings and beliefs just to stay employed, FtE appreciates FtM's efforts. If only she were more efficient!

Many of my friends are progressive writers, artists, and activists who have the same manager/employee split personality. The employees are always whining about something: Why don't we have (any/better) health insurance? A 401(k)? And when are we going to get a raise? The managers keep threatening to close the "factory" and throw us at the mercy of the market. The employees point out the socially responsible nature of their work. The managers mumble, *As if anyone gives a damn.*

The managers and employees are united on one front. We need more money. And more of a clue how to earn and use it.

Many of us are suspicious of money, not surprising when many of the people with surplus use it to screw other folks over. But I believe the intellectual critiques of capitalism among many progressives actually have deeper and more personal roots.

Were your mother and father paid a fair wage? Could they even get a job? Could they keep it? Money is not just about numbers. How we use or abuse it depends on our emotional, political, and historical perspectives.

During our childhoods, in particular, we develop ideas about whether money is a force to be feared or loved, and how likely we are to be able to control it.

This is how I remember the Reagan '80s: schoolchildren in Baltimore cheering when Reagan got shot; jokes about government cheese, usually coming from folks who ate it; the acceleration of the steep decline in urban public schooling; the constant longing to buy a brand-name anything that could provide a veneer of self-worth. Now that Reagan has slipped into the haze of Alzheimer's, his hagiographers have gotten even more insistent. He wasn't about Iran-Contra and choking the life from cities. He built the perfect America.

Not mine.

The Bush Zeroes will divide America's memory as well. Did Bush II bring a return to values or an emphasis on the value of killing? Was that tax cut the beginning of the end of the American Empire or simply a reward for the people who make this country great?

Too many progressives look at money as inherently tainted. We play a game of keep-away, bragging about who's broke. Meanwhile, urban pop culture has no compunction about acknowledging the value of money. Money can get you cars, clothes, sex, and what passes for respect. Money, specifically the U.S. dollar, is the world's lingua franca. Many activists who presume to speak for the urban "underclass" talk about up-ending the economic system, as if that's what most people want. If our economy is a sinking ship, many would settle for a berth on the upper decks.

One of the most revolutionary things artists and activists could do is conduct their lives not as poverty crusades, all sackcloth and ashes, but as crusades to end poverty, including our own. Learning how to manage money—and sharing that information with others—is transformative. As I struggle to learn more about money, I also learn how much of my identity I've sold. One of my unpaid jobs is filling out all the forms from healthcare providers, banks, and credit agencies telling me I can only preserve my privacy rights if I explicitly say so in writing. In other words, your social security number, the medications you take, and the videos you rent are all accessible by clicking a mouse unless (and maybe even) if you ask them not to be.

Understanding money means understanding America.

The revolution needs accountants.

Dude, Where's My Tax Cut?

May 29, 2003

Dude, I'm feeling majorly shafted. Like, I was reading the newspaper—well, not really *reading* it, I was, like, watching *Fantasy Island* (Mr. Roarke is SO boss) and dropped my pepperoni slice right on top of my roommate's paper. Oops.

Anyway, I ate this 'roni off of this headline about "A Tax Cut Without End." The government is giving away all this money, see? And it might be, let me look at the paper again, $320 billion over ten years. Or it might be, like $800 billion, 'cause, y'know, once you're gettin' all the free loochie, why stop?

I was doin' my end-zone dance cause I figured I'm a millionaire now, right? That's mucho zeroes to split—$800,000,000,000!!!!! Then my roommate came home.

I call him Dr. Doom because to him, everything sucks. *He* sucks. He's always bugging me to take out the empties and saying if I don't recycle the world's going to end.

So I told him I'm a millionaire! Uh huh, uh huh!

Dr. Doom totally harshed my high. He was, like, you're not gettin' any of this money, dude. First off, he said, you're on unemployment, remember? I told him it wasn't my fault I got fired from the copy shop, and he said, no, listen, that even if I got back on the nine-to-five groove, I wouldn't be seeing any serious cash.

Why not? I said.

'Cause, he said. 'Cause it's not for people who work, it's for people who make all this money off of stocks. Take the Doomster, for example. He's making good loot for a patchouli-smelling guy, almost fifty G's for writing stupid articles. And he's going to get back, like, $300 a year.

He got all bitter, see. Three hundred bucks a year! He pays three hundred bucks a *month* for health insurance. And then he went off on how he had to live with a pig like me so he could save money for his own place, but he didn't want to be home it stinks so bad, and why was the kitchen full of empties?

I said, dude, calm down, don't get all personal and stuff. But I really wanted to know where my million dollars was going.

Dr. Doom said that that heart attack guy, the vice president, is the kind of guy who gets the cash. The vice prez was the tiebreaker vote on this tax cut, and he was gonna get eighty-five extra G's just the first year, even more the next. The prez was getting back $33,000.

So, like, the Prez and Heart Attack Dude are getting my money? I said. Whoa.

Dr. Doom said they were getting back *his* money. He got all pissed again, saying how he was working and my parents were paying my rent. For him to get back the four grand he paid for health insurance each year as a tax cut, he'd need to make over two hundred and fifty grand. And then, y'know, he wouldn't care if he had to pay for insurance. Plus, 25 percent of people who aren't geezers on Social Security don't have insurance at least part of the year. If only we had nationalized health care, Doom said. That would be a friggin' tax cut.

I said what was nationalized health care?

The Doomster just sighed. He pulled up this site on the Internet, the Freelancer's Union. It's this thing he just joined so his healthcare would cost less. He said that 30 percent of the people who work in NYC are freelancers like he is. But unless you make over a hundred grand a year, you can't afford decent insurance. So these guys, the union, are trying to make a stink about it. They call working and not having insurance "middle class poverty."

My roommate said a lot of other stuff too, about how the schools are screwed up now but just wait till there's even less money 'cause of the tax cut, and raising the cost of the subway was like taxes too, and, y'know—when was I going to take out the empties?

Fine! I can take a hint. Is raising the cost of beer like taxes, too? If so, I was thinking—and I hate to say it—Dr. Doom might be right.

Media and Technology

You've Got News!

January 11. 2000

Beware the smell of synergy in the morning.

With the merger of America Online and Time Warner in a deal valued at $350 billion, American consumers can be assured of top-quality info-tainment about every single Time-Life-Warner-Turner-CNN-TNT-HBO-Cinemax-*People*-*Sports Illustrated*-*Entertainment Weekly*-*Money*-*Fortune*-New Line-Atlantic-Electra-Sire-AOL book, movie, magazine, online feature, or news event in the world. Just don't be too picky about hearing a wide range of voices and opinions from this or any other big info conglomerate.

I suppose, being an occasional contributor to *Time*, I should look at the good news in all this. AOL Time Warner will be surfing on top of the broadband wave. Soon, not only will you be able to watch an editor from *Sports Illustrated* interviewed on CNN on your Time Warner cable hookup, you'll also be able to watch the whole thing on a flawless broadband connection over AOL! Now that, my friends, is service. It only raises one question: what will you be watching?

The short answer is that you'll be watching whatever the handful of big boys who own the big media companies tell you to. Despite being a wired kinda gal—online since '94—the AOL-Time Warner merger shocked me. It slapped me in the face and said, "Honey, I know you write books about things like race relations. Books are good, as long as there's a web tie-in. The reality is that we're going to be making most of our money off of chat rooms from now on, so tighten your bra and start pretending to be a fourteen-year-old girl who likes Christina Aguilera."

Sorry, I must have drifted. The serious answer lies in Internet lingo itself. At one time, we used to call the Internet the "web," because each site linked to a network of information by other people. Now, in the age of e-commerce, content is "sticky." (Think of those glue traps we use to catch poor little mice.) Companies like AOL Time Warner want you to come to them for news and entertainment and "stick" there—using only other sites, services, and companies that they own.

With the "sticky" theory of media, it becomes a waste of time and waste of money for companies to get new voices into the news. Why have an independent economist chat on AOL when you can use someone from *Fortune*? Why use an independent child psychologist on CNN when you can use someone from *Parenting* magazine? The flawed *Time*/CNN Tailwind story on nerve gas in Vietnam proved that synergy doesn't always make for better news. But who cares? It got great distribution.

Let's get one thing straight. The merger of AOL and Time Warner is a 2+2=500 combination. Cable television is small potatoes compared to the broadband universe. With broadband in full effect, herky-jerky net-video will be a thing of the past. And we'll have complete freedom of choice, as long as someone on the other end has provided video for us to look at. Just think about it. We'll be able to catch any episode of *The Dukes of Hazzard* that we missed, at any time, anywhere we're logged on!

All of this technology is well and good, but American media today is suffering from a lack of imagination. Media merger mania means that more and more of America's news looks and sounds alike. If you're one of the handful of dealmakers who control half the media outlets in America, you can join the mutual admiration club and appear for free on every major morning, noon, and evening news broadcast in the country. Meanwhile (and I speak from years of experience at companies like *Newsweek* and ABC News) working journalists have to kick and scream to do stories about people who are young, poor, rural, nonwhite, or just plain nonglamorous.

It would be bad enough if America really wanted more pablum. But in recent years, the number of Americans who read the newspaper or watch television news on a daily basis has been dropping faster than the Dow after a bad word from Greenspan. My profession, once considered crusading and noble, is now just slightly less disreputable than dealing used cars.

With its 20 million users and its myriad online "channels," AOL had a chance to introduce America to a whole new broadcast medium. It seems like yesterday—wait, maybe it *was* yesterday—that the "broadband revolution" promised an infinite variety of programming from fresh voices and upstart companies. But with AOL at the helm, how soon before we cry "3,573 channels and nothing on?"

***

Update: The AOL-Time Warner merger was a spectacular failure. Stock in the combined company lost roughly two-thirds of its value by 2003. That year, the company dropped "AOL" and returned to the Time Warner name. In broader news, a coalition of organizations and politicians from across the political spectrum fought back changes in the FCC's media ownership rules, which would have favored more media mergers.

The Uncertainty Principle of Reporting

December 12, 2000

In physics, the Heisenberg Uncertainty Principle states, "The mere act of observing something changes the nature of the thing observed." I wonder if physicist Werner Heisenberg was really a reporter.

Take my trip to northern Florida to interview nonvoters about why they didn't vote and what they thought of the "constitutional crisis." It had nothing to do with the story crackling just beneath the surface on black voter disenfranchisement. But nothing is ever simple in a state like this, a state where convenience stores bear the name "Dixie," blacks and whites live in the same towns close together but very far apart, and our need to communicate sometimes trumps all.

I have an addendum to Heisenberg's principle. "The nature of the observer changes the nature of the thing observed." First of all, I'm black. Second, I'm a woman. Third, I look younger than my thirty-one years. All of those things can work for or against me, but I can't change any of them when I do face-to-face interviews. When I went to the small town of Havana, Florida—a town divided between a well-off white section and a much less affluent black section—race cut both ways.

Let me put things in context. Picture this: two black women, both younger-looking than their years. (Dani, the assistant editor of my website, still gets hit on by high school kids.) Picture this: two young-looking black women, both with cameras and reporter's notebooks, going door-to-door in a relatively affluent white neighborhood, asking people if they voted in the last election. Most were at work. The ones who we found had voted. One, clearly worried about who we were, said, "Don't you think this is strange?"

Picture this: two black women in a different part of the same town, a dim community center where a dozen black men play checkers, cards, and pool. Several of them have criminal records. In Florida, convicted felons can't later clear those records and vote. While the African-Americans who voted are at work, some right next door, these men pass their days until something better comes along. We find out that the schools in town are almost all black; the white families send their children to private schools. The town is segregated cleanly down an invisible line. Over the course of our time in town, we also find out that those further from power have a tougher journey to the ballot box. In another part of the Tallahassee area, we found black voters who'd never gotten the registrations or absentee ballots they signed up for and—common to both blacks and whites—lower-income voters who'd failed to register or vote because they'd moved locations.

Later on, we went to a RV camp between Havana and Tallahassee where all the residents we met were white, split Bush/Gore, and were happy to talk about who they voted for. The nonvoters were slightly more wary of our motives. One Bush supporter missed the chance to vote because of a family illness and was glad to share her disappointment with us. She did ask to see ID. I thought that was fair and was happy to show her my official NYPD press pass, which is harder for freelancers to get than a parking space in Times Square. Others seemed more wary of the government on principle. One would only speak off the record, and another man, who had a confederate flag sticker on his RV door, wouldn't expound on that sentiment at all. If I'd looked a bit more like those last two nonvoters, could I have cajoled them into a deeper conversation? Broken down the barriers of unspoken wariness and distrust? Perhaps not, but I suspect so.

There are times that subjects just won't say things to me they think I don't want to hear, whether it's about race, gender, or personal taste. Other times, I develop a perceived intimacy with my subjects that is so close that I have to remind them that I'm working and we're not friends and, in some cases, millions of people will see or hear the result of the work I do. Sometimes I don't ask the right questions myself.

At historic junctures like these, journalism creates a common American narrative, but it always comes with caveats. That includes the fact that both reporter and subject are individuals with histories, cultures, and backgrounds that may make them uncomfortable allies in the search for truth.

Reality Bites: As the News Industry Shrinks, "Reality TV" Gains Ground

February 12, 2001

Have you ever heard of *When Chefs Attack*? According to the latest TV ratings, this look inside "America's Scariest Restaurants" did fairly well on the third-tier UPN network but not as well as *Cheating Spouses Caught on Tape*. I confess I haven't ever seen this exposé on good-food-gone-bad. The name alone conjures up a Mortal Kombat–style game where one chef throws Ginsu knives and the other counters with a lethal spray of salmonella. Frankly, I bet that's more entertaining than the reality.

These days reality, or at least "reality" TV, is the name of the game. Shows like the raunchy *Temptation Island*, the long-running *Cops*, and the wildly popular *Survivor Part Deux* are blanketing the airwaves, kicking aside traditional sitcoms and series. Never mind that reality TV is never quite what it seems, the situations often set-up, overedited, and semiscripted. We know it, too, and we don't care. We willingly buy into the illusion.

There used to be only one big hit in the reality TV genre. It was called the news, and almost everyone watched it. Today, only about half of Americans watch the network news, and the three major cable news channels—CNN, MSNBC and Fox—have been fighting over their modest but well-informed audiences. As a result, the past few months have been a season of bloodletting at both the cable and network news channels.

CNN, part of the new AOL Time Warner conglomerate, has taken one of the hardest hits. While its newer competitors are still gaining viewers, the twenty-year-old network lost 8 percent of its viewing audience in the past year. CNN made the decision to cut four hundred employees, including some veteran reporters. More significantly, they've changed how they're structuring the news, cutting the number of stories they do each day by a third, from sixty to forty, and pumping up the talk. (That led to some awkward moments, like one anchor joking she "should have taken the buyout" and others sitting uncomfortably on couches, their legs visible for the first time in years as they emerged from the veil of newsdesks.)

The networks aren't immune either. ABC News is releasing fifteen correspondents as their contracts expire and merging the daily and weekend news divisions. Last month NBC announced plans to cut up to 10 percent of its staff, not sparing strong ratings winners like *Dateline*. Having worked for ABC and CNN and appeared on many of the other networks, I know that this business is a lot harder than it looks. Just like reality TV, the news is a mix of verité and entertainment, and the folks who work in the biz are expected to work obscene hours, get all their facts straight, then, just as they're dropping from exhaustion, slather their faces with makeup and smile (or frown seriously) on cue. You want reality? Show a correspondent in her office with five empty coffee cups, a pile of notes, and hair sticking out in every direction.

Doing the hard work of television journalism is very different from what people think reporting should be like. Reporters often do the leg work by telephone, or sitting in endless committee meetings, or drinking endless cups of java during stakeouts. None of these are what you'd call glamorous. Correspondents and producers are constantly under edict to watch the budget, even when they can count on using some library b-roll. The part where the reporter talks into the camera is called a "stand up"—the journalist perfectly coiffed; if outdoors, hair blowing in the breeze; a line or two memorized in order to set the right tone for the rest of the piece. One good ninety-second piece can easily take twenty or fifty or even more hours to prepare.

Television news is like that line about the duck: on the surface, it's all glide; underneath, furious paddling. And perhaps that's the problem: recent efforts have been about the surface. Striving to produce a friendlier news product, the networks and cable news outlets have stopped paddling so hard, stopped offering national and international news. Reality TV has claimed the low ground, the news has claimed a superficial high ground, and information pays the price.

The New Face of News

May 30, 2001

Last month, a bomb—a *very* smart one—was dropped in the ink-stained halls of the newspaper industry. One of the most powerful men in the business, *San Jose Mercury News* publisher Jay Harris, quit his job citing executives' pressures to focus on fixed profit goals. In a speech to his fellow editors this month, he said, "The high salaries many of our leaders receive—in newsrooms and newspaper business offices as well as corporate headquarters—have turned into golden handcuffs. . . . Today, we hear a growing chorus of brave souls—both inside and outside the industry—protesting vigorously, and an audible grumbling of discontent from within the ranks of journalists and readers alike. They are all concerned about the current drift away from quality. . . ."

Harris's bombshell was notable for even more than his courage and candor. He is one of a growing number of African-American journalists and journalists of color to leave the profession just as America is mapping its diversity through census results. For example, while this nation is over 12 percent African-American, the ranks of black newspaper journalists actually dropped from 5.31 to 5.23 percent last year according to the American Society of Newspaper Editors. It's pretty ridiculous that we have to mark newsroom diversity in such micro-increments, a sign of how little progress (or regress) has been made since the industry promised to match the nation's diversity in the year 2000. Instead, in the past year, the overall representation Latino, Asian, and Native Americans dropped (to 3.66, 2.30, and 0.44 percent respectively), and the number of newspapers with no non-white reporters rose to 44 percent of the total.

Why is this happening? It's been a brutal year for the media business overall, from the cuts at the networks to vows of poverty by the newspaper companies, who are cutting costs by shrinking the size of their newsprint. Some of the journalists of color who are leaving the business are casualties of last hired/first fired policies. But others are simply fed up with hearing readers and viewers beg for news that accurately represents the community, and not getting support from the top brass to deliver. After all, a recent study of broadcast news found that black criminals were four times as likely to be shown in mug shots; but only 1 percent of network soundbites on foreign affairs were uttered by African-Americans. If anyone is going to hear what Harris calls the "audible grumbling of discontent" from America's readers and viewers, journalists of color will—and are.

In the absence of general-interest media that reflects the diversity of America, audiences are turning to other sources. First, there is the ethnic press: the Independent Press Association has just published a guide listing 198 New York City magazines and newspapers published in thirty-six languages. Alternative weeklies like New York's *Village Voice* are striking new ground on gritty hard-news topics, winning a Pulitzer for covering AIDS in Africa. And the growing youth media movement is attracting a young demographic to news written and broadcast by, for, and about teens.

While many news organizations are tightening their belts to achieve profitability, their audiences and staff are leaving in order to find what they consider more relevant information. But the general interest press plays a critical role in our society—at best using the First Amendment protections to deliver news without bias to all, acting as a town hall of sorts. Of course, these lofty goals have always co-existed with, sometimes struggled with, the ethics of business, perhaps never more than now. Editors and publishers would do well to remember that their businesses can't succeed without talent that knows America inside and out. The success of journalists of color is critical to the long-term future of the industry—and it's good business as well.

What Value Media and Democracy?

June 29, 2001

Could we see a day where one of the three major network newscasts is cancelled, a sliver of its content folded into a show like *Dateline* or *Primetime*, if not *Survivor*?

Are we headed towards a de facto oligarchy, as fewer and fewer voters participate in presidential elections, while the average voter income keeps rising?

The first scenario started out as a nervous joke inside network newsrooms years ago, but now many top broadcast employees, buffeted by cutbacks, believe one of the big three will fold. Over the past fifteen years, the nets have gone from jointly reaching 90 percent of America's viewing public to just under half.

Likewise, in the past election the percentage of voters flatlined at just over 50 percent—buoyed only by the increased black turnout—while the percentage of working and middle-class voters plunged in relationship to high-income voters. While Americans making $50,000 or less are 80 percent of the population, they were less than half of all voters, compared to 63 percent as recently as 1992.

What do these two trends share in common? A shortsighted view of who the "audiences" are for two of the most powerful and interlinked "products" in American society—media and democracy. Our concept of the market economy influences everything, whether that's a business that also serves a public service mission like journalism or public service itself. The question today is whether the business practices we've chosen are actually helping or hurting both the business owners and society at large.

For those who care about the news business, the past few years have been painful. Aside from loving the free books, CDs, and shrimp we get, most of us went into the field in order to deliver some value to society, to connect people to information and often to each other. Under our current economic models, the average American is a low-value proposition. So the networks people-metered America to determine with minute-by-minute accuracy what viewers wanted to watch on television, and whether or not they are "in the demo"—which for news means middle-aged, upper-middle-class, white, and suburban. The mission of news as a public service for Americans of all races and income levels around the world began to go the way of the brontosaurus.

In politics, the same thing happened, with a tweak. The "demo" became a mix of the voter base and the donor base, and when the needs of the two diverged, the former sometimes became an afterthought. There is only so much time you can spend on the campaign trail, and you can either do it on the streets or at rubber chicken fundraising dinners. We all love to feel loved by someone powerful, even if we have to pay for the privilege. But many voters, nurtured by incidents like Karl Rove's insider deal with Intel and the failure of a Democratic response, worry that the two parties are more interested in feeding at the trough than serving the public. When I talk to young and working-class voters these days, the number one description I get of politicians these days is "crooked"—and that crosses party lines.

The only way to reverse the trend of the Incredible Shrinking Media and Democracy is to prove that it can be a market success. Perhaps we need a new model. I paid a recent visit with a group of Swiss and American businesspeople and politicians to the prestigious University of St. Gallen, described as the equivalent of Harvard Business School. President Peter Gomez posted a Powerpoint slide of their management model, a nimbus of interlocking interests including not only investors but employees, the environment, and the public. Taking into account societal norms and especially "stakeholders"—a much wider range of individuals than the U.S. "shareholder" model—produced greater gains in American companies according to the Dow Jones Sustainable Development Index. The American response to our host was largely the polite equivalent of "homey don't play that."

The European model of growth is hardly flawless. (Just think of Parisian garbage strikes.) But our current shareholder-based approach is certainly failing the news business and, arguably, democracy as well. Network news narrowcasting has produced an ever-smaller, ever-more homogeneous audience with less to offer as a common forum for civic discourse. Politicians are doing the things they know best—speaking back into that echo chamber with high-priced television ads and an increased willingness to flaunt their desire for corporate cash to pay for them.

If we want long-term success, we should at least begin to evaluate what an American stakeholder-based approach to media and democracy would look like. First, we would have to evaluate who America's stakeholders are. Certainly, that would mean acknowledging the media's phantom limbs—all of the potential viewers who had been lost and written off over the years, not only unwittingly. Research by former ABC News executive Av Westin found that stories about black, Latino, and Asian-American subjects were turned down more often by executives who feared that they wouldn't please white viewers and used people-meter evidence to prove it. Now that America is nearly 30 percent black, Latino, Asian American, the networks have to realize that their efforts to attract one audience have alienated others—and, more important, realize that their business practices go against the tenets of good journalism.

Likewise with democracy, we should consider stakeholders including not only missing voters, but also nonvoters. Among America's citizens are 12 million poor children who will never be a voting bloc. Solving the problems of child poverty will require long-range solutions that could involve a mix of workplace, social service, and educational programs for parents and children.

Otherwise, we can fold the news into *Survivor* and resign ourselves to a fraction of Americans showing up at the polls.

This is *Survivor*, of a different sort.

When Is a Good Liar
Better Than a Good Reporter?

May 12, 2003

When I heard about Jayson Blair, the twenty-seven-year-old black reporter at the *New York Times* who made up at least half of his recent articles, I knew that the spin would be about race. Blair was a minority recruit. Now, according to some critics, he's a poster boy for the repeal of affirmative action.

To its credit, the *New York Times* hasn't published such drivel. Editors claim that race wasn't a part of the problem. On that score, I think they're wrong.

Race is always an issue—one that, if you live long enough, will work both for and against you. As America gets more diverse, the total number of black and of-color newspaper reporters has stagnated from year to year, in some cases dropping. The failure of America to have a truly integrated media does two things: 1) reinforces racial essentialism (e.g., all black reporters are held accountable for the sins of one; not so for whites) and 2) gives people who really want to play the race game a wide open field in which to do it.

Racial essentialism means that whites are thought of as having no race, and blacks (and to a lesser extent, other nonwhites) are thought of as *only* seeing the world via race. This skewed perspective leads to the assumption that whites are "objective" when covering race (because they are somehow neutral, or raceless) and blacks are biased. It also means that white people don't have to apologize for famous plagiarists like the *Boston Globe*'s Mike Barnacle and Ruth Shalit (who penned a controversial article on race in the newsroom for the *New Republic*). Blacks apparently do.

Journalism is like any profession. There are a smattering of people who make us look bad, including the reporter caught stealing gold from Iraq and the two paid $10,000 each by the *National Enquirer* for lying about Elizabeth Smart's family. Many examples of journalistic misconduct never make it public. One minority reporter I know received a severance package because his boss, who was white, plagiarized his work. The supervisor was not fired, and the incident was not made public.

Now that we've established journalists aren't perfect, let's get to the bigger issue. News organizations—hell, *all* organizations—like their employees to fit into the culture. That's not bad when there's some flexibility. But too much conformity leads into the trap that Harvard Business School professor Rosabeth Moss Kanter describes in her now-classic *Men and Women of the Corporation*. The people who advance the quickest in a company tend to look and act the most like their superiors, who are usually white and male. Blair wasn't white, but I suspect he was a skillful mimic who used his knowledge of the corporate culture to get by.

Liars like Blair are shapeshifters who spend at least as much time ingratiating themselves with others as they do on their work. Since his days on the college paper, Blair was known as someone who used his charm to get by. (One wonders, given the outrageousness of the stunts he pulled, exactly how much ass-kissing he had to do.)

This type of charming liar possesses qualities that, at least in the short term, are very appealing to editors. No assignment is too difficult, no request off-base. Real reporters get stuck or at least find out that the story they uncover is different from the one assigned. Liars don't have this problem.

The best reporters today, including the best black reporters, follow the story, not the assignment. This tends to be problematic for many black reporters whose editors challenge their independence, particularly on stories of race. Talented reporters of color who see important story suggestions get shot down too often are branded "troublemakers" and leave the business. That's one reason that the biggest diversity challenge news organizations face is not hiring reporters of color, but retaining them.

There are countless reporters of color with proven track records looking for new opportunities. The question is whether outspoken, honest journalists of color are a better fit than con artists like Blair.

The New York Times' Much Ado About the Wrong Thing

June 5, 2003

On the morning of Thursday, June 5, the leadership of the *New York Times* called together their staff for the second major town hall meeting in as many weeks. The first time, editors Howell Raines and Gerald Boyd fell three-quarters of the way down their swords—dispensing mea culpas but, in executive editor Raines' case, stating he would not resign.

This time, they resigned.

I've got one simple question. Why?

This is not a trick question. It strains belief to think that that one ludicrously megalomaniacal liar, Jayson Blair, could topple this paper. If so, it may well be that he was simply one domino who started a chain reaction.

Take the first town hall meeting. Raines said, "You view me as inaccessible and arrogant. You believe the newsroom is too hierarchical, that my ideas get acted on and others get ignored. I heard that you were convinced there's a star system that singles out my favorites for elevation." According to one reporter in the room, this self-denunciation didn't mollify the assemblage as much as inspire bloodlust. Now that heads have rolled, what kind of newsroom will emerge?

My prediction is that there will be a final round of mea culpas, and then it's back to business as usual. No, I don't mean letting liars run wild—that was never typical. I mean getting rid of the autocratic management style that stifles real innovation and creativity. Raines's fiefdom was called "the republic of fear." It will take tremendous courage, including the willingness to experiment and fail, for this institution to become more democratic. If the *Times* became more open to the needs and contributions of its reporters, it could set a tremendous precedent for the industry.

Unfortunately, the business right now resembles a herd of sheep. Many editors assign pieces more to impress their fellow editors than to serve the needs of the public. When I read the pile-on of attack pieces about the *New York Times*, I hear a distant *baaa*.

Most media institutions would be better served looking at scandals closer to home: the gaps in their own coverage. My nominations for the top media scandals of the year:

Why didn't news organizations have the courage to challenge the Bush administration's flimsy, now discredited,
rationales for war?

Where are the follow-up investigations on spectacular
business debacles like Enron? Where'd the money go, and
how can we prevent corporate fraud in the future?

Why did we only learn of the loopholes cutting poor families from the tax cut after it was passed?

Why isn't there more innovative reporting on critical but
not sexy issues like public education and the growing debt
spiral facing American families?

Why isn't there more innovative reporting on successes in
citizen action, like the California referendum mandating
treatment for nonviolent drug offenders, which has
shrunk the country's largest prison system?

And why doesn't the media question its own reporting on
the 2000 election debacle and the current election?

The biggest challenge facing the news industry today is not any single
fraud, but whether journalism itself is relevant to the lives of Americans.
That's one town hall meeting I'm still waiting for.

Internet Kills the Television Blahs

April 14, 2003

A few days after the start of the war, I was sitting in a hotel restaurant having breakfast. At night, the eatery was a sports bar. But that morning, fifteen television sets, some as large as five feet square, broadcast war coverage.

Over my eggs, toast, and coffee, I watched the last night's bombing raids, big red blooms of fireballs. Interspersed were animated graphics of military maneuvers and equipment resembling a sophisticated, nihilistic video game.

As hard as I tried, I couldn't look away. Television is mesmeric, engaging, and according to scientific research, addictive. Last February in *Scientific American*, award-winning researchers Robert Kubey and Mihaly Csikszentmihalyi presented their findings on television addiction. It's a term they reluctantly came to accept because the viewing patterns of Americans (who average three or more hours per day) fit the classic definition. No shocker here: we feel relaxed while we're channel surfing. But Kubey and Csikszentmihalyi were surprised that "the sense of relaxation ends when the set is turned off, but the feelings of passivity and lowered alertness continue." In other words, we end up feeling sapped and powerless right after a big TV binge.

But online news consumers have found a very different—and highly active—way of getting their information. Some of the most sophisticated news consumers, including progressives worldwide, have become the "blog"-era equivalent of news editors. By both receiving and distributing information via email, they vote with the click of a mouse on what information matters.

"It's nice to have these 'intelligent agents'—my friends and list neighbors—passing along the worthiest columns and news stories," says musician and radio producer David Gans. He receives information via e-mail lists, discussion boards, and the online community the Well, whose media conference he hosts. Individuals like Gans, informed and discerning about what they send out, become hubs in this distributed information network.

Net use has grown exponentially since the first Gulf War—the "television war"—a decade ago. Says Australian writer Richard Evans, "I prefer [online news] to watching television as I have more control of the kinds of images and stories I read. I also use the Google news service as a way of getting a quick overview of a variety of sources." Studies also show that Americans find the web outlets of major media (like CNN.com) more trustworthy than their parents.

Print and online publications that make it easy for readers to forward material have seen a jump in traffic. The *New York Times* sends out 3.7 million headline alerts each day. But their Most E-mailed Articles feature, which allows online readers to see what other readers have forwarded, has come into its own. New York Times Digital spokesperson Christine Mohan says that in March, the highest-traffic month so far, the average number of articles emailed was about 75,000 per day. But in the days preceding the war, readers emailed up to 120,000 stories daily. "When you send something to your colleague, the person is much more likely to open it. It's that inherent trust," says Mohan.

Novelist Danzy Senna (*Caucasia*) uses the *New York Times*'s system to email articles to friends and family. She also passes on alerts about upcoming peace marches and acts of civil disobedience. Judging by online outreach for recent peace rallies, the ability to customize and control the flow of information produces action as well as education. And alternative news sources may have benefited from the online news surge even more than major-media ones. In my admittedly unscientific survey of individuals who received and forwarded war-related news, most (including Senna) sent and received more independent than major-media coverage.

The downside? Not all information is credible. Web producer Emily Gertz finds some people on progressive e-mail lists passing on bad information. "As part of harnessing the power of networked information," she says, "there needs to be a steady level of education about net resources and etiquette from those of us who've been online for a long time (in my case, over ten years)."

People who forward too much volume or too little of interest find people begging off their lists. And unique or "sticky" information, like Tamim Ansary's letter about Afghanistan after 9/11, travels the world lightening quick, which opens the door for clever hoaxes.

The system is largely self-correcting, however—and growing. The only thing that could block news "intelligent agents" from their mission is the question of revenue. For now, most outlets don't charge for accessing or forwarding information, happy simply that they're getting more eyeballs. In this world, readers and publishers share the burden of distribution. Online information fans have turned Fox News's slogan on its ear, telling outlets "You Report, the World Decides."

Getting Ashcrofted

April 30, 2003

I stood in a dim basement office facing a rack of electronic equipment. An employee in the ID card office grasped my thumb and pulled it toward the glass top of a small scanner. "Your hands are wet," she said, turning on a miniature fan. I forced myself to breathe deeply while my hands dried out.

My fingers always get clammy and cold when I'm scared, which I suppose I shouldn't have been. I've never been arrested. And I've never been finger-printed—until now.

I work for a nonprofit in space donated by other companies. Next week we move to the offices of one of the biggest corporations in America. They happen to fingerprint all their tenants.

I tried my best to talk my way out of it. I even considered working from home. But it wasn't going to fly. I respect the work I do, and if I wanted to continue it (not to mention eat and pay rent), I was going to have to put civil liberties on the back burner. But I was still scared. And as it has ever since I was a child, my body revealed the fear I tried to mask.

Once my hands dried out, the employee rolled my fingertips over the scanner of the Electronic Fingerprint Capture Station (ECFS) 2100. The loops and whorls that make up my prints appeared as oversized black patterns on a computer screen in front of me. Who needs ink?

The company that developed the ECFS recently changed its name to Integrated Biometric Technology. Everybody wants to cash in on the marketability of biometrics, the technology of identifying people based on biological traits. Biometrics extends far beyond electronic fingerprinting to retinal scans and, perhaps most controversial, face recognition from video surveillance. Biometrics is Big Brother, Inc.

There are some proven successes in this field. Fingerprint databases helped crack the D.C. sniper case. The FBI got a print from a shell casing left behind in a fatal liquor store shooting in Montgomery, Alabama. Agents ran it through the Integrated Automated Fingerprint Identification System (IAFIS) and pulled alleged teen sniper John Lee Malvo's print. Malvo and his mother had been fingerprinted by the INS. They then found police records connecting Malvo's mother and forty-one-year-old suspect John Allen Muhammad.

But fingerprint evidence is not infallible. In cases where prints are smudged, IDs are a judgment call made by individual law enforcement agents. A year ago in the case *U.S. v. Plaza*, a Philadelphia court even ruled that fingerprints were not scientific evidence, but an art. That judge would love the early feedback on face recognition

This month, researchers from the Department of Defense and other government agencies released the "Face Recognition Vendor Test 2002," mandated by the Patriot Act. Their headline cheered systems that could identify 90 percent of people caught on tape, but that only counted the top contenders; the worst company only identified 34 percent of faces correctly in indoor lighting, with an average score among systems of just 68 percent.

All the products worked miserably on outdoor pictures, and all produced false positives. Those in the hip hop generation beware: even the top surveillance systems had their worst ID rate with young Americans. The top three had less than a 65 percent accuracy rate for people between eighteen and twenty-seven years old.

The bad news about face recognition hasn't stopped the Washington, D.C., police department from building a high-tech command center to watch dozens of surveillance cameras placed around the downtown. The system, first activated on September 11, 2001, has been bashed by the city council. But a March 10 article by David Fahrenthold in the *Washington Post* depicts residents of a crime-plagued neighborhood asking for cameras. They're tired of their cars being stolen and their tires being slashed.

The residents of Benning Ridge have a point. It's not enough to protest surveillance. The same people who are at risk of bad surveillance also bear the brunt of street crime. Civil libertarians need to expand their mission to ensure the people whose liberty they're trying to protect get decent police protection as well.

Meanwhile, I feel like a suspect for some crime I haven't committed. A private company may have gathered my fingerprints, but the government's new Total Information Awareness system will allow virtually unfettered access to private databases for "anti-terror" purposes. A friend of mine says I've been "Ashcrofted"—forced to give up my privacy for pretty much no reason at all. Maybe as more of us are Ashcrofted, we'll ask how we can balance liberty and safety instead of giving up rights for no return.

***

Update: The government changed the program's name from "Total Information Awareness" to "*Terrorism* Information Awareness," presumably to make it sound just a tad less Big Brother–ish.

Virus Problems on the 'Net Are SoBig

August 28, 2003

"Hey—is there a new virus out there?"

Last week I sent that e-mail to the webmaster of TheBeehive.org, the site where I work. I pointed out the signs. I'd been getting lots of spam-type email (no surprise) with suspicious attachments (particularly the .pif extension).

By the afternoon, we knew there was a virus, or, more precisely, a worm. A worm culls all of the emails from the computer it's accessed (when you open the extension) and then uses them as both the To and From addresses for its attack. By now, hundreds of millions of emails generated by the latest worm, SoBig, have circulated the 'Net. I guesstimate that I've gotten fifty or so a day for the past five days. My worm alter-ego has also sent them out, judging by the bounced messages I got from computers that rejected e-mails using my address.

Avoiding viruses and worms has become a necessary survival tactic for the 58 percent of Americans who use the Internet. I altered my POP email download program to recognize certain phrases that the worm uses as a subject line. Please don't send me anything personal with "Your Application," "Thank You," or "Wicked Screensaver" as a header, 'cause that stuff's going straight in the trash.

Which brings me to the downside of all this mishegoss: it's turning the Web into the equivalent of a booby-trapped jungle, which people only enter if they're totally strapped and ready. Nobody who got an account to do online banking or get pictures of their grandchildren bargained that the 'Net would be such a swamp. My grandmother, God rest her soul, went online at the age of eighty-two. Shortly thereafter she was solicited to buy Viagra and see nude Russian girls lick their daddies. But porn solicitations, at least for the moment, do not crash your hard drive. Under the assault of SoBig, sites from the BBC to small mom and pop shops were inaccessible. Other current viruses will flat out smash your hard drive, specifically if it's using Microsoft software.

This year, the number of people in the U.S. who stopped using the Internet matched the number of people who started using it. Some lost access to a computer. Many more didn't like it or had technical problems. Theoretically, it's just fine not to be online. But living digitally is becoming more like credit cards. I remember the day that, outraged, one of my professors found he could not rent a car without a credit card. The same thing is happening with online transactions, but it's much sneakier.

Companies wear down consumers with fifteen-minute telephone wait periods before you reach a customer service representative. Sometimes it's the equivalent of a regressive tax, where people who can't book online or get e-tickets incur extra fees (as with airlines). One of the most ridiculous ploys came from United Airlines, which directed phone callers who could not get through to an actual human being, to a website offering a 5 percent discount on bookings. When not a single person is left in United's office to field complaints, the mission will be complete.

Part of my job at TheBeehive.org is creating content for low-income families. On the one hand, I want to tell them that life online is everything it has been promised—a portal to more choice, more freedom, more self-expression. And the other part of me wants to send them a free bumper-sticker: My Problems with the 'Net are SoBig!

Race and Justice

Taxi Wars: New York's Perception and Reality

November 7, 1999

Last week the actor Danny Glover filed a complaint with the Taxi and Limousine Commission because several cabs passed him and one gave shoddy service, and now New York is abuzz with talk of just how racist cab drivers are. Thank God that someone famous finally made a fuss. The thousands of New Yorkers who are routinely passed by, harassed and mistreated by this city's yellow cabs wouldn't have found much recourse on their own.

This February a New York City cabbie called me a "cheap mother [expletive] nigger" because he wouldn't take me to Newark Airport and I wouldn't pay him a couple of bucks for driving me four blocks in no particular direction. I did what all good New Yorkers are supposed to do: I got his medallion number and took him to taxi court, the Taxi and Limousine Commission's process for arbitrating disputes and fining cabbies if necessary.

What happened? Well, it's now November and I'm due for my fourth, and hopefully final, appearance before the court. In what may be simply a misunderstanding or an elaborate ruse, a driver did not show; then the wrong driver came; then the apparently right driver did not show. He has been fined nearly $800 in absentia for refusing to take me to my destination; abuse of passenger; and two other taxi-land abuses. Nonetheless he has another chance to appeal so I must go back to taxi court once more.

Of course, most people denied a taxi don't do what I do. They don't get the medallion number and call the TLC because they assume the driver will never be punished. I wish I could tell them differently, but it's been nine months and I haven't been any closer to justice than the inside of the TLC hearing room.

The feeling, perhaps warranted, that these abuses will not be punished drives some people to do truly stupid things. A man I know—a young dreadlocked magazine editor who I would not ordinarily describe as "rough, rugged, and raw"—says he ended up punching out a cab driver who refused to take him to his destination. I chewed him out for letting his anger get the best of him and reinforcing stereotypes of blacks, but I wonder how many young black folks have done the same thing in the same circumstances.

When black people react to racism with fury, we become "angry black people." In other words, we become the problem, not the ones who are experiencing problems. Reverend Al Sharpton has begun organizing around the taxi issue, as he does around every issue of racism that arises in this city. (Nota bene: He only has a monopoly on the issue because there is no competition.) Anything that Rev. Sharpton touches tends to piss white New Yorkers off. Partly for that reason, and partly because of our deep denial about the pervasive nature of institutional racism, I bet most white New Yorkers view the taxi cab controversy as yet another example of black folks carping and moaning.

Perception drives a wedge into civic debates. Some people see racial complaints against New York taxis (or the NYPD, for that matter) as a simple statement of fact; others see them as race-based exaggeration. For better or worse, our understanding of racial issues is often visceral. If you've never been denied a cab—or more important, never been called a nigger—your perception of the world as fair and just is likely to remain untarnished. Secondhand knowledge counts, too. If your black friend, who you know and trust, tells you about his or her experiences, it is a far cry from reading about racism in paper or seeing a ninety-second spot on the news.

While New York is in a period of incredible prosperity, we are also ignoring some fundamental demographic rifts that could tear New York apart. New York is becoming a city with a mostly white plutocracy (based on Wall Street and Silicon Valley), a tightly squeezed multiracial middle class, and a largely black and brown underclass. Issues like the taxi controversy are the little signal fires that should warn us that our overall economic prosperity alone is not enough to make New York a liveable city, a good city, a great city.

Mayor Giuliani has hardly set a tone for crossracial dialogue. (It was eleven months ago, wasn't it, that he simply refused to meet with the Manhattan borough president, a black woman?) The only way we're going to end issues of structural racism—smaller ones like the taxi problem; bigger ones like police brutality—is if we want to. The only way we will want to is if we understand each other. And in that, I'm afraid, we are getting not closer but further apart.

The Brothers Bush and Florida's "Fairness" Firefight

March 18, 2000

In the past week, Bush has faced a firestorm of criticism for alleged intolerance and racism. But, you may ask, are we talking about Presidential candidate George W., or his brother, Florida governor Jeb?

Either one, actually. Dubya got soundly thrashed in the Michigan and Arizona primaries after bowing so low to kiss the feet of the Christian right that he spoke at Bob Jones University—with its history of racism, anti-Catholicism, and anti-George Bush, Senior-ism. And now there's a new scandal at hand: *Southern Exposure* magazine has dug up records listing GWB as a donor to the Richmond, Virginia, Museum of the Confederacy, which holds its annual ball in a former slave hall festooned with Confederate flags. Sure makes Dubya's waffling over the South Carolina flag look tame, don't it?

But Dubya's been getting plenty of ink these days. Let's turn our attention to his baby brother, who these days is getting called the likes of a "plantation master." Why? At Jeb's urging, Florida just became the first state to voluntarily ban race and gender considerations in college admissions.

Jeb Bush is, of course, not only the governor of Florida, but the man whose children were described as "the little brown ones" by their very own grandfather, George, Sr. With his Mexican-born wife and his early efforts to reach out to black and Latino lawmakers, Jeb was supposed to be a true compassionate conservative, a Republican racial healer. At least that was the story when he ran and won in '98. He ran a losing campaign in '94, as a hard-line conservative. When asked then what he would do for black Floridians if elected governor, he replied succinctly: "Probably nothing."

But in the face of a threat to affirmative action, Governor Jeb did worse than nothing—he ended the program by fiat, and hastily put together a new plan with just enough promise to antagonize advocates for real change. When affirmative action arsonist Ward Connerly rode into town this fall with the intention of putting a referendum on the ballot as he had in California and Washington, Governor Jeb took evasive action. Unfortunately, that meant ending affirmative action and starting a program called "One Florida," which guarantees state college admission to all Florida high school seniors graduating in the top 20 percent of their class. This will definitely keep state campuses from becoming all white but, among other flaws, may distribute black and Latino students to less selective state colleges.

Floridians have reacted to this executive fiat by staging old-school civil rights protests, including two state representatives who took over Jeb's executive office. Cameras caught the governor on tape yelling "Kick their asses out!" and threatening to make somebody's life—probably the representatives'—"a living hell."

Citizens across the state will make Jeb's life a living hell on March 7, the thirty-fifth anniversary of the Rev. Martin Luther King Jr.'s march in Selma. On that day, as Bush delivers his State of the State address, they plan to mass outside of the state capitol. The NAACP is even threatening a boycott of the state if "One Florida" is implemented.

Why is holding on to traditional affirmative action so important? Because you cannot change the entrenched problems of race with race-blind methods alone. Studies by the likes of former heads of Princeton and Harvard Universities, William Bowen and Derek Bok, show that affirmative action is effective, helping in ways ranging from familiarizing whites with a multiracial workplace to growing the black middle class. When we decry affirmative action's "fairness," we leave untouched all the other forms of privilege that go into college admissions: wealth, family connections, geography, athletic ability, "legacy" or alumni status. We always legislate against race and gender, two of the most legitimate reasons to level the playing field, and leave the other factors untouched.

You think Jeb Bush would know that. Just think of the young rich white boy with a SAT score of 1206 who got into Yale as a double legacy (dad and grandpa were alums), then coasted through with a C average. That kid, of course, was Jeb's brother George W. Affirmative action for rich kids will continue unabated, while our legitimate desire to provide racial equality suffers a blow.

The Thin White Line

March 19, 2000

If you're young, dressed casually, and black, it might just be better to be a drug dealer than an honest man. Honor can get you killed.

Patrick Dorismond's job was to make New York tourists feel safe, patrolling the area near Macy's in a police-like uniform. But after work last week, a man in plainclothes asked him where to buy drugs. Outraged, Dorismond scuffled with the man—an undercover cop—who subsequently shot the father of two dead at close range. Had Dorismond been a dealer, he would simply have been arrested. But his righteous indignation at being targeted as a hoodlum—no doubt because of his skin color—cost him his life.

Will white Americans embrace the cause of Patrick Dorismond, or see him as necessary collateral damage in the war against crime? Replace this one man's name with any of the dozens of people killed in police shootings in America each year, and we get to the crux of the issue of excessive police force—the response, or lack thereof, of the mainstream public. While black and brown Americans reel from the news of each new shooting, most people try their hardest to ignore the racial divide in policing. The "thin blue line" of police protecting Americans from crime has an ugly underbelly: a thin white line of public apathy toward the targeting of black and brown men, often for no worse crime than dressing casually, walking or driving in working-class neighborhoods, or having dark skin.

Make no mistake, this issue crosses all state and local lines. Louisville, Kentucky, is riven by the decision to give officers who killed an unarmed black teen awards for "exceptional valor." The mayor fired the police chief who granted the honors, and police countered on Friday by staging a massive demonstration against the mayor. Los Angeles is staggering under the weight of a police corruption and brutality scandal so severe that it may cost the city up to $300 million to settle charges of police shooting, framing, and abusing suspects. Even if white Angelenos do not feel the bite of a bullet, their wallets will pay the price. How sad that we have to rely on the enlightened self-interest of money to highlight how police brutality hurts all of us. But nothing else seems to be working.

The Big Apple is the center of the police brutality issue these days. The city is still reeling from the acquittal last month of the four officers who fired forty-one bullets at Amadou Diallo, leaving a man armed only with a wallet to soak his own stoop in his blood. Days after the acquittal, another unarmed black man was shot and killed, and now Dorismond. This latest case highlights yet another critical issue: the targeting of black men in America's drug wars. African-Americans are 13 percent of the population; 15 percent of those who use drugs; 35 percent of those arrested for drug crimes; and 50 percent of those convicted. Many white users exchange merchandise for money behind closed doors, and even if they buy on the street, their skin color gives them camouflage in a world where cops use dark skin as probable cause. It is what got Patrick Dorismond killed and what keeps the jails disproportionately filled with blacks and Latinos in a War on Drugs which is merely a war on urban America.

And therein lies the heart of the problem: police brutality in America really does hit communities of color far harder than others, means far more to some of us because of our race and class. Is white America turning a deaf ear to the sobs and the sighs of black mothers because the streets are safer? In truth, the decline in crime is largely a function of the improved economy. There is absolutely no evidence that the relentless intimidation, persecution, even murder of unarmed blacks and Latinos has lowered the crime rate. Quite the opposite: it has caused a deep and abiding resentment that could poison American race relations for years to come.

***

Update: The police officers who killed Dorismond were cleared of criminal charges. The city agreed to pay the Dorismond family a $2.25 million settlement. In 2004, the NYPD agreed to pay $3 million to the family of slain immigrant Amadou Diallo. Haitian immigrant Abner Louima, who was tortured by police, received an $8.75 million settlement. While the police are rarely held legally accountable in these brutality cases, the taxpayers are held accountable for paying the settlements.

Cincinnati, Race, and the Rest of Us

April 17, 2001

Cincinnati knew it had a problem. In early May, Mayor Charlie Luken ranked improving race relations as the area's number one problem, bar none, stating, "The future of this city depends more on our ability to treat one another fairly than on any single economic issue, and I think we have a long way to go."

A month later, the city was in flames.

Many folks in Cincinnati wish the mayor had put his money where his mouth is. Resident Joan Siegel, whose father helped integrate the city's real estate business, says "He [Luken] was aware of it, but of course he should have done more. It's going to take a long time for the anger to die down and people to communicate." America is getting more and more diverse, but in cities like Cincinnati, blacks and whites are living further and further apart.

After police shot and killed the fifteenth unarmed black male in five years, the city erupted. But even days of fires and riot gear and curfews don't measure up to the effects of the real problem: the all-American color line. Cincinnati is one of the most segregated cities in America and is in the middle of a continuing period of white flight. White Americans are actually the most segregated group in American society—according to the Census, white Americans are likely to live in 83 percent white neighborhoods—and one of the effects of white flight from urban centers is to withdraw resources and a tax base from the city. One report estimated that "80 percent of poor blacks live in poor, inner-city neighborhoods, while 70 percent of poor whites live in middle-income, suburban neighborhoods." Lower-income white kids end up in better schools, safer neighborhoods, and with better social services than their black counterparts. Race leads to economic segregation as well.

Segregation helps create the police problem. White flight has left a cadre of mostly white officers policing mostly black neighborhoods. The reality is that the residents of black neighborhoods, like the residents of every neighborhood, need the police. But young black men in particular, unlike the residents of white neighborhoods, now routinely fear the police harming them. It creates a terrible duality even for the most law abiding of citizens: wanting to be protected, on the one hand—after all, you pay taxes—and resenting the Boys in Blue because they harassed you, or your uncle, or your father, on the other. Until America deals with the full implications of what racial profiling does to law enforcement, policemen and citizens won't feel truly safe.

Mayor Lukens has formed a race relations commission, a suspiciously dull-sounding enterprise to combat the fires of the past week. Similar efforts following the Rodney King verdict in Los Angeles largely got bogged down in bureaucracy. Building consensus won't be an easy task when some business leaders are already lambasting him for being too easy on the rioters, and other community leaders are chastising him for letting race relations go into freefall. Hopefully the business, civic, and government leaders here will realize and produce real change.

A month ago, the mayor of Cincinnati said that race was the number one problem in his city. The question now is what is he going to do about it. And what will we do to help?

A Silver Lining to a Whole Lott of Nonsense

December 19, 2002

In the week since Senate Majority Leader Trent Lott confessed to dreaming of a really White Christmas, I've been through all five of Dr. Elisabeth Kübler-Ross's stages of grief. I've been in denial that the media could write so many times that Lott's words "appeared" to embrace segregation; angered when half of the rebukes (like J. C. Watts's) sounded like apologies; bargained that if we got into a good debate on race and politics, we might learn something; got depressed that the story was reduced to "segregation happened, it really happened"; and finally accepted, once again, that this is just America, God bless us every one.

Trent Lott, a man who can shout "smaller government" while shoveling defense industry pork into his district, is hardly a model of honesty. Then again, is the man he praised so generously, Strom Thurmond? As South Carolina governor, Strom Thurmond used the most powerful "n" words of the time "nigger" and "never"—as in, never would African-Americans take a place in an integrated South.

In 1948, Thurmond ran for president on the segregationist Dixiecrat ticket, which Senator Lott endorsed post facto. But at the same time, Thurmond was paying for the college education of Essie May Washington, a student at all-black South Carolina State College. Washington was openly considered by fellow students to be Thurmond's daughter. Despite being questioned many times by several reporters, neither Washington nor Thurmond has ever denied nor confirmed their relationship. You can find more in an article from the *South Carolina Point* and in the book *Ol' Strom*, co-written by *Washington Post* reporter Marilyn W. Thompson.

Segregation has always been a farce, morality a veil for economic gain and social insecurity. And slavery, its genesis, was the most unfair labor policy in the world, where bargaining led to mutilation or death. But during their days of enslavement, some African-Americans did amazing things.

The Capitol Dome is crowned by a bronze statue of an Indian maiden representing Freedom. That statue was cast by an enslaved man named Philip Reid, who supervised some of the many enslaved people who worked on the very buildings where Trent Lott works. In fact, most of the men who built the Capitol and the White House were African-American and enslaved. During the last session of Congress, House Continuing Resolution 368 called for "Establishing a special task force to recommend an appropriate recognition for the slave laborers who worked on the construction of the United States Capitol." It was referred to the Senate Committee after being passed by the House, but representatives took no further action.

Now's the time. Lionizing the glory days of segregation may get Lott tossed out of the Senate leadership, if not voted out of the Senate itself. But even if he sticks around a while, let's revive the work on this memorial, and give him something to think about. Providing a positive reminder of how this nation was built will be a fitting silver lining to this ugly incident.

***

Update: Trent Lott resigned as Senate majority leader but continues to serve in the U.S. Senate.

Email your representatives and ask for the resurrection of H.CON.RES.368. You can go to http://www.congress.org and enter your zip code to find and email your representatives.

Do Segregationists Have a Heaven?

July 1, 2003

If *The Lovely Bones* is right about heaven, Strom Thurmond has just appeared in a glorious version of the white South, where the clock stopped no later than 1948. In the bestselling book about a murdered girl, heaven is divided into neighborhoods of like-minded people (or spirits). If my version of heaven was, say, running a college radio station, and your version of heaven was having your own ska show, we might end up as eternal neighbors.

So here's my question: do segregationists have a heaven? If so, the senator is probably planning a picnic with Nathan Bedford Forrest, founder of the Ku Klux Klan, or enacting legislation with Orville Faubus or doing a Civil War exercise with General Robert E. Lee. Think of the fun! Senator Thurmond, no doubt in his younger form, can spend his day vanquishing the Northerners. Afterwards, the kindly negras will fetch him and his new friends their footstools and pipes. (If no kindly negras choose to appear in the segregationist heaven, maybe the boys can take turns in blackface, like *Birth of a Nation*.) Of course, they'll keep a seat warm for Trent Lott.

The passing of America's longest-serving senator raises a whole heavenly host of questions. Yes, the afterlife is described in major religious texts, but do any of us share an exact concept of what it is? Do we get a cookie-cutter heaven, a prefab cloud and a new white robe, or is the great beyond customizable? And what about the entry requirements? Hey, slavery was condoned by the church. Are all the slaveowners upstairs, chillin'? Or is morality retroactive—they were admitted to heaven, but once the church flipped on slavery, they were kicked down to hell? Or, as many theologians posit, is time an illusion? If so, some people who did their best to live by the morals of the day will show up at the pearly gates only to get the Celestial Gong.

This doesn't even get into the question of religious difference. Is there one heaven (and hell) for people of all faiths? Or, much as the world is divided into countries, is the afterlife divided by religion? What if you're a Jewish Buddhist? Do you commute?

It's all fun to think about, particularly given the complexities of Ol' Strom's life. Like, that black daughter of his, when she passes, will they have a family reunion? Will Thomas Jefferson and his black kids show up to welcome her home? Or will Strom spend his eternal sunset among spirits who, throughout the ages, have championed the separation of the races?

God willing, when I go, I'll end up on the other side of town.

***

Update: Shortly after his death, Strom Thurmond's black daughter, Essie May Washington-Williams, told the news media about their relationship. She said she did not want to go public while he was alive. But as early as the 1940s, black newspapers were reporting on the black Thurmonds, who include not only Washington-Williams but an uncle (Thurmond's father's half-brother) and two cousins.

Integrity Breeds Dissent

June 24, 2003

My grandmother, Mary Catherine Stokes, is one of my heroes. She is also very sick now. Much later than I should have, I started audiotaping some of the stories that make up her life. One of them is the tale of how she challenged employment discrimination on her job, the price she paid, and the gains she won.

My grandmother only went to work—and started taking college classes—after the youngest of her six children was in school. She began working at the Social Security Administration as a GS-2, an entry-level employee. In her words:

"I went to work with a determination to get promoted as soon as possible. One of the things that hurt so much was the fact that there was a black man who had reached a grade four. At that time, a grade four was great for a black person. When he found out I had put in for GS-5, he said, 'You know you're wasting your time—a black middle-aged woman trying to get a job of that nature.' When I retired, he was still a GS-4, and I was a GS-11," she said.

"When I applied for a promotion, the white girl got the promotion. They told me she was more qualified. I had a high school degree and had gotten A+ on college classes. She had to get a GED in a hurry so [she could qualify for the job]. One of the reasons that she got it was because I had refused to accept [my supervisors'] attitude about a group of young black women who were eligible for promotion who were being bypassed."

My grandmother insisted that the black employees be evaluated fairly, by the same measures as white ones. They did well on every test, but management was not pleased. "They called me into the office, and they said, 'This could mean your future.' I said, it would just have to mean it," my grandmother said.

She didn't receive a promotion for four years. "I just kept plodding along. Eventually I wrote to the commissioner and I told him what I'd done. They nominated me for the commissioner's citation. As soon as I got nominated for the commissioner's citation, I got nominated for a Grade 11. It was only after I received that citation—the highest citation that Social Security can give—that I got promoted to a job you could really say you took a look a lot of effort with."

My grandmother is an extraordinary woman not only for her integrity, but for her deep compassion. She mentored and befriended white employees as well as black. She also remained loyal in the truest sense to the institution she served—by bringing them kicking and screaming into the era of the integrated workplace.

In a small-minded world, loyalty and integrity are enemies. Conservative proponents of the New Patriotism call anyone who disagrees with the Bush administration a traitor. This leaves no room for the very American principle of dissent, the thesis-antithesis-synthesis of ideas that undergirds all social progress. The expression of the ideals in the Declaration of Independence only became meaningful with dissent—dissent against slavery, against the inability of women to vote, against legalized employment discrimination. Without dissent there is no democracy.

Who dissents? In every case of major social change, people of integrity made a very hard decision. They chose to stand up for principles that, at the time, were illegal or considered immoral. I met a gentleman named "Skip" Barner who, in the 1950s, promoted black employees and treated the black woman who worked for his family like a human being. When she stayed late, he would drive her home. When she ate lunch, she sat at the table with his wife. This so outraged the local Ku Klux Klan that they threatened his wife. Skip Barner took a gamble that leaving documents about the threats in a safe deposit box, should anything happen, would keep them safe.

That takes integrity.

It's easier to look at examples of integrity from the past than from the present. But one current example stands out for me—the whistleblowers at Enron. Greed and a misplaced sense of loyalty to a corrupt corporation kept many top officials from telling the truth. But Sherron Watkins blew the whistle on the phony accounting. She didn't save the company, or its reputation. But she can be assured, in addition to sleeping better at night, that her obituary will not tout her as someone who squandered billions and put thousands of people out of work.

Loyalty and integrity are not enemies. When we place loyalty to the power structure of an institution or government above loyalty to its people, we undercut the ideals we claim to serve.

Integrity is one of the most important, and most threatened, of American values. Of course, "values" is a fighting word, particularly to progressives and liberals who have seen morality used as a weapon. But values can be—and for many of us have been—a healing balm that soothes the injustice of everyday life. One of the challenges of our experiment in American democracy is how to express values in public life. We can learn a lot from those who have had to make hard decisions before us.

***

Update: My grandmother passed away in July 2003, leaving behind a legacy of individuals whom she mentored and championed.

Beyond Our Borders

AIDS in America and Africa: Dollars and Denial

July 10, 2000

At the start of the Eighth International AIDS Conference in South Africa, the first to be held in a developing nation, hundreds of researchers and health care workers walked out of a speech by President Thabo Mbeki. In recent months, the South African leader has repeatedly questioned whether HIV causes AIDS, the pandemic that currently infects over 25 million people across the continent. Citing a World Health Organization report, the president's key message was that "extreme poverty is the world's biggest killer, and the greatest cause of ill health and suffering around the globe."

Mbeki's refusal to focus on HIV was bitter medicine indeed for the thousands of health professionals gathered in South Africa to slow the ravages of AIDS, if not stop it. For doctors struggling to institutionalize preventative measures like condom use, Mbeki's words were two giant steps backward. In a decade, the U.S. Census Bureau predicts, life expectancy in several African countries including Botswana, Swaziland, and Zimbabwe— my paternal family's home—will hover near thirty. Without AIDS, the life expectancy would be near seventy. But that is Africa. America is a different story, right?

Lest we get complacent, the numbers in our country are shocking as well. Yes, we've developed new treatments and lowered the overall death rate. But for whom? In America, as in Africa, the wealthy usually stay well while those in poorer communities face much higher risks of infection. A new Centers for Disease Control report found that 2.5 percent of African-American adults in Jersey City, New Jersey, are infected with HIV, and the figures are virtually identical in nearby Newark. "These are figures that were similar to what we were seeing in Africa 15 years ago," said the CDC's director of HIV/AIDS prevention, Dr. Rob Janssen. Both Newark and Jersey City are hardscrabble, though reviving, urban centers, with more than their share of poverty, crime, and drugs. As the patterns of infection in this country are becoming more class-based, and more black and brown, white Americans may find AIDS easier to ignore.

For example, since poverty correlates with drug use, communities of color have borne the brunt of IV drug transmissions and their collateral damage. Years ago, I lost a relative to AIDS who learned she had been infected by the IV drug using ex-husband she had already divorced. "A lot of the older women who got infected, they were with men who they didn't know until later on were using IV drugs," says Michael Saunders, director of Education and Social Support for the organization Gay Men of African Descent (GMAD). Today, women of color between the ages of sixteen and twenty-four are the female demographic hardest hit, and gay men of color are increasingly bearing the brunt of the male AIDS crisis. Saunders faults a lack of discussion of sexuality in communities of color, as well as inadequate health care and access to long-term treatment with AIDS drugs. "We go to the emergency room to deal with chronic illnesses," he says.

America needs a more equitable health care system, one that will offer coverage to the 44 million citizens without insurance. With health care, more poor and working-class Americans infected with HIV would be diagnosed during routine checkups; just as important, they would receive top-notch AIDS drugs, which are prohibitively expensive without medical coverage. Throughout Africa, the issue is far starker. The price of AIDS drugs is simply out of reach for most citizens, and U.S. and multinational pharmaceutical companies have only grudgingly met a small portion of the need for treatment. Groups like the Nobel Prize–winning Doctors Without Borders constantly press the drug giants to treat all AIDS sufferers, not just the wealthy.

"I do think the epidemic affects us across the board," says GMAD's Saunders. "The level of poverty in Africa is greater than it is here, but I don't think it changes what the epidemic looks like. Families are decimated; communities are falling apart; there needs to be a dialogue about how economic structures affect the epidemic here and abroad." Thus Thabo Mbeki is partly right—poverty is a huge factor in AIDS. It affects who's at risk, who gets treated, and how the world reacts. But he is dead wrong when he waffles about the cause of AIDS—HIV—and the need to call its name aloud. Lack of dollars is one problem facing AIDS workers; denial looms just as large.

Free Trade, Free Cuba

May 14, 2001

I always thought the most popular drink on the island just south of Miami would be the rum and Coke *Cuba libre*, or Free Cuba. While visiting Cuba (legally, unlike most of the 100,000 Americans who visit the island per year) I found that tourists at least tend quaff the minty *mojito*. But there won't be a surge of American tourists to Cuba anytime soon. Despite widespread evidence that the U.S. embargo against Cuba is out of line with our global policies, Bush administration officials don't seem inclined to lift travel and trade bans anytime soon. In fact, since the United States was voted off the United Nations Human Rights Commission—arguably due to the U.S. stance on Cuba—the administration may have hardened its position.

America has built what techies might call a financial firewall against Cuba, one of our closest neighbors and the former site of all sorts of glitzy *Americano* gangster mayhem. After all, there's the Helms-Burton Act blocking trade with Cuba. It includes a provision that hasn't yet been enacted, but soon may, allowing lawsuits in the U.S. against the European firms busy pumping billions into joint Cuban enterprises. They, of course, could choose to countersue us. But while we bar trade with Cuba, we are trying to give U.S. businesses a leg up with the recent free trade summit on Latin America.

Trade rights are a fickle thing. America rails against Cuban human rights abuses, but we trade with China, which harvests the organs of executed prisoners. (Some organs may have, according to a recent investigation by the *Village Voice*, ended up in American bodies.) We trade with Burma, which has put a Nobel Prize winner under arrest, and with countries that do not allow women the vote. And we've staged several unsuccessful assassination attempts against Castro. But despite the pleas of the agriculture sector, among others, trade with Cuba remains among the most restricted in the world, affecting not just luxury items but basic foodstuffs and even medicines.

The effect on the flow of people is the most profound. A couple of million Americans, both Cuban expats and tourists, would likely flock to the island if the embargo were lifted. Somehow, an increasing number of Americans are ducking under the fading red curtain of the embargo—which Cuban officials call the "blockade." In Havana last week, I met fresh-faced New Englanders who were spending a semester abroad at the University of Havana. Then a friend in New York told me her son's school, a public school, did a week exchange in Cuba. "I wish they went for longer," she said.

And at the glitzy Hotel Nacional, where wealthy Cubans bring their daugh-
ters for *quinceanera* photographs and foreigners smoke Cohibas and drink
rum, photographs of Che and Fidel hang on the wall across from photographs of Naomi Campbell and Francis Ford Coppola.

This is not nirvana, to say the least. Some of the tourists come especially
for the *jineteras,* or the women and men whose range of special services slide on
a payment scale. As the Soviet Union collapsed, so did the Cuban economy.
Only recently have ordinary Cubans, according to government statistics,
begun again eating enough food to keep them alive. And, as a *Habanero* named
Julio Cesar put it, "An American and a Cuban are having a fight about
democracy. The American says, I can go to the White House, knock on the
door, ask for George W. Bush, and tell him what I think about him. The
Cuban says, 'Yes, it is the same. I can go to the Plaza de Revolution, knock on
the door, ask for Fidel, and tell him what I think about George W. Bush.' "

One official said the government was examining the impact of the tourist
economy on their dream of what the French think of as *liberté, egalité, fraternité.*
In America, we prize liberty—you can walk down the street naked covered in
chocolate sprinkles, but don't ask for health care. In Cuba, they prize *egalité.*
Every neighborhood has a doctor. Of course, she or he is paid $20 U.S. per
month and has few medicines with which to treat patients, due in part to the
ramifications of U.S. policy. Nonetheless, the Cuban infant mortality rate
is lower than America's, and its literacy rate is higher.

America could learn something from Cuba. And Cuba, which has often
been portrayed as being too proud or too foolhardy to change, is certainly
learning something from America.

***

Update: In 2003, both chambers of Congress seemed poised to remove
some of the travel restrictions to Cuba. But the Bush Administration successfully lobbied against the move. It also tightened travel restrictions in
2004, a move that divided the powerful Cuban immigrant community.
Meanwhile, 85 percent of Americans favor easing or ending the embargo
against Cuba.

The Colonial Filter:
America Looks at Africa

May 19, 2001

The country where half of my family lives is going to hell. In America, where we pretend to live as a classless society, we are at least divided into rough chunks of poor, working- and middle-class, and rich. In Zimbabwe, the poor, whether subsistence farmer or city-dwellers, make up the majority of the population. Better-off suburbanites like my eighteen-year-old brother are a much smaller group. My brother, who hoped to go to the national university now roiled by strikes, has a grim sense of humor about the chaos. "People came in and stole the television so most nights all we do is sit around and look at each other," he says.

It troubles me that Zimbabwe only makes headlines now that it's in trouble. It even hit the pundit shows this weekend, as the *McLaughlin Group*'s Tony Blankley predicted Zimbabwe's descent because of lack of respect for the rule of property. He was talking about the actions of Robert Mugabe's government no doubt, and on an immediate level he was right. But modern Africa as we think of it was founded on a lack of respect for the rule that the people living there deserved the property on which they lived or, sometimes, even to live. Today, an unwillingness to treat African lives as equal to our own taints our perspective on issues ranging from land disputes to the global AIDS crisis.

When I visited just three years ago, Zimbabwe was still known as a tourist destination, a lovely place to honeymoon at the stunning Victoria Falls or gaze at the centuries-old remnants of the Mwene Mutapa empire, the Great Zimbabwe. Now we hear about internecine battles between political parties; fuel shortages; government censorship of the press and manipulation of the courts; and this winter, the killings of white farmers.

I deplore the headlong slide of the country into anarchy, and think the nation's president, Robert Mugabe, has largely pushed it to the brink. But the coverage of Zimbabwe's problems (and Africa's in general) often reflects a lack historical perspective. Call it the colonialism filter.

Take the headlines about five white farmers killed this winter. The white farmers make up 1 percent of the population but own half of the arable land. Zimbabwe's president, who could have advocated for peaceful land reform years ago, dispatched thugs to rough them up and throw them out in order to raise support for his embattled presidency. At the same time, a new political opposition party called the Movement for Democratic Change (MDC) mounted a spirited challenge to Mugabe's leadership. Dozens of MDC supporters were killed. But their deaths didn't make headlines here in the states. The colonialism filter blocked that.

The filter seems to have blocked a serious discussion of land reform as well. (Many members of the international community support it, as long as it's done peacefully, with financial compensation.) Even less serious discussion is given to the role of Western multinational corporations, particularly in the oil and diamond industries, in supporting corrupt leaders to ensure maximum access to raw materials. The war in the Congo and Rwanda has been fueled largely by the immense diamond wealth there.

In another question of property—intellectual property—we see African nations like Zimbabwe dominating news of the global AIDS crisis. Western drugs manufacturers blocked other companies from making low-cost generic medicines for poor AIDS sufferers. Only in the past couple of years have we even debated the issue seriously. Before that, as millions sickened and died, we simply said "no pay, no way."

Finally, under domestic and international pressure, the U.S.–based drug manufacturers agreed to sell AIDS medicines at cost to poor countries. The Merck drug Crixivan will cost $600 per year in Africa, one-tenth the cost in the United States; a Bristol-Meyers Squibb AIDS drug Zerit will cost $54 per year in poor nations, versus over $3500 in the U.S. That says a lot about the markups Americans pay.

In our increasingly diverse and global nation, we can't afford to think of ourselves as isolated. Today I stepped into a taxicab with a driver from Ghana who recognized me from television. We discussed Zimbabwe and Kwame Nkrumah, who brought independence to Ghana and helped influence a generation of African leaders. Then he added, "It's a shame we don't spend more time on news from other than this side of the Atlantic. There's a lot to discuss."

Raising the Question of Disarmament, Again

December 17, 2002

Hiroshima, Japan—Inside the building there is a soft shuffling sound amid the silence. People look down as if entering a wake. In some sense, they are. The Hiroshima Peace Memorial Museum commemorates the hundreds of thousands of people who died in the first nuclear catastrophe. In some sense, it also mourns our loss of innocence as a species, when we learned we had the power to completely destroy ourselves.

The museum tour begins with footage of the mushroom cloud and a pastiche of facts. The first heat blast was 900 times hotter than the sun. Eighty thousand people died instantly when the U.S. Enola Gay dropped "Little Boy" on August 6, 1945. Approximately 200,000 people died by 1950 from injuries and radiation poisoning. Another 100,000 may have died from bomb-related causes since.

On August 9, another U.S. plane dropped a larger bomb, "Fat Man," on Nagasaki. Because of the mountainous terrain, fewer people died: 70,000 by the end of the first year.

Burnt baby clothes. A warped metal lunch tin still filled with its incinerated contents. More gruesome mementos: the hair that fell out, warped nails, keloided skin. One homemade wooden sandal, the only object that identified a dead girl. We visitors peered at each remnant behind glass, fragments of the lives that were lost.

I was sickened at the description of students burnt so badly that the skin on their arms slipped off and forward, hanging from their fingertips like loosened gloves. I finally started to cry when I saw the placard by a little rusted tricycle. One month shy of his fourth birthday, Shinichi Tetsutani was riding his tricycle in his front yard when the bomb hit. Burned beyond help, he spent the day in agony and died that night. Shinichi's father buried him in the backyard with the body of a girl he used to play with and his tricycle. Forty years later, the family re-buried the remains, and donated the rusted tricycle to the museum.

My mind flipped to an image of the Raggedy Ann doll found in the rubble of the World Trade Center and then to the story of Juliana Valentine McCourt. The four-year-old was flying with her mother to visit Disneyland on September 11. A family friend, also traveling from Boston, was supposed to meet them there. McCourt and her mother Ruth boarded

United Airlines Flight 175, which hijackers steered into the south tower of the World Trade Center. Their friend, Page Farley Hackel, was on American Airlines Flight 11, which crashed into the north tower. When I cried for Shinichi I cried for Juliana and many other children who have died in conflicts they can't understand.

The people who filled the museum were mostly Japanese, from babies in their mothers' arms to an old man walking with two canes. I wondered if any were *hibakusha*, or A-bomb survivors. Would they want to see the vivid reminders of what they'd lived through? Among the many Westerners were crew-cut U.S. military men from local bases, solemnly absorbing what the endgame of war might mean.

Hiroshima's peace museum is filled with exhortations never to relive the "evil" of this day. From the Japanese perspective, the bombings of Hiroshima and Nagasaki were evil. From the American perspective at that time, they were heroic military actions taken to end the war and prevent further suffering.

Japanese citizens I spoke with during my trip were shocked that the Smithsonian Museum exhibited the Enola Gay on the fiftieth anniversary of the bombing. That exhibit became one of the most controversial in the museum's history. Veteran's groups objected to materials that they said made them look bent on vengeance. Because of their protests, the plane was exhibited with almost no historical material, and the director at the time resigned.

"The past isn't dead. It isn't even past," said William Faulkner. And even today, our country and Japan are reliving the legacies of World War II. We, as the victors, have largely retreated into the comfortable haze of laudatory war movies about the greatest generation. Japan not only lost the war, but its ability to occupy and control territories throughout Asia, particularly China and Korea. The rebuilding of postwar Japanese society has come with constant soul-searching about the place and meaning of the past, with some defiant neo-nationalists beginning to mix their opinions with the general remorse and regret for actions like the 1937 Nanjing Massacre.

Our leaders can't seem to get enough of the word "evil" these days. During the State of the Union speech in which President Bush named Iran, Iraq and North Korea an "axis of evil." "Evil is real, and it must be opposed," he said.

Today humans across the world can arm themselves with weapons fit for gods, point them at each other, and cry "evil." But evil, at least on this earth, is still a flexible and subjective term. Our concept of it bends to public opinion, nationalism, fear, and historical perspective. What the majority condones at one moment—slavery, the Holocaust—may become the evils of the next age.

Perhaps the greatest challenge of our time is to draw the clarity of historical perspective ever closer to the present day. What is happening now that will seem evil in forty years time or least unbelievably stupid and self-destructive? My long personal list ranges from the tacit acceptance of the global AIDS epidemic to the U.S. prison-industrial complex. At the top, a point so depressingly obvious I can't bear to think about it often: we will never be safe so long as multiple countries and possibly unknown free agents have the power to end the world at any moment.

I am a nuclear baby. I grew up at the end of the duck-and-cover age, doing silly drills in my first-grade classroom, seeing those radiation signs leading us to a basement that would never protect us from a blast. Watching TV during dinner in the Reagan 1980s, I felt the tensions of a Cold War I couldn't fully understand and read fatalistic novels about what would happen after a nuclear strike. And then the Soviet Union crumbled under glastnost. We had earned a blessed respite.

But our plans to disarm went awry. Even Ronald Reagan said in 1982 that nuclear war "cannot be won and must never be fought." Under pressure from disarmament advocates, he implemented treaties with the Soviet Union. But President Reagan also initiated the plan for a "Star Wars" national missile defense initiative, or bombs that would explode enemy bombs in the sky.

Today, although the United States has spent over $120 billion testing the system, it point-blank does not work. But President Bush increased the fiscal year 2002 budget 60 percent to roughly $8 billion per year. He also stated, "Now is the time not to defend outdated treaties but to defend the American people."

Because we are spending money we don't have on a program that doesn't work, we risk inflaming the nuclear threat rather than decreasing it. Russian president Vladimir Putin remarked that if the United States unilaterally violates anti-ballistic missile (ABM) treaties with "Star Wars" technology, Russia would then consider all arms agreements void. But this economically hard-pressed country may not be able to protect the arms it has, which, like its biological weapons, could pass into the hands of terrorists. We'd be better off devoting our efforts to making sure they decommission their nuclear weapons, and lessening ours.

And a Pentagon report called "Foreign Responses to U.S. National Missile Defense" states that if the U.S. builds a shield, China will expand its long-range nuclear arsenal tenfold, from 20 missiles to 200. In other words, if we get new guns, so will the other guys. And just as the Cold War bankrupted the Soviet Union, a War on Terrorism that relies on overblown military spending could empty U.S. coffers.

At a conference in Switzerland last year, I ate dinner with a U.S. military official working on "Star Wars." He tried to convince me that the $60 billion or so price tag was a bargain. He also gave me a gray missile defense sticker featuring a variety of little bomb-like icons. I suppose if I put that on my window, like an alarm system label, the nukes will avoid me. (The stickers, by the way, are extremely ugly. If nothing else, the federal government could have shaved a few dollars on that.) Another person at the table gave me a look of disgust, reserved for traitors, because I didn't support the missile plan.

I have no desire to burn to death, explode, melt, vaporize, or die from radiation poisoning. I don't think President Bush and his advisors want to either, but I question their means of keeping us safe.

President Reagan began disarmament in large part due to pressure from citizens, scientists, and policymakers who saw the dangers of the arms race. These dangers are hidden in the silos of middle America and the Rockies, while the nuclear devastation Japan lived through is now concealed by skyscrapers.

When I stepped outside the peace museum, I found it hard to believe Hiroshima had ever seen tragedy. A toddler in a shirt with red, white, and blue stars stomped up to me, took my hand and led me a few steps through the plaza. Folk musicians sang along a bridge by the water. Their backdrop was the Atomic Dome, the ghostly shell of the only building left close to the blast epicenter. Most of the central city and its occupants were vaporized.

Today, Hiroshima is beautifully rebuilt, clean and new, filled with shops and tourists. It is a phoenix risen from the ashes. Of course, the bombs we have built since 1945 are much, much stronger. We will also have to be stronger not to use them.

Poor Rich Africa

September 8, 2003

This July, on my birthday, I strolled through Portobello Road market in London. Along the curving thoroughfare, people sell all manner of things, from shiny silver flasks to long leather coats and fresh lychee nuts.

At one stall selling old maps, I fingered a map of Africa from the 1920s, with pale colors tinting huge colonial African states. Many of them had different names than they do today—an understandable phenomenon given the way these countries were hacked out of the populous continent with little regard for the needs of the occupants. Overlaid on each state or region the names of natural resources. Gold, copper, iron. Ivory and oil. Everything that modern society runs on could be found in Africa. It still can today.

So why is Africa so damned poor?

First, let me backtrack a bit. The current political debates over Africa have a sly tone of censure, as if the continent had brought all its misery upon itself. (And these fifty-plus countries are always just "Africa," as in *Survivor Africa* and "the President's Africa Trip.") I mean, for God's sakes, these Africans are a permanent fixture on the charity drives and late night infomercials, their children crusty-cheeked and covered in flies. Beggars can't be choosers and Africans, judging by their constant state of incivility in the news, don't even choose to get along.

It's against this backdrop that Africa's poverty takes on added significance. We believe that poor people, here and abroad, are sort of like the developmentally disabled. They just don't make smart decisions. A couple of years ago, the director of the United States Agency for International Development said Africans couldn't benefit from advanced drug therapy because they don't use clocks and "don't know what Western time is." As it turns out, in a study released this week, Africans do a better job of taking their AIDS medications on time than folks from the United States—90 percent of Africans as opposed to 70 percent of Americans. Fancy that.

Why is *the way* that AIDS survivors take their medication a big international issue, anyway? Well, it's because the U.S. has steadfastly fought lowering the price of AIDS drugs to anything that an average citizen of an African country could pay. We have markets to protect. AIDS medications, patented by U.S. companies, cost an average of $10,000 per year. The per capita income of Uganda, hit hard by the virus, is $1,200 per year.

In the time since the AIDS virus was identified, over 18 million sub-Saharan Africans have died from the disease. Because of the exponential infection rate of the virus, most have died since the United States began producing antiretroviral drugs to battle the disease. We may have maintained our profit margins, but we have blood on our hands.

Today, although we've agreed to either provide or allow low-cost AIDS drugs in Africa, we still seek to preserve our control over African's lives. The key initiative that came out of the president's trip to Africa earlier this year was funding for the fight against AIDS. Now that funding is in jeopardy.

George Bush supposedly allotted the AIDS initiative $15 billion over five years—an annual allocation of $3 billion a year. However, he only submitted a budget request of $2 billion dollars to Congress. The president loves the photo ops on Goree Island—a place where he called slavery "one of the greatest crimes in history." But he does not or will not realize that AIDS is enslaving the continent today.

Senator Richard Durban (D-Ill.) is now fighting to restore the funds. This fight is a perfect opportunity for Americans to join their voices with those of Africans and advocate for the best interest of the continent. Yes, there are Africans—diplomats like U.N. Secretary General Kofi Annan, and statesmen like former South African President Nelson Mandela—who speak eloquently on behalf of their people. But there are many more voices clamoring to be heard.

New York University professor Manthia Diawara's new book, *We Won't Budge*, addresses the silencing of Africans on African issues. His personal account of a life spent in Mali, France, and the United States unsparingly criticizes unsavory African traditions like clitoridectomies, the false non-racialism of the French, and the blatant racism of America. Diowara writes, "I am now unhappy wherever I go in the world. I cannot stand the stereotypes Europeans have of Americans or Africans, and vice versa. I cannot discuss Israel with Europeans, or Palestine with Americans. How did the world decide that we Africans have nothing meaningful to say about these important issues facing us: democracy and human rights. Lest our oppressors forget, we Africans have eyes to see, ears to hear, heads to analyze and mouths to judge."

Perhaps the rest of the world is afraid of Africa's judgment, afraid that after all these years of being silent, the citizens of the continent will stand and cry, "J'Accuse!" We Africans accuse you of murder, coercion, complicity in the death of our people, first by military force and now by withholding medication. Since free speech is quite often expensive, it isn't surprising that those with few funds remain silent. We Americans, however, in the richest country in the world, are not barred from speaking. We simply refuse.

African nations could, of course, pay for their needs if they had access to their own resources. But the production of gold, diamonds, and the columbite-tantalite used in cell phones largely benefits Westerners. These resources have also become battlegrounds in civil wars, as rebels force civilian labor to reap the rewards of diamond (Sierra Leone) and columbite-tantalite (the Democratic Republic of the Congo) mining. In other nations, like Nigeria, multinational corporations barter with dictators, doing an end-run around the nation's people.

Ah, Africa! So rich, and yet so poor. If its resources were free—and its people as well—African nations could do anything. Anything.

Fortress America

January 6, 2004

I'm glad I got to see the world before it closed up shop.

In the past decade, I've been lucky enough—blessed enough—to travel to four continents. The countries I've toured are a literal A to Z, as I road-tripped from coast-to-coast in America and hiked through the mountains of Zimbabwe. And now, both within and without our nation, prospects for mind-expanding travel are narrowing to the aperture of a pin, or perhaps to the invisible width of a bit of data.

Today, the United States began photographing and fingerprinting non-U.S. citizens as they entered the country. The program, US-VISIT (United States Visitor and Immigrant Status Indicator Technology) is budgeted at $380 million. An estimated 24 million individuals each year will have to pass two finger scans and have their photographs taken as they enter the United States. The government's hope is that it will catch terrorists and those who overstay their visas.

In the words of Homeland Security director Tom Ridge, "As the world community combats terrorism . . . you're going to see more and more countries going to a form of biometric identification to confirm identities." Biometrics is a developing, and lucrative, arena of technologies that map and quantify the body digitally.

Ironically, the International Biometric Industry Association had scheduled its annual conference for September 11, 2001, in Orlando, Florida. The association rescheduled the conference, with a keynote called "Homeland Security and Biometrics," for February 2002. Since then, the financial prospects for biometrics firms have soared. In much the same way that the war on Iraq has improved the fortunes of military outsourcing firms like Halliburton's subsidiary Kellogg, Brown and Root, our nation's response to the September 11 attacks is feeding the coffers of biometrics firms for an uncertain reward.

This holiday season, the United States blocked or delayed several international flights into the country because of security concerns. Ultimately, no arrests were made, and the government admits there may have been no terrorist plot to begin with. In fact, some of the flights had spelling errors on their passenger manifests that caused the delays. More specifically, a test of the US-VISIT program in Atlanta screened over 20,000 passengers and found just 21

people with suspicious records. None of them were suspected terrorists—
rather, they had been convicted of offenses including statutory rape.

On the one hand, no one wants criminals entering the United States.
But at a cost of $380 million dollars a year, this program is wildly expensive
and does not seem to net its target of terrorists (who may well have sophisticated ways of foiling the system). Instead, it may deter legitimate tourists
and hurt an already ailing airline industry.

And moves like this one do not just affect non-*estadounidenses*. The tightening of global travel restrictions sends a message to Americans that the
world is as closed to us as the United States appears to be to those on the
outside. They add to the already rampant paranoia that the world is merely a dangerous (and not also a wondrous) place and the only safe haven is a
gated community within a shuttered nation. Our country is becoming a
fortress of our own devising, both psychologically and tangibly. For example, last week Brazil began fingerprinting and photographing American
visitors as a tit-for-tat.

"At first, most of the Americans were angered at having to go through all
this," said Wagner Castilho, a press officer for the Brazilian federal police.
"But they were usually more understanding once they learned that Brazilians
are subjected to the same treatment in the U.S."

We can't expect special treatment on the global stage. If we restrict access
to the United States, others will restrict our access to the world. And that
would be a devastating shame. In an era of terror, anger, and recrimina-
tions, one of the healing balms is a one-on-one connection with people of
other nations. We cannot heal the rifts in this fractious world by hiding in
our domain. No screening program will make us absolutely secure. And if
we retreat—attempting to become an island fortress—we will endanger not
only our humanity, but our long-term security as well.

Epilogue: Rebuilding Trust

It was a fresh, clear March day. My friends and I gathered at the broad steps of the New York Public Library at Forty-second Street. A group of dancers captivated the growing crowd, which ranged from parents pushing strollers to a group of women (and one man!) in hot-pink wigs and fishnets.

We were all gathered for the same reason: to mark the one-year anniversary of America's war on Iraq with a peaceful protest. At noon, we began walking towards Madison Avenue. The crowds got thicker until, in the Thirties, we couldn't move at all. A solid wall of thousands of people stood, marking their hopes for our nation's future with their bodies.

The year before it was bitterly cold. Protesters bundled up and braved subfreezing wind chills to mark their discontent. The mood was grim. America had just gone to war.

This time, despite the daily body count from Iraq, the mood was sober but not somber. Parents of enlisted men and women carried signs saying "Support Our Troops: Bring them Home." A group of New York City public schoolchildren marched to demand education funds, not war funding, take priority. A group of college professors and students did the same.

It struck me then that we were not marching against something, but marching *for* something: a better, safer America. Whether we achieve that goal will largely depend on the outcome of election 2004.

What we need now even more than answers is questions. Why do people that we know and respect and love refuse to participate in politics? Where did this loathing for an important part of our lives come from? Why is politics shameful and sad? Why is poverty shameful and sad? What do we owe Americans who work full-time? What is success? Why did we go to war? What does war mean to us? What does prosperity mean to us? Who's an American? How do we make this country better? For whom? Why? How long will it last? Will it all last?

There are three simple actions we can take to make America better. First, we can vote, whether it's for the best, for the least-worst, or just because it registers that we exist in the political life of our nation. Second, we need to research our options for political participation, which include not only voting but attending city council meetings, letter-writing, joining community groups and PTAs, peaceful protest, and joining interest-based coalitions. All of these mean we have to put ourselves out, just a little bit, to help the country along. Last, we can trust our instincts. Most people have some innate sense of where we should be headed, but many of us are too discouraged to voice an opinion. Voice your opinion. The worst you can do is be wrong and learn from the experience.

America needs all of our wisdom, strength, attention, and experience to thrive and grow. The lockout of half the population from American politics will not change unless we change it: not just the parties, not just the activists, but ordinary Americans who reach out to their friends, families, and neighbors.

Endnotes

Preface

1 Edmund L. Andrews, "The Job Picture: The Data; In the Latest Numbers, Economists See the Cold, Hard, Truth About Jobs," *New York Times,* 6 March 2004. Retrieved electronically from NewYorkTimes.com, March 2004.

1. Trust

1 Frances Fox Piven and Richard A. Cloward, *Why Americans Still Don't Vote: And Why Politicians Want It That Way* (Boston: Beacon Press, 2000), 2–3.

2 Amie Jamieson, Hyon B. Shin, and Jennifer Day, "Voting and Registration in the Election of November 2000," U.S. Census Bureau (February 2002).

3 "Public Trust in Government is Going Up In Recent Years," *Reinvention Express,* Vol. 4, No. 5 (11 May 1998). Retrieved electronically 19 April 2004, http://govinfo.library.unt.edu/npr/library/express/1997/vol4no5.html.

4 "The 2004 Political Landscape: Evenly Divided and Increasingly Polarized (Part 6)," Pew Research Center for the People and the Press. Retrieved 16 April 2004, http://people-press.org/reports/display.php3?PageID=755.

2. A Brief History of Voter Turnout

1 Piven and Cloward, *Why Americans Still Don't Vote,* 247.

2 Michael Holt, "Zachary Taylor (1849–1850)," Americanpresident.org. Retrieved 20 March 2004, http://www.americanpresident.org/history/zacharytaylor/biography/AmericanFranchise.common.shtml.

3 "Prairie View: The Full Story," RocktheVote.com. Retrieved 20 March 2004, http://www.rockthevote.com/rapthevote/rap_pv_story.php.

4 Piven and Cloward, *Why Americans Still Don't Vote,* 45.

5 Kate Tuttle, "Voting Rights Act of 1965," Encarta Africana. Retrieved 20 March 2004, http://www.africana.com/research/encarta/tt_393.asp.

6 Gregory Palast, "Florida's Flawed 'Voter Cleaning' Program," *Salon*, 4 December 2000. Retrieved 20 March 2004, http://archive.salon.com/ politics/feature/2000/12/04/voter_file/print.html.

7 Sheldon S. Shafer, "GOP to put challengers in black voting precincts" *Louisville (Kentucky) Courier-Journal*, 23 October 2003. Retrieved 20 March 2004, http://www.courier-journal.com/localnews/2003/10/23ky/wir-front-votes1023-9144.html.

8 Micah Sifry, "From the Author's Note," *Spoiling for a Fight: Third Party Politics in America* (Routledge Press, 2002). Retrieved 20 March 2004, http://www.spoilingforafight.com/introduction.htm.

9 Piven and Cloward, *Why Americans Still Don't Vote*, 135–136.

10 Ibid., 261.

11 Steven J. Rosenstone and John Mark Hansen, *Mobilization, Participation, and Democracy in America* (Essex, UK: Pearson Longman, 1993), 145. Cited in Piven and Cloward, *Why Americans Still Don't Vote*, 267.

12 Piven and Cloward, *Why Americans Still Don't Vote*, 272. Emphasis mine.

3. The 2000 Election

The 2000 election sidebar from "Election 2000-The Recount," HistoryCentral.com. Retrieved 20 Mar. 2004, http://www.multied.com/ elections/2000recount.html.

1 Ann McFeatters, "Chapter Five: A Wild Election Night," *Pittsburgh Post-Gazette*, 17 December 2000. Retrieved 20 March 2004, http://www.post-gazette.com/election/20001217chap5.asp

2 "Newspaper: Butterfly Ballot Cost Gore White House," CNN, 11 March 11, 2001. Retrieved 21 March 2004, http://www.cnn.com/2001/ ALLPOLITICS/03/11/palmbeach.recount/.

3 Pew Research Center, "2004 Political Landscape (Part 6)."

4 Council for Excellence in Government, "You Need to Know . . . Voter Turnout is Falling," TakeYourKidstoVote.org. Retrieved 20 March 2004,

http://www.takeyourkidstovote.org/intro.htm; Nebraska Secretary of State, "Why the Youth Citizenship Survey is a Program of National Significance," State.NE.us. Retrieved 20 March 2004, http://www.sos.state.ne.us/ YouthProjects/NatlMock.htm.

5 "Havana, Florida," City-Data.com. Retrieved 20 March 2004, http://www.city-data.com/city/Havana-Florida.html.

6 "The Sentencing Project," Human Rights Watch (1998). Retrieved 21 March 2004, http://www.hrw.org/reports98/vote/usvot98o.htm.

7 Rebecca Perl, "The Last Disenfranchised Class," *Nation*, 24 November 2003, 13.

8 Ibid, 14.

9 "Almost a Third of All Convicted State Felons Were Sentenced for Drug Trafficking or Possession," U.S. Department of Justice, January 12, 1997. Retrieved 22 March 2004, http://www.ojp.usdoj.gov/bjs/pub/ press/fssc94.pr.

10 John Lantigua, "How the GOP Gamed the System in Florida," *Nation*, 30 April 2001. Retrieved 22 March 2004, http://www.thenation.com/ doc.mhtml?i=20010430&c=5&s=lantigua.

11 Grant Hayden, "Will the New Help America Vote Act Prevent a Repeat of the 2000 Florida Fiasco?" Findlaw.com, 5 November 2002. Retrieved 20 March 2004, http://writ.news.findlaw.com/commentary/20021105 _hayden.html.

12 Farhad Manjoo, "Voting into the Void," *Salon*, 5 November 2002. Retrieved 20 March 2004, http://archive.salon.com/tech/feature/ 2002/11/05/voting_machines/print.html.

13 Allen Breed, "Uncovering What Went Wrong in the Miami-Dade Election Fiasco," Associated Press, 16 September 2002. Retrieved 20 March 2004, http://www.govtech.net/news/news.phtml?docid= 2002.09.16-30300000000022816; Louise Witt, "More Calls to Vet Voting Machines," *Wired*, August 2003. Retrieved 20 March 2004,

http://www.wired.com/news/politics/0,1283,59874,00.html?tw=wn_story
_related.

14 Dana Milbank, "Tragicomedy of Errors Fuels Volusia Recount," *Washington Post*, 12 November 2000, A22. Retrieved from WashingtonPost.com, 22 March 2004.

15 Kim Zetter, "How E-Voting Threatens Democracy," March 29, 2004. Wired.com. Retrieved 16 April 2004, http://www.wired.com/news/evote/0,2645,62790,00.html?tw=wn_story_page_prev2.

16 Farhad Manjoo, "Bad Grades for a Voting-Machine Exam," *Salon*, 15 October 2003. Retrieved 20 March 2004, http://archive.salon.com/tech/feature/2003/10/15/riverside_voting_machines/print.html.

17 John Schwartz, "New Economy: Computerized voting machines are secure and efficient, their makers say. Skeptics are demanding a paper trail," *New York Times*, 15 December 2003. Retrieved electronically from NewYorkTimes.com, February 2004.

18 Associated Press, "Diebold Appears to Have Conflict," *Ohio Beacon Journal*, 29 August 2003. Retrieved 20 March 2004, http://www.ohio.com/mld/beaconjournal/business/6646063.htm.

19 Elise Ackerman, "Electronic Voting's Hidden Perils," *San Jose Mercury News*, 1 February 2004. Retrieved 22 March 2004, http://www.mercurynews.com/mld/mercurynews/7849090.htm.

20 Ben Tripp, "Welcome to the Machine," *CounterPunch*, 20 February 2003. Retrieved 18 April 2004, http://www.counterpunch.org/tripp02202003.html.

21 "California's Secretary of State Announces Electronic Voting Directives," Government Technology, 24 November 2003. Retrieved electronically 18 April 2004, http://www.govtech.net/news/news.php?id=78499.

22 Ian Hoffman, "Diebold Apologizes for Failure," *Oakland Tribune*, 22 April 2004, 1; Greg Lucas, "State bans electronic balloting in 4 counties," *San Francisco Chronicle*, 1 May 2004, A1.

4. The Red and the Blue

1 Steplock, "Zogby—America Still Culturally Divided; Blue States vs. Red States, Democrats vs. Republicans," Free Republic.com. Retrieved 6 June 2004, http://www.freerepublic.com/focus/f-news/1052538/posts.

2 John Zogby, "Introduction," *O'Leary Report/Zogby International Values Poll 2004*, (New York: Zogby International, 2004), 2.

3 "2004 Political Landscape: Evenly Divided and Increasingly Polarized (Overview)," Pew Research Center for the People and the Press. Retrieved 16 April 2004, http://people-press.org/reports/display.php3?PageID=749.

4 James Pinkerton, "The New New Deal Coalition," Tech Central Station, 20 January 2004. Retrieved 20 March 2004, http://www.tech-centralstation.com/012004I.html.

5 Robert G. Kaiser and Ira Chinoy, "Scaife: Funding Father of the Right," *Washington Post*, 2 May 1999, A1. Retrieved 22 March 2004, http://www.washingtonpost.com/wp-srv/politics/special/clinton/stories/scaifemain050299.htm.

6 Thom Hartmann, "Healthcare Reveals Real 'Conservative' Agenda—Drown Democracy in a Bathtub," CommonDreams.org, 25 February 2003. Retrieved 22 March 2004, http://www.commondreams.org/views03/0225-10.htm.

7 Paul Byrnes, "Head of State" (review), *Sydney Morning Herald*, October 16, 2003. Retrieved electronically 6 June 2004, http://www.smh.au/articles/2003/10/151065917477362.html?from=storyrhs&oneclick=true.

8 Pew Research Center, "2004 Political Landscape (Overview)."

9 Sifry, "Author's Note."

10 Senate Governmental Affairs Committee, "Homeland Security Bill Clears Senate in Resounding, Bipartisan Vote," Senate.gov, 19 November 2002. Retrieved 20 March 2004, http://www.senate.gov/~gov_affairs/111902press.htm; Kellie Lunney, "Employees uncertain about proposed homeland security agency," GovExec.com, 11 October

2001. Retrieved 20 March 2004, http://www.govexec.com/dailyfed/1001/101101m1.htm.

11 "Congress approves US security body," BBC News, 20 November 2002. Retrieved electronically 2 May 2004, http://news.bbc.co.uk/2/hi/americas/2493929.stm.

12 Coleen Rowley, "Coleen Rowley's Memo to FBI Director Robert Mueller (edited)," *Time* , 21 May 2002. Retrieved 20 March 2004, http://www.time.com/time/covers/1101020603/memo.html.

13 "Bush Begins Push for Security Plan," CBSNews.com, 8 June 2002. Retrieved 20 March 2004, http://www.cbsnews.com/stories/2002/06/08/attack/main511579.shtml.

14 Michael Tackett, "Bush's speech drowned out his critics," *Chicago Tribune*, 6 June 2002. Retrieved 2 May 2004, http://www.thestate.com/mld/thestate/3416845.htm.

15 "Ex WorldCom CEO Ebbers Indicted," Associated Press, 2 March 2004. Retrieved 22 March 2004, http://msnbc.msn.com/id/4428124/.

16 Steven Thomma, "Democrats' support fading, poll finds," Knight Ridder Newspapers, July 2003. Retrieved 20 March 2004, http://seattletimes.nwsource.com/html/politics/2001295371_outlook29.html.

17 David Brooks, "The Triumph of Hope Over Self-Interest." *New York Times*, 12 January 2003. Retrieved electronically from NewYorkTimes.com.

18 "Despite Social Security, Some Seniors Live in Poverty," National Center for Policy Analysis. Retrieved 6 June 2004, http://www.ncpa.org/pi/congress/pd092499b.html.

19 Julie Appleby, "43.6 million don't have health insurance," *USA Today*, 30 September 2003. Retrieved 20 March 2004, http://www.usatoday.com/money/industries/health/2003-09-30-insurance_x.htm; "The 2003 HHS Poverty Guidelines," U.S. Department of Health and Human Services, HHS.gov, last updated 27 February 2004. Retrieved 20 March 2004, http://aspe.hhs.gov/poverty/03poverty.htm.

20 Dave Lindorff, "Dishonerable Discharge: Bush administration slashes veterans' benefits," November 26, 2003. VeteransforPeace.org. Retrieved 20
March 2004, http://www.veteransforpeace.org/Dishonorable_discharge
_112603.htm.

5. Pop and Politics

1 Robert D. Putnam, *Bowling Alone: The Collapse and Revival of American Community*
(New York: Simon & Schuster, 2000), 27.

2 David Boaz, "A Snapshot View of a Complex World," Cato Institute (July
15, 1999). Retrieved 6 June 2004, http://www.cato.org/research/articles/
boaz-990715.html.

3 Glenn Augustine, "Most Research Misses the Facts: Americans use twice as
much media as they say," Ball State University (25 February 2004).
Retrieved 20 March 2004, http://www.bsu.edu/news/arti-
cle/0,1370,7273-850-18107,00.html; "Media Use in America,"
(Universal City, Calif.: Mediascope Press, 2003). Retrieved 20 March
2004, http://www.mediascope.org/pubs/ibriefs/mua.htm.

4 "Cable and Internet Loom Large in Fragmented Political News Universe," Pew
Research Center for People and the Press, 11 January 2004. Retrieved 20
March 2004, http://people-press.org/reports/display.php3?ReportID=200.

5 "Chuck D. Takes His Act to Air America," Reuters, 8 April 2004. Retrieved
6 June 2004, http://msnbc.msn.com/id/4697119.

6 Mos Def, "Hip Hop," *Black on Both Sides* (Rawkus Records, 1999).

7 Renuka Rayasam, "Rappers, Wrestlers Push Vote Campaign," *Atlanta Journal-
Constitution*, 23 September 2003. Retrieved 20 March 2004,
http://www.hiphopsummitactionnetwork.org/Content/Main.aspx?PageId=17.

8 "The Campaign for Young Voters Survey Research Projects," Center for
Democracy and Citizenship, 2004. Retrieved 20 March 2004,
http://www.youngcitizensurvey.org/.

9 Julie Meyer, "Age: 2000," U.S. Bureau of the Census (2000 Census). Downloaded February 2004 as an Adobe Acrobat file from http://www.census.gov/prod/2001pubs/c2kbr01-12.pdf.

10 50 Cent, "P.I.M.P.," *P.I.M.P.* (Universal, 2003).

11 Dilated Peoples, "Worst Comes to Worst," *Expansion Team* (EMD/Capitol, 2001).

6. The Future of Political Parties

1 Bill Hillsman, *Run the Other Way: Fixing the Two-Party System, One Campaign at a Time*, (New York: Free Press, 2004), xv.

2 Karlyn H. Bowman, "Quarter of Americans Have Voted Third Party for President," *Roll Call*, 5 November 2003. Retrieved 20 April 2004, http://www.aei.org/news/newsID.19425,filter./news_detail.asp.

3 Lynette Clemetson, "Younger Blacks Tell Democrats To Take Notice," *New York Times*, 8 August 2003, A1.

4 "Success of Rhode Island's Vote for America Results in Development of National Organization," Vote for America, 9 July 2002. Retrieved 20 March 2004, http://www.voteforamerica.org/our_states/rhode_island/ripress.cfm.

5 Sifry, "Author's Note."

6 Piven and Cloward, *Why Americans Still Don't Vote*, 63.

7 Ibid., 65.

8 Elizabeth A. Hodges, "Igniting the Fuse: Opening Up Third Party Politics," *Z Magazine*, April 1997. Retrieved 6 July 2004, http://zena.secureforum.com/znet/zmag/zarticle.cfm?URL=articles/apr97hodges.html.

9 "Timmons v.Twin Cities Area New Party," *Oyez: U.S. Supreme Court Multimedia* (April 1997). U.S. Citation; U.S. 351 (1997). Retrieved 6 July 2004, http://www.oyez.org/oyez/resource/case/830/print.

10 Sifry, "Author's Note."

11 Eric Beohlert, "Radio's Big Bully," *Salon*, April 30, 2001. Retreived 2 May 2004, http://dir.salon.com/ent/feature/2001/04/30/clear_channel/ index.html?pn=1.

Voter Registration
(And Mail-In Ballot)
Resources and Deadlines

Election rules and procedures vary by state. In most states you can obtain voter registration forms and mail-in ballot request forms by phone or via the Internet.

Via the Internet

For mail-in ballots request forms, visit www.firstgov.com/Citizen/Topics/Voting.shtml and click the "Absentee ballots" button in the "Register to Vote and Go Vote" section. Check out regulations for your area.

For voter registration forms, try any of these nonpartisan Web sites: **YourVoteMatters** (www.yourvotematters.org), **League of Women Voters** (www.lwv.org/voter/register.html), **Rock the Vote** (www.rockthevote.org), **Sojourners** (www.sojo.net), and **Declare Yourself** (www.declareyourself.org). In most cases, you will be able to fill out the form online and print it out. Then sign it and mail it to the address provided.

By Phone

Call your secretary of state's office at the number listed below to request 1) a voter registration form or 2) a mail-in ballot request form. You can also ask about where you cast your ballot in person.

State	Secretary of State Contact	State	Secretary of State Contact
Alabama	334-242-7200	Montana	406-444-2304
Alaska	907-465-4611	Nebraska	402-471-2554
Arizona	602-542-4285	Nevada	775-684-5708
Arkansas	501-682-1010	New Hampshire	603-271-3242
California	916-653-6842	New Jersey	609-989-1900
Colorado	303-894-2596	New Mexico	505-827-3600
Connecticut	860-509-6000	New York	518-474-4750
Delaware	302-739-1111	North Carolina	919-807-2000
District of Columbia	202-727-2525	North Dakota	701-328-2900
Florida	850-245-6500	Ohio	614-466-2655
Georgia	404-656-2881	Oklahoma	405-521-3912
Hawaii	808-453-8683	Oregon	503-986-1500
Idaho	208-334-2300	Pennsylvania	717-787-6458
Illinois	217-782-2201	Rhode Island	401-222-2357
Indiana	317-232-6531	South Carolina	803-734-2170
Iowa	515-281-5204	South Dakota	605-773-3537
Kansas	785-296-4564	Tennessee	512-463-5770
Kentucky	502-564-3490	Texas	800-252-8683

Louisiana	225-925-1000	Utah	801-538-1041
Maine	207-626-8400	Vermont	802-828-2363
Maryland	410-974-5521	Virginia	804-371-0017
Massachusetts	617-727-7030	Washington	360-902-4151
Michigan	517-322-1460	West Virginia	304-558-6000
Minnesota	651-296-2803	Wisconsin	608-266-8888
Mississippi	601-359-1350	Wyoming	307-777-7378
Missouri	573-751-4936		

Deadlines for Voter Registration and Mail-in Ballot Requests and Submission

If your questions are not answered by the table below, call your secretary of state's office at the number listed above. Or visit fec.gov (the Federal Election Commission).

State	Voter Registration Deadline	Mail-in Ballot Deadlines
Alabama	10 days before an election.	Request an absentee ballot until 5 days before an election.
Alaska	30 days before the election.	Mail-in ballot applications must be received seven days before an election.
Arizona	29 days before the election.	Requests for absentee ballots may be made up to 90 days prior to the election, but ballots are only mailed 33 days prior to the election.
Arkansas	30 days before the election.	One-stop voting occurs on the Saturday 10 days before the election. Mailed-in ballots must be received by the day before the election.
California	15 days before the election.	Request an election ballot beginning 29 days and ending 7 days before the election.
Colorado	29 days before the election. If the application is received in the mail without a postmark, it must be received within 5 days of the close of registration.	Request an absentee ballot up to 2 days before the election.
Connecticut	14 days before the election.	Request an absentee ballot until the day before the election. County officials will mail ballots out 31 days before a general election and 21 days before a primary.
Delaware	20 days prior to the general election and 20 days prior to any primary election.	One-stop voting is available until noon the day before an election. Mailed-in ballots are due by the

		close of polls on Election Day. Requests for mail-in ballots must be received 4 days before the election.
District of Columbia	30 days before the election.	Submit a request for an absentee ballot no later than 7 days before an election. Vote in person at the Board of Elections and Ethics beginning 14 days and ending 1 day before election day.
Florida	29 days before the election.	Call the Supervisor of Elections office to ask about an absentee ballot as soon as possible. Contact the election officials for more information.
Georgia	The fifth Monday before any general primary, general election, or presidential preference primary, or regularly scheduled special election pursuant to the Georgia Election Code. The fifth day after the date of the call for all other special primaries and elections.	Apply for an absentee ballot as early as 180 days before an election, and up to the day before the election.
Hawaii	30 days before the election.	Submit your application for an absentee ballot starting 60 days before the election. The last day to submit an application is 7 days before election day.
Idaho	25 days before the election, 24 day before for in person or register in person at the polls.	Request an absentee ballot by mail up until 6 days before the election. Vote absentee in person at the county clerk's office up until 5:00 p.m. the day before the election.
Illinois	29 days before the primary, 28 days before the general election.	Request an absentee ballot by mail beginning 40 days and ending 5 days before the election. Request and vote the absentee ballot in person starting 40 days before the election and no later than the day before the election.
Indiana	29 days before the election.	Request an absentee ballot starting 90 days before the election. Request an absentee ballot in person up until noon on the day before an election at the county elections office.

Iowa	Must be delivered by 5 p.m. 10 days before the election, if it is a state primary or general election; 11 days before all others. A postmark 15 or more days before an election is considered on time.	Request an absentee ballot by mail or in person 70 days before the election.
Kansas	Delivered 15 days before the election.	Request your absentee ballot at any time. County elections officials start sending out ballots 20 days before the election.
Kentucky	29 days before the election.	Absentee balloting is available upon application at least 7 days before date of election. Certain conditions on the application must be met.
Louisiana	30 days before the election.	Vote in person the week prior to the week of the election at the Registrar's office in your parish.
Maine	Delivered 10 business days before the election (or voter may register in person up to and including election day).	Request an absentee ballot 90 days prior to the election. You may also vote absentee in person 30 to 45 days before the election at your municipal clerk's office.
Maryland	Postmarked 25 days before an election or received in the elections office by 9 p.m. no later than 21 days before an election.	Absentee balloting is allowed on Maryland under specific conditions.
Massachusetts	20 days before the election.	Apply for an absentee ballot for all elections in a year using one absentee ballot application. You may vote absentee in person at the county clerk's office 2 or 3 weeks before the election depending upon the type of the election.
Michigan	30 days before the election.	Absentee ballot requests must be in before 2:00 p.m. the Saturday before the election.
Minnesota	Delivered by 5:00 p.m. 21 days before the election (there is also Election Day registration at polling places).	Vote absentee in person on the Saturday and Monday before election day.
Mississippi	30 days before the election day.	Request an absentee ballot 45 days before the election in person at the voter registrar's office. Absentee

		ballots can only be requested in person.
Missouri	28 days before the election.	Absentee ballot is available by application. (Online application is available.) In-person absentee voting begins 6 weeks prior to the election.
Montana	30 days before the election.	During the period beginning 75 days before the Election Day, and ending at noon the day before the election, you may apply to your Election Administrator for an absentee ballot.
Nebraska	The third Friday before the election (or delivered by 6 p.m. on the second Friday before the election).	Vote absentee ballot 120 days before the election. Vote absentee in person at your county elections office starting 35 days before and ending the day before the election.
Nevada	9:00 p.m. on the fifth Saturday before any primary or general election. 9:00 p.m. on the third Saturday before any recall or special election, unless held on the same day as a primary or general election. Then it remains on the fifth Saturday.	Vote absentee in person at the county clerk's office starting 12 days before and ending 4 days before the election.
New Hampshire	Voter registration forms must be received by city or town clerk by 10 days before the election, Register at polls on Election Day. (New Hampshire officials will only accept the National Voter Registration Form as a request for their own voter registration form.)	Absentee ballots are available from the town or city clerk 30 days prior to an election.
New Jersey	29 days before the election.	Mail-in absentee voter applications must be received by the county clerk at least 7 days prior to the election, or vote in person by 3:00 p.m. the day before election day.
New Mexico	28 days before the election.	Vote in person at your county clerk's office 20 days prior to the election.
New York	25 days before the election.	Request an absentee ballot

		beginning 30 days before and ending 7 days before the election day.
North Carolina	Postmarked 25 days before an election or received in the elections office or designated voter registration agency by 5 p.m.	Request a mail-in ballot beginning 50 days before and ending no later than the Tuesday prior to election day. Ballots are due by 5:00 p.m. the day before the election. Vote absentee in person up to 17 days before election day.
North Dakota	North Dakota does not have voter registration.	Request an absentee ballot any time before an election. The ballots will be made available to you starting 40 days prior to the election.
Ohio	30 days before the election.	You can vote absentee if you will be absent on election day, are 62 or old, you or a family member are hospitalized, have a disability, are an elections official, are in jail, and for other reasons.
Oklahoma	25 days before the election.	Request an absentee ballot at anytime up until the Wednesday before the election.
Oregon	21 days before the election. (There is no deadline for applications for change of name, change of address, or to register with party.)	No absentee voting in Oregon since all ballots are mailed to registered voters.
Pennsylvania	30 days before an election or primary.	Absentee ballot application requirements vary. Contact local officials.
Rhode Island	30 days before the election.	Absentee ballot requests must be received by the local board of canvassers no later than 21 days before the election.
South Carolina	30 days before the election.	County voter registration office must receive your voter application by mail no later than 4 days prior to the election, or apply and vote in person up until 5:00 p.m. the day before an election.
South Dakota	15 day before the election.	Vote absentee in person up until the day of the election at the county auditor's office.
Tennessee	30 days before the election.	Vote absentee at the county election office between 20 days and 5 days

State	Registration Deadline	Absentee/Voting Information
		before the election. Mail-in absentee ballots must be requested from county elections office.
Texas	30 days before the election.	Vote anytime starting 17 days before an election through the fourth day before election day. Request absentee ballots by mail 60 days before the election through the seventh day before the election.
Utah	20 days before an election.	The county clerk should receive absentee ballot applications no later then the Friday before the election.
Vermont	Delivered to the town clerk before 12:00 noon, postmarked, or submitted to DMV on the second Sat. before an election.	Absentee ballot requests must reach the town clerk no later than 17 days before the election to receive a ballot.
Virginia	Delivered 29 days before the election.	Vote absentee in person at the office of the general registrar up until 3 day prior to the election.
Washington	30 days before the election by mail or delivered in person at the specified county location up to 15 days before an election.	Request an absentee ballot up to 90 days before an election.
West Virginia	20 days before the election.	Vote absentee in person between 15 and 3 days before the election at the circuit clerk's office. If you've requested an absentee ballot, you can also vote at the polls.
Wisconsin	For municipalities where voter registration is required, 13 days before an election; or completed at the local voter registration office 1 day before an election; or completed at the polling place on election day,	Applications must be received by the municipal clerk's office no later than 5:00 p.m. the Friday before the election day, or requested in person no later than 5:00 p.m. the day before election day.
Wyoming	30 days before an election or register at the polling place on election day. Wyoming does not accept the National Voter Registration Form, which means you must use the state form.	Call or write the county clerk for details. Absentee ballots must be returned immediately.

Sources of Nonpartisan Candidate Information

Project Vote Smart (www.vote-smart.org)

Researches candidate positions and voting records, and provides links for state-specific information. You can also call 1-800-VOTE-SMART.

The League of Women Voters (www.dnet.org)

Collects information from campaigns and sorts it by issue.

Farai Chideya was courted by political journalism, jilted by political journalism, considered a divorce, and gave it a second chance. She's been married to political journalism for fifteen years—her whole working life. She's hoping they reach their golden anniversary together and don't fight too much.

Chideya has worked for media outlets including *Newsweek*, Oxygen Media, CNN, ABC News, and MTV. She's written two previous books: *Don't Belive the Hype: Fighting Cultural Misinformation About African-Americans* and *The Color of Our Future*. She's been to at least thirty of the fifty United States, and to four continents as well. Despite that, she still doesn't quite understand how people or governments work. There's still time, and hope.

Farai Chideya loves old school hip hop, her family, her country, and anything barbecued. Visit her in cyberspace at www.faraichideya.com. And check book news and appearances: www.trustthebook.com.